APPEARANCE, DISABILITY AND THE LAW

People with disfigurements often face prejudice, exclusion and discrimination in employment and across other life contexts. Law's response to this evidence is flawed both by its own limited and illogical scope and its failure to understand the perspectives of those people who may need to use it. Drawing on interviews with people with lived experience of disfigurement and employers, the book sketches out different approaches to the complex social problem of discrimination against people with visible differences. It also asks whether, in our changing social context, law should widen its protection beyond disfigurement. Would a protected characteristic of appearance offer viable legal rights to the many millions of us who do not have a disfigurement but who are prone to a few spots, whose ears stick out more than we would like, or who are carrying an extra stone in weight?

HANNAH SAUNDERS leads the policy and education work of an international alliance of not-for-profit organisations working to secure greater recognition of the rights of people with visible differences. She is also a Visiting Fellow at Queen Mary University of London.

CAMBRIDGE BIOETHICS AND LAW

This series of books – formerly called Cambridge Law, Medicine and Ethics – was founded by Cambridge University Press with Alexander McCall Smith as its first editor in 2003. It focuses on the law's complex and troubled relationship with medicine across both the developed and the developing world. In the past twenty years, we have seen in many countries increasing resort to the courts by dissatisfied patients and a growing use of the courts to attempt to resolve intractable ethical dilemmas. At the same time, legislatures across the world have struggled to address the questions posed by both the successes and the failures of modern medicine, while international organisations such as the WHO and UNESCO now regularly address issues of medical law. It follows that we would expect ethical and policy questions to be integral to the analysis of the legal issues discussed in this series. The series responds to the high profile of medical law in universities, in legal and medical practice, as well as in public and political affairs. We seek to reflect the evidence that many major health-related policy and bioethics debates in the UK, Europe and the international community over the past two decades have involved a strong medical law dimension. With that in mind, we seek to address how legal analysis might have a trans-jurisdictional and international relevance. Organ retention, embryonic stem cell research, physician-assisted suicide and the allocation of resources to fund health care are but a few examples among many. The emphasis of this series is thus on matters of public concern and/or practical significance. We look for books that could make a difference to the development of medical law and enhance the role of medico-legal debate in policy circles. That is not to say that we lack interest in the important theoretical dimensions of the subject, but we aim to ensure that theoretical debate is grounded in the realities of how the law does and should interact with medicine and health care.

APPEARANCE, DISABILITY AND THE LAW

HANNAH SAUNDERS
Queen Mary University of London

CAMBRIDGE
UNIVERSITY PRESS

CAMBRIDGE
UNIVERSITY PRESS

Shaftesbury Road, Cambridge CB2 8EA, United Kingdom

One Liberty Plaza, 20th Floor, New York, NY 10006, USA

477 Williamstown Road, Port Melbourne, VIC 3207, Australia

314–321, 3rd Floor, Plot 3, Splendor Forum, Jasola District Centre, New Delhi – 110025, India

103 Penang Road, #05-06/07, Visioncrest Commercial, Singapore 238467

Cambridge University Press is part of Cambridge University Press & Assessment, a department of the University of Cambridge.

We share the University's mission to contribute to society through the pursuit of education, learning and research at the highest international levels of excellence.

www.cambridge.org
Information on this title: www.cambridge.org/9781009605045

DOI: 10.1017/9781009605076

When citing this work, please include a reference to the DOI 10.1017/9781009605076

First published 2025

A catalogue record for this publication is available from the British Library

A Cataloging-in-Publication data record for this book is available from the Library of Congress

ISBN 978-1-009-60504-5 Hardback

CONTENTS

ACKNOWLEDGEMENTS

I am in the debt of many people for their help in writing this book. First, I thank the participants who volunteered their time to be interviewed and to attend focus groups at different stages of the research, and the charities who have supported this process. It would not have been possible without them.

I am very grateful to the late Professor Aaron Baker, who passed away shortly after my PhD viva and whose guidance, commitment and good humour during that journey was second to none. My special thanks also go to Professor Kate Malleson of Queen Mary University of London, for her unwavering energy, enthusiasm and excellent guidance. I am also grateful to many others who have generously given their thoughts on earlier drafts and ideas, including Di, Lizzie, Roger, Phyllida and the Labour Law discussion group.

Finally, thank you to my family for their belief in this project.

TABLE OF CASES

UK Case Law

A Kinlay v Bronte Film and Television Limited [2021] ET/2200251/2020 (18 July 2021, unreported, ET).

Bickerstaff v Butcher (2015) IT92/14 (3 February 2015, unreported, NIIT).

Blyth v Historic Scotland [2001] ET/S/4000514/00 (14 February 2001, unreported, ET).

Britlief v Birmingham City Council [2020] ICR 653 (EAT).

Campbell v Falkirk Council [2008] S/136261/07 (9 April 2008, unreported, ETS).

Cosgrove v Northern Ireland Ambulance Service [2007] IRLR 397 (NICA).

Cromwell Garage Ltd v Doran [2011] UKEAT/2011/036 (8 April 2011, unreported, EAT).

Dhillon v Leeds Teaching Hospital NHS Trust [2019] ET/1800222/19 (18 December 2019, unreported, ET).

Ellen Mart v Assessment Services Inc [2019] UKEATS 0032/18/SS (16 May 2019, unreported, EAT).

English v Thomas Sanderson Ltd (2009) ICR 543 (CA).

EOC v Secretary of State for Trade and Industry [2007] ICR 1234 (QBD).

Finn v British Bung Manufacturing Company Ltd [2022] ET/1803764/2021 (11 May 2022, unreported, ET).

G v Head Teacher and Governors of St Gregory's Catholic Science College [2011] EWHC 1452 (Admin).

Goodwin v Patent Office [1999] IRLR 4 (EAT).

Griffiths v Lancashire County Council [2009] (17 April 2009, unreported, ET).

Hand v The Police Authority for Northern Ireland [2002] NIIT 1691/01 (2 August 2002, unreported, NIIT).

Hartley v Foreign and Commonwealth Office Services [2016] ICR D17 (EAT).

Hussain v Sky In-Home Services Ltd [2017] ET/2300908/16 (10 January 2017, unreported, ET).

Hutchison 3G Ltd v Edwards [2014] UKEAT/0467/13/DM (4 August 2017, unreported, EAT).

Insitu Cleaning v Heads [1995] IRLR 4 (EAT).

J v DLA Piper LLP [2010] ICR 1052 (EAT).

Johansson v Fountain Street Community Development Association [2005] NIIT 311_03 (4 July 2005, unreported, NIIT).

Leighton v VR Music Limited and Others [2020] 2301546/2018 (17 April 2020, unreported, ET).

London Underground v Edwards (No2) [1988] IRLR 364 (CA).

M O'Reilly v (1) BBC & (2) Bristol Magazines Ltd [2011] ET2200423/2010 (10 January 2011, unreported, ET).

McNicol v Balfour Beatty [2002] IRLR 711 (CA).

Paterson v The Commissioner of the Police of the Metropolis [2007] IRLR 763 (EAT).

Pepper v Hart [1992] 3 WLR 1032 (HL).

Primmer v Mayflower Kebabs Ltd [2007] (unreported, ET).

R (on the application of UNISON) (Appellant) v Lord Chancellor (Respondent) [2017] UKSC 51 (SC).

Riam Dean v Abercrombie and Fitch [2009] (August 2009, unreported, ET).

Rugamer v Sony Music Entertainment UK Limited [2001] IRLR 644 (EAT).

Smith v HM Prison Service [2004] ET/2406059/03 (10 August 2004, unreported, ET).

Smith v Rees [2013] EqLR 74 (ET).

Taylor v Ladbrokes Betting and Gaming Limited [2017] IRLR 312 (EAT).

The Chief Constable of Norfolk v Coffey [2018] IRLR 193 (EAT).

The Chief Constable of Norfolk v Coffey [2019] IRLR 805 (CA).

Vatcher v Kelly Services (UK) Ltd [1999] UKEAT 595/99/0510 (5 October 1999, unreported, EAT).

Walker v Sita Information Networking Computing Limited [2013] UKEAT/009/12 (8 February 2013, unreported, EAT).

West Midlands Passenger Transport Executive v Singh [1988] IRLR 186.

Whyte v First Capital East Limited [2005] UKEAT/0686/04/DM (22 March 2005, unreported EAT).

ECHR Case Law

I.B. v Greece App no 552/10 (ECtHR, 3 October 2013).

Kiyutin v Russia (2011) ECHR 439, para 64.

EU Case Law

C-188/15 *Bougnaoui v Micropole SA* [2016] 7 WLUK 275.

Case C-395/15 *Daouidi v Bootes Plus SL* [2017] 2 CMLR 21.

Case C-354/13 *FOA v Kommuneres Landsforening (Kaltoft)* [2015] 2 CMLR 19.

C-335/11 and C-337/11 *HK Danmark, acting on behalf of Ring v Dansk almennyttigt Boligselskab and HK Danmark, acting on behalf of Lond Skouboe Werge v Dansk Arbejdsgiverforening, acting on behalf of Pro Display A/S (Ring and Skouboe Werge)* [2013] 3 CMLR 21.

Case-C-270/16 *Ruiz Conejero v Ferroser Servicios Auxiliares and Ministero Fiscal* [2018] 2 CMLR 27.

US Case Law

Gerdom v Continental Airlines, Inc., 692 F.2d 602 (9th Cir. 1982).
Superior Min. Co. v Industrial Commission (1923) 309 Ill. 339, 141 N.E. 165.
Wilson v Southwest Airlines Co., 517 F. Supp. 292 (N.D. Tex. 1981).

TABLE OF LEGISLATION

British Primary Legislation

Worker Protection (Amendment of Equality Act 2010) Act 2023
S1

British Secondary Legislation

Equality Act 2010 (Disability) Regulations 2010 SI 2010/2128
Reg 3
Reg 5
Equality Act 2010 (Specific Duties) Regulations 2011 SI 2260/2011
Reg 2
Reg 3

International Legislation

Universal Declaration of Human Rights 1948 UN (10 December 1948) General Assembly Resolution 217A (III)).
UN Convention on the Rights of Persons with Disabilities (12 December 2006) A/RES/61/106
Preamble
Art 1
Art 3
Art 3 (7)
Art 3 (8)
Art 8
Art 27
Optional Protocol

France

Code du Travail
Art 1132-1
Art 1133-1
Art 1121-1
Law No 223-451 (9 June 2023)
Art 5

Norway

Marketing Control Act 2009 (as amended by Inst. 146L, 2020–2021)
s2

US[1]

District of Columbia Code
§ 2-1401.01
Elliott-Larsen Civil Rights Act, No 453 of 1976, Michigan
art 1 § 372202(1)
Harford County, Maryland, Code
chap 95 § 95-3
chap 95 § 95-5
Howard County, Maryland, Code
title 12 subtitle 2 §12.200 (ii)
title 12 subtitle 2 §12.201 (xv)
Madison, Wisconsin, Code of Ordinances
chap 39 §39.03 (1)
chap 39 §39.03 (2)
New York City Administrative Code
title 8 chap 1 §8-107 (1)
Prince George's County, Maryland, Code
subtitle 1 div 12 Subdiv 1 §2-185
subtitle 1 div 12 Subdiv 1 § 2-186 (21)
Regulations to Implement the Equal Employment Provisions of the Americans with Disabilities Act
29 CFR 1630.2(h)
Santa Cruz Municipal Code
chap 9.83 §9.83.010
chap 9.83 §9.83.020 (12)
chap 9.83 §9.83.030
San Francisco, California, Administrative Code
chap 12A §12A.1
Urbana, Illinois, Municipal Code
chap 12 art 3 div 1 § 12-37
chap 12 art 3 div 1 §12-39

[1] References in this section are believed to be correct as of 5 February 2024.

ABBREVIATIONS

Act	Equality Act 2010
art	Article
CA	Court of Appeal
chap	Chapter
CRPD	UN Convention on the Rights of Persons with Disabilities
div	Division
EAT	Employment Appeal Tribunal
ECHR	European Convention on Human Rights
ECJ	European Court of Justice
ECtHR	European Court of Human Rights
EDI	Equality, Diversity and Inclusion
EHRC	Equality and Human Rights Commission
ET	Employment Tribunal
EU	European Union
HC	High Court
HL	House of Lords
HR	human resources
Ill	Illinois
NHS	National Health Service
s	Section
SC	Supreme Court
subdiv	Subdivision
UN	United Nations
US	United States

1

Introduction

Awareness is growing about how physical appearance affects life experiences. In 2021, the House of Commons Women and Equalities Committee's inquiry into body image concluded that 'people face appearance-based discrimination on a daily basis, at work, in schools and in public spaces. In addition, a decade of soaring social media use, increased exposure to online advertising and a persistent and pervasive diet culture, mean that concerns about the way we look start younger, last longer, and affect more people than ever before'.[1] The impact of appearance on the way that others treat us, and on the way we feel about ourselves, is fast gaining recognition as a societal problem.

Against this backdrop, it is surprising that there is only one provision in the Equality Act 2010 ('the Act') which deals with appearance concerns – those affecting people with 'severe disfigurements'.[2] And even this limited provision has remained stubbornly consigned to the shadows. Since it was introduced in 1995,[3] it has produced few reported cases and has been largely ignored within academia. Moreover, many people living with a disfigurement are not even aware that this act exists,[4] despite surveys consistently indicating that they suffer elevated levels of discrimination, hate crime and socioeconomic disadvantage.[5] This suggests a mismatch; high instances of reported disfigurement discrimination relative to very low numbers of disfigurement discrimination

[1] House of Commons Women and Equalities Committee, *Changing the Perfect Picture: An Inquiry into Body Image* (Sixth Report of Session 2019-21, HC274) 5. Contains Parliamentary information licensed under the Open Parliament Licence v3.0.

[2] Equality Act 2010, sched 1 s3.

[3] Disability Discrimination Act 1995.

[4] Changing Faces, 'Disfigurement in the UK' (*Changing Faces*, 2017) 37. Nearly half of the respondents in this survey did not know that severe disfigurement was included within the scope of the Act.

[5] Ibid 12–41.

claims. Using this mismatch as a starting point, this book evaluates the law on disfigurement and appearance equality.

The evidence presented here will show that people with disfigurements often face prejudice, exclusion and discrimination across life contexts, including in employment in Great Britain,[6] which is the focus of this book. It will argue that the law's response to this evidence is flawed – both by its own limited scope and its failure to understand the perspectives of those people who may need to use it. And it will begin to sketch out different approaches to the complex social problem of discrimination against people with disfigurements.

1.1 About This Book

The first few chapters survey the relevant law on disfigurement equality and construct an evaluative framework of equality objectives. After this introduction, Chapter 2 explores an important premise which underlies this critique of the law: it examines the idea that disfigurement inequality is a problem which merits a *legal* response – namely the granting of protective rights under the Act. It concludes that, despite some uncomfortable distinctions, there is a compelling case for a legal response in this area. The nature of law's current response is then laid out. Relevant parts of the international legal framework – including EU law, the UN Convention on the Rights of Persons with Disabilities ('CRPD') and decisions of the European Court of Human Rights ('ECtHR') applying the European Convention on Human Rights ('ECHR') – are explained by reference to the models of disability which implicitly inform them.

Chapter 3 probes the meaning of the word 'equality'. It outlines a multidimensional, substantive conception of equality, as adopted by the UN Committee for the Rights of Persons with Disabilities. But it notes the Act's lack of engagement with some aspects of this ideal. The Act's scope is both more limited and more individualised than this substantive concept might demand. Making sense of what law *might* intend to contribute to meeting equality ideals is difficult but necessary, as it can provide a benchmark against which to evaluate the law. With this in mind, the chapter proposes five potential objectives, which are guided by the Act's scope. These range from changing attitudes and shaping perceived social norms through to influencing behaviours or compensating victims of

[6] The Act does not apply in Northern Ireland.

negative treatment. These potential objectives are used as a framework for assessment of law's contribution throughout the rest of the book.

The middle chapters scrutinise the law on severe disfigurement equality doctrinally and empirically to establish its limited impact, and the reasons for this. Drawing on original interview data about both life with a disfigurement and employer responses to it, they interrogate the gap between real life and the working of the law. Chapter 4 draws on both existing research and semi-structured interviews with people with visible differences to explain what we know about the human experience – both psychological and social – of having a disfigurement. For instance, are particular types of disfigurement more vulnerable to discrimination than others? Are certain life contexts impacted more acutely? Are coping mechanisms commonly used? It considers the link between physical appearance and perceived personality traits. And it challenges common assumptions – like the idea that more severe disfigurements are always worse to live with (an erroneous assumption which lives on undaunted in the law). Despite methodological difficulties in researching such a dynamic and underexplored area, the chapter identifies significant disadvantage in looking different. With this in mind, the chapter probes how people with lived experience of visible difference understand their experiences and relate them to the law. Exploring the legal consciousness of this group of people provides a partial insight into the low numbers of claims brought under the relevant part of equality law. It interrogates the gulf between what the law says on paper and how it works in real life, revealing tensions and mixed messages which undermine law's potential for effectiveness.

Chapter 5 addresses the application of the law on disfigurement from the point of view of employers. It analyses the findings from interviews with HR and equality, diversity and inclusion (EDI) professionals about their approaches to disfigurement equality at work. It explores employer approaches to visible difference in a variety of contexts – from recruitment to workplace culture to making reasonable adjustments. The chapter reveals considerable uncertainty amongst employers about how to address the social barriers of looking different. This uncertainty is addressed by guidance in Appendix 1. Moreover, drawing on literature about the legal consciousness of human resources departments, it also uncovers tensions in the daily reality of HR practice which may impact both their ability and motivation to create appearance-inclusive workplaces.

Chapter 6 uses doctrinal analysis to ask what the word 'disfigurement' means, and whether we can justify treating disfigurement differently from the related concepts of appearance and obesity. It identifies significant gaps created by a law which only protects a small subset of people experiencing appearance disadvantage – those with severe disfigurements – and which may exclude many of those many of those disabled by social barriers because of other aesthetic differences, such as those experiencing hair loss, those whose bodies are differently sized or those with facial movement impairments (such as facial palsy or synkinesis). It doubts whether these inconsistencies and mixed messages can be justified. It also considers whether other protected characteristics – such as sex or age – can be drafted in to fill the gaps in legal protection but concludes that this may amplify the inconsistencies within the law.

Chapter 7 considers the severity threshold in the Act. Examining how the law establishes severity, it asks whether the threshold can be justified – particularly given that the Act's standard definition of disability (which is based on functional deficit) applies a lower threshold of substantiality. It argues that the severity threshold is out of step with the lived experience of visible difference and explores whether the concept of perceptive discrimination can be used to bypass this problematic threshold. The chapter also addresses the problem of complex conditions – those which include both an aspect of disfigurement and of function – and concludes that, mirroring academic debate about the rigidity of models of disability, the law's approach is not flexible enough to encompass all types of disabling barrier holistically.

Chapter 8 draws on sociological literature in debating whether law – however drafted – is capable of solving the complex problem of discrimination against people who look different. It argues that, although we should not expect too much of law in tackling the complex social problem of appearance bias, strategically targeted laws can sometimes play a part in changing attitudes, norms and behaviours. While prohibitions on discrimination are important for remedial purposes, other types of legal and social reform may be better placed to create the conditions for greater inclusion of people with visible differences.

The final chapters consider how relevant equality objectives might be better achieved. Chapter 9 draws on the evidence outlined earlier in the book to evaluate a range of possible legal interventions. Structured according to the five potential equality objectives outlined earlier, the measures include steps to increase the positive visibility of people with disfigurements in daily life, methods of motivating employers to become appearance-inclusive and changes to influential institutions outside the employment context. They also include a range of legislative reforms to replace the severe disfigurement provision with a better remedial mechanism, such as the creation of a new protected characteristic of disfigurement or the reformulation of the definition of disability.

Chapter 10 questions whether law should widen its lens to address general appearance discrimination too. Would a protected characteristic of appearance offer viable legal rights to the many millions of us who do not have a disfigurement but are less-than-beautiful in some way? For example, is appearance objective enough to be adjudicated in law? Is a clear distinction between mutable and immutable aspects of appearance important – or even possible given increasing medico-cosmetic opportunities to change the way our bodies look? Do we have an unobjectionable nomenclature to describe appearance and attractiveness in legal terms? And could we swallow well-meaning employers' attempts to measure the attractiveness of their staff for the purposes of diversity monitoring? The discussion draws on examples of comparative laws in France and America. Both countries have adopted wider conceptions of appearance equality (despite the US having draconian ugly laws in place until the 1970s which prevented 'unsightly' beggars – such as those with disfigurements – from being seen in public).[7] And America's laws have seen a recent period of growth, with Binghampton, New York, the latest to vote such a law onto its statute books in 2023.[8] However, both sets of laws remain little used so far, despite evidence showing that appearance discrimination remains prevalent.[9] How could we ensure that a protected characteristic of appearance in the UK avoided a similar fate?

1.2 Key Claims

Three key claims will be developed throughout this book. The first, which is fleshed out in Chapter 2 primarily, is that there is an ideological tension about the meaning of disability in both the Act, and the international legal framework which has shaped it. That tension stems from whether disability should be conceptualised as an individual, functional limitation resulting from impairment, or as the result of the interaction between impairment and wider social barriers. The Act's main definition of disability epitomises the former approach, because it seeks to identify adverse effects on someone's ability to carry out activities resulting from

[7] On this, see Susan M Schweik, *The Ugly Laws: Disability in Public* (New York University Press 2009).

[8] New York City Administrative Code, Title 8 Chap 1 §8-107 (1).

[9] See Deborah Rhodes, *The Beauty Bias* (Oxford University Press 2010); and further Chapter 10.

impairment.[10] The severe disfigurement provision, on the other hand, represents the latter; the barriers resulting from looking different are usually rooted in society and the attitudes of others, not in function. The severe disfigurement provision is therefore a rare expression of social model principles in the Act. Despite this, the detail of the Act and case law under it still serve to reinforce the primacy of the individual, medical model of disability. For example, as Chapters 6 and 7 explore, narrowness in the way the disfigurement provision has been both drafted and interpreted undermines its social model logic.

The second claim, explored primarily in Chapters 4 and 5, is that this conceptual tension is also present in the lived experiences of both people with visible differences and HR managers within employers. The internalisation of medical model concepts shapes the way that these two different groups of actors perceive, apply and use the law, serving to undermine it even further. For example, many people with visible differences do not self-identify as disabled because they understand disability in purely functional terms. This impacts the way they feel about the law. And HR managers often see their role in supporting disabled employees in functional terms only, without anticipating the social barriers of looking different, or knowing how to create appearance-inclusive workplaces.

My third claim is that the rights to non-discrimination granted to people with severe disfigurements under the Act appear largely ineffective. There are few signs of the kinds of changes which the Act, judged by its own scope, might seem to aim for. There is sparse evidence of attitudinal or behavioural change towards people with visible differences in the workplace since severe disfigurement was first protected by disability equality law[11] and there are considerable limitations in the remedial mechanism which it offers to people who are discriminated against because of visible difference. I argue that, while changes to the Act hold some promise, we may be asking too much of even a reformed equality law, unless accompanied by other legal and policy interventions designed to address the social barriers of different appearances.

1.3 Scope and Limitations

As this area of law has received very little academic attention to date, there is a lot of ground to cover. As such, I have not been able to do

[10] Equality Act 2010 (n 2) s6.

[11] The Disability Discrimination Act 1995, sched 1 s3.

justice to everything which could be relevant and difficult choices have been necessary. These exclusions are not a reflection on the importance of the issues, but more on the practicalities of squeezing everything into one book. One exclusion relates to personal styling and image choices – hairstyles, make-up, piercings, clothing, tattoos and so on – as a form of self-expression. These choices matter to many people. The extent to which organisations should legitimately be able to control these appearance features as part of the worker/hirer relationship is debatable, especially when expecting workers to conform to a set appearance standard can place a greater demand to assimilate aesthetically on some groups of people than others[12] and can force people to engage in dangerous practices such as dieting and cosmetic surgery. Beyond a few brief mentions, this book does not set out to contribute to that debate.

Another exclusion relates to the overlap between appearance and other protected characteristics, such as sex, race, age and religion. This overlap can be found in the law itself – such as when hairstyles common among certain racial groups are banned, or when policies preventing the wearing of any religious symbols are imposed at work. The book makes a few brief allusions to this regulatory overlap but does not attempt the systematic analysis of gaps and inconsistencies which this topic deserves. The overlap can also be found in researching lived experiences. For example, although it is often assumed that visible difference matters less as you get older, studies show that this is not always the case, and other factors – such as job type – may impact too. A book on the complexity of appearance intersectionality would be valuable, but that is not a task undertaken here.

The last exclusion worthy of specific mention relates to appearance laws internationally. Notwithstanding a few brief forays in Chapters 2, 9 and 10 the book does not attempt to map visible difference laws internationally, concentrating instead on Britain. There are many unknowns in the international context. I am not aware, for example, of any resource which maps those countries that treat visible difference as a disability. Or indeed any research which seeks to understand the impact of disability status on the availability of healthcare or social security benefits for people affected by visible difference globally. Studies exploring the definitions and terminology relating to appearance globally would also be

[12] Kenji Yoshino, 'The Pressure to Cover' *New York Times magazine online* (New York, 15 January 2006) <www.nytimes.com/2006/01/15/magazine/the-pressure-to-cover.html> accessed 25 October 2023.

useful, particularly those which have found expression in the law. These gaps deserve to be written about, but I do not attempt to do so in this book.

Finally, I should stress that my two interview studies in this book were qualitative and small-scale by design, so no claim is made as to statistical representativeness. We would have much to learn from wider consultation with the visible difference community, and from long-term research measuring changes in attitudes and behaviours in response to legal changes and other interventions. I hope that this book will provide a foundation for future research to narrow the gaps in existing knowledge.

1.4 Terminology

Finally, a word about terminology. Some people and representative organisations in this area are reluctant to use the word 'disfigurement' to describe their appearance. 'Visible difference' is a frequently used alternative, but this is not straightforward in the context of legal research, not least because 'disfigurement' is the word used in the Act itself. The phrase 'visible difference' can also lack clarity, meaning different things to different people at different times. One might conclude, for example, that a broken leg is a visible difference because it is a physical variance which can be seen – but few of us would class a broken leg as a disfigurement. The same goes for hair which has been dyed purple. There are both points of overlap and points of difference between the terms 'visible difference' and 'disfigurement'. There are strong arguments to suggest that law's terminology should reflect the language adopted by the relevant community themselves, rather than imposing labels which are convenient for lawyers. But in this area and many others, law has not done so. As it is not possible to critique the legislation without engaging with its wording, the two terms ('disfigurement' and 'visible difference') are used interchangeably in this book, with visible difference intended as a synonym for disfigurement.

The concept of large body size also raises difficult terminological problems. There are many words used to describe people to whom this concept applies: fat, obese, overweight, large, corpulent and so on. Feelings run high about the correct term(s) to use, and views can change rapidly. 'Obese' tends to be favoured in medical contexts, but many people prefer not to use this word to describe themselves.[13] At one

[13] Deborah McPhail and Michael Orsini, 'Fat Acceptance as Social Justice' (2021) 193 *Canadian Medical Association Journal* E1398.

conference which I attended, the 'e' in the word 'obesity' was replaced by an asterisk for this reason. The fat acceptance movement, particularly in the US, seeks to reclaim the word 'fat' in a descriptive sense, to free it from the negative social connotations commonly attributed to it.[14] But again, many people feel uncomfortable with this choice of word. A recent study found that, where a discussion is necessary, many people prefer talking about variations in 'weight'.[15] Given the lack of a clear consensus on this issue, I have chosen to use a mixture of terms throughout the book.

The terminology of 'law' is also more complex than at first it might appear. As this book sets out to evaluate the effectiveness of a particular provision in the Act, law here refers to legislation, and the case law, regulations and guidance which accompany it. However, to end the definition there suggests that law is wholly separate from society; an authoritative source which exists independent of the way we use it. As the empirical work summarised in this book progressed, this interpretation became increasingly difficult to sustain; discussions with participants revealed different social understandings of law in real life, which often had a much greater impact on their choices than whatever the statute book said. Once they slide off the page of the statute book into real life, rights under equality law become tangled with issues of identity, workplace customs and social meanings. As Catherine Albiston and Gwendolyn Leachman argue, 'institutions, actors on the ground, and widely shared cultural beliefs shape what law will mean in practice',[16] leading to '[t]he insight that law can be found not only in the courts and legislature, but also in bureaucratic organizations like workplaces and schools, in prosecutorial and police discretionary decisions and in lawlike social customs and legal understandings that permeate everyday life'.[17] This book draws in aspects of both perspectives. It critiques the Act and accompanying decisions as a set of rules and considers the practical implications of using these in the courtroom. But in places it also turns its gaze on the juncture between law and real life to understand the meanings of law to employers and people with visible differences at work.

14 Ibid.

15 Adrian Brown and Stuart W Flint, 'Preferences and Emotional Response to Weight Related Terminology Used by Healthcare Professionals to Describe Body Weight in People Living with Overweight and Obesity' (2021) 11 Clinical Obesity 3.

16 Catherine R Albiston and Gwendolyn M Leachman, 'Law as an Instrument of Social Change' in James Wright (ed) *International Encyclopaedia of the Social and Behavioural Sciences* 13 (2nd edn, Elsevier 2015) 543.

17 Ibid.

2

Law's Response to Disfigurement Inequality

2.1 Justifying a Legal Response

This chapter addresses two related questions. First, it asks why disfigurement inequality is a problem which merits a *legal* response – namely protection under relevant legislation. Second, after setting out law's current response, it questions the logic of law's chosen form.

The answer to the first question – whether disfigurement inequality justifies a legal response – sounds obvious; as will be demonstrated, people with disfigurements can be unfairly disadvantaged financially, socially and emotionally by their appearance. But it doesn't automatically follow that law should intervene, because there are plenty of group disadvantages which equality law does not address. Legal measures may sometimes not be particularly apt; the disadvantage caused by poverty, for example, would seem better served by political measures to redistribute resources than by legal measures to promote equality and recognition. But other forms of group disadvantage – such as social class[1] or perhaps obesity – might seem apt for a legal response but remain outside the scope of equality law. Hence group disadvantage is not enough on its own to engage equality law; something more – disadvantage *plus* – is needed.

The search for 'disadvantage *plus*' criteria by which to assess groups calling for inclusion within equality law has generated a significant body of debate. Among them, three proposed criteria – immutability, dignity and stigma – have gained prominence in the discussion. Turning to the first of these criteria, immutability is the idea that rights under equality

[1] Campaigners have argued that social class should become a protected characteristic. See, for example, British Psychological Society, 'BPS Launches #Makeit10 Campaign' (2022) <www.bps.org.uk/psychologist/bps-launches-makeit10-campaign> accessed 25 October 2023. Cf Lizzie Barmes and Kate Malleson, 'The Case for Caution in Making Social Class a Protected Characteristic under the UK's Equality Act 2010' (Oxford Human Rights Hub, 3 August 2023) <https://ohrh.law.ox.ac.uk/the-case-for-caution-in-making-social-class-a-protected-characteristic-under-the-uks-equality-act-2010/> accessed 3 August 2023.

law should extend to protect those traits which are innate within the individual, rather than traits she has chosen. Focusing on disadvantage beyond the control of the individual has a lot of attraction in principle, but the reality is far from simple. Pregnancy, for example, is a characteristic which can't comfortably be categorised as either chosen or immutable,[2] despite meriting protection. The recognition of growing numbers of philosophical beliefs also puts strain on the dividing line between chosen and immutable characteristics. Ethical veganism is a case in point; its recognition as a philosophical belief sits uncomfortably with the fact that 84 per cent of people in that group choose to return to eating meat at some point in their lives.[3] Conversely, other characteristics such as height, intelligence, left-handedness and genetic predisposition would appear to be permanently immutable yet remain out of reach of equality law.

Where disfigurement is concerned, immutability is easily satisfied. Most disfigurements result either directly from a medical condition or injury (such as a cleft lip or a burn injury) or indirectly (such as scars from self-harm resulting from depression) and are therefore immutable. There is an exception though: tattoos. Tattoos are not immutable but are (almost)[4] always a deliberate acquisition. This logic is mirrored in the Act, which excludes unremoved tattoos and piercings from the scope of protection.[5]

But it might be going too far to say that getting a tattoo is mutable in the sense of being *chosen*. The concept of choice implies being able to exercise free will to select between options.[6] To sustain an argument that tattoos are always 'chosen' ignores the impact of social context on the options available. Research from Australia suggests that tattoos are more prevalent among those with lower levels of education (and, for men, among those practising a trade rather than a professional role).[7] If our personal

[2] Sandra Fredman, *Discrimination Law* (2nd edn, Oxford University Press 2011) 131.

[3] Humane Research Council, 'Study of Current and Former Vegetarians and Vegans: Initial Findings' (Faunalytics, 2014) <https://bit.ly/43qxBZq> accessed 19 December 2023.

[4] Examples exist of people being tattooed against their will, in contexts ranging from gang membership, to oppressed minorities, to drunken stag nights.

[5] Equality Act 2010 (Disability) Regulations 2010, SI 2010/2128, s5.

[6] Sandra Fredman, 'Substantive Equality Revisited' (2016) 14 International Journal of Constitutional Law 712, 730.

[7] Bruce Tranter and Ruby Grant, 'A Class Act? Social Background and Body Modifications in Australia' (2018) 54 Journal of Sociology 412. A similar correlation can be observed between social class and deaths from alcoholism. See Charlotte Probst and others, 'Socioeconomic Differences in Alcohol-Attributable Mortality Compared with All-Cause Mortality: A Systematic Review and Meta-analysis' (2014) 43 International Journal of Epidemiology 1314.

context determines the personal narratives open to us, the idea that traits are chosen – and therefore mutable – starts to feel uncomfortable.

Interestingly, though, the law takes an uncharacteristically expansive stance on people who choose to have their tattoos surgically removed; the exclusion of tattoos under the Act only applies to unremoved inkings. (You may wonder why anyone would need anti-discrimination rights relating to a tattoo which has been removed. The answer could be that tattoo removal rarely succeeds in completely taking away the tattoo, but instead fades it, often leaving it visible to some degree, sometimes with scarring from the removal process too). Roughly 30 per cent of people regret tattoos they got when they were younger,[8] but the cost of tattoo removal is prohibitive for many. This means that only those with sufficient resources will stand a chance of buying their way back into the scope of the Act if tattoo regret sets in down the line. This can be contrasted with the Act's approach to addictions,[9] where the exclusion from scope is permanent; a recovered alcoholic can forever be treated less favourably without legal redress under the Act, no matter how long she has been sober for. If the choice and budget to remove a tattoo can be recognised by equality law, one might wonder why the choice and strength to stay sober in the long term cannot. With distinctions like this, mutability as a justification begins to creak at the seams.

The second disadvantage *plus* factor proposed as a justification for the scope of equality law is dignity. Under this concept, discrimination is more than just different treatment; it is different treatment for a reason which touches on the essence of the person. This moral touchstone helps to prevent equality being reduced to its lowest common denominator[10] by treating everyone equally badly. In other words, dignity helps to ensure that the way people are treated respects what it means to be human.

But dignity has its challenges. As a concept, it can be hard to pin down,[11] making it easily manipulable and open to abuse.[12] Rory O'Connell argues that dignity is sometimes conceptualised as materialistic justice: ensuring that the people most in need receive social

[8] Charles Bankhead, 'Tattoo Me: Tales of Regret and No Regrets' (Medpage, 2013) <www.medpagetoday.com/meetingcoverage/aad/37730> accessed 25 October 2023.

[9] Equality Act 2010 (Disability) Regulations 2010 (n 5) s3. Note the exception of addictions arising from medical treatment or medically prescribed drugs.

[10] Fredman, 'Substantive Equality Revisited' (n 6) 724.

[11] Christopher McCrudden, 'Human Dignity and Judicial Interpretation of Human Rights' (2008) 19 *European Journal of International Law* 655, 655.

[12] Fredman, 'Substantive Equality Revisited' (n 6) 725.

goods.[13] At other times, it refers to the place of the individual in society, and their right to feel valued and make autonomous decisions.[14] Or to the idea of protecting an ethical, good way of life, free from immorality.[15] This 'plasticity'[16] of meaning may be why dignity can be hard to reconcile with the current scope of domestic discrimination law; as an example, why does differential treatment because of age touch on human dignity while differential treatment because of personality does not? Is it really a greater affront to individual dignity to be refused a job because you are deemed too old than because you are deemed too boring, shy or annoying?

But while the exact parameters of dignity may be uncertain, there is little room for debate about its application to the concept of disfigurement. If we interpret dignity as a right to feel valued as a human being, physical appearance is key. The way we look is intricately connected with our self-esteem and our sense of who we are. This is particularly true in our increasingly image-based digital culture, in which curating a visual display of one's life is front and centre to many people in feeling valued. If dignity means materialistic justice or personal autonomy, looking different can affect how other people treat us and judge our worth, affecting our ability to get a fair share of social goods and to exercise free will in our life choices.[17] And if dignity is conceptualised in ethical terms emphasising the moral worth of the human condition, it is salient that disfigurement is often a physical representation of a significant life event – such as an accident, an illness, a war, or being the victim of a crime – the impact of which should not be trivialised. Dignity justifies a legal response to disfigurement discrimination too.

The final disadvantage *plus* factor to consider as an underlying rationale for equality law is stigma. Iyiola Solanke draws on Erving Goffman's work[18] in arguing that stigma is, in essence, 'a mark' or the 'potentially persistent social approbation which it triggers'.[19] The presence of stigma underlying discriminatory behaviour can be keenly felt on occasion. Solanke argues that an anti-stigma principle enables the law to focus

13 Rory O'Connell, 'The Role of Dignity in Equality Law: Lessons from Canada and South Africa' (2008) 6 *International Journal of Constitutional Law* 267, 274.
14 Ibid 273.
15 Ibid 272.
16 Ibid 284.
17 See Chapter 4.
18 Irving Goffman, *Notes on the Management of Spoiled Identity* (Penguin 1963).
19 Iyiola Solanke, *Discrimination as Stigma* (1st edn, Hart 2016) 36.

on the stigma attaching to a trait rather than issues of group identity.[20] This is important in relation to disfigurement because there does not (yet, at least) appear to be a clear collective identity of people with disfigurements in the same way that there is for some other marginalised groups of people. Solanke recognises that not all stigma merits protection, however; a mechanism (which she formulates as a series of questions[21]) can be used to divide rightly stigmatised characteristics from those which merit protection. She argues that while tattoos fall within the former camp, justifiably excluded from protection, disfigurements fall within the latter.

However, defining stigma in legal terms, with all its changing contextual variations, is troublesome. We might know it when we feel it but proving it could be difficult – perhaps the territory of unconscious bias testing. Goffman regarded stigma as affecting most people from time to time,[22] indicating a widespread and fluid concept incompatible with fixed labels. There is also a risk that the same stigma which makes a trait deserving of protection under equality law might prevent those experiencing it from wanting to wear that label as a badge.[23]

Stigma is different from both immutability and dignity in focusing its gaze on societal reactions to a trait, rather than on the origin or nature of the trait itself. This is useful because societal reactions are not always objectively proportionate to the trait. By way of example, Chapter 4 will show that, on occasion, people with minor disfigurements experience worse harassment than people with objectively more severe disfigurements. Using stigma as a litmus test of disadvantage *plus* helps to ensure that legal protections mirror the real scope of disadvantage. This has become even more important now that, for many of us, interactions are no longer restricted to the people we meet locally. With technology now enabling vast numbers of interactions within minutes from a worldwide audience, the potential for stigma to manifest in harassment and abuse is multiplied exponentially.

To sum up, none of the three rationales discussed – immutability, dignity or stigma – individually offers a fail-safe way of sifting all traits deserving legal protection from other characteristics. But their combined potential is greater, recognising that different justifications underlie particular characteristics and their contexts. Whichever rationale(s) we

[20] Ibid 134.

[21] Ibid 20.

[22] Goffman, *Notes on the Management of Spoiled Identity* (n 18) 152.

[23] Tom Shakespeare, *Disability Rights and Wrongs Revisited* (2nd edn, Routledge 2014) 95.

apply, though, it is clear that disfigurement does *matter* legally and its inclusion within the scope of equality law is justified.

Regrettably, deciding that disfigurement inequality is worthy of a legal response doesn't guarantee that the legal response which follows will be effective. Protection under equality law is not an end in itself, and its ability to be a means to an end is still a moot point. Later chapters will explore this further in considering what type of law – if any – might stand the best possible chance of reducing the problem of disfigurement inequality. But first I will consider the approach to disfigurement inequality which has already been adopted in legislation.

2.2 Law's Response

2.2.1 Equality Act 2010

In Britain, discrimination against someone with a visible difference is, at least to some extent, prohibited by disability provisions in the Act. The main definition of disability is contained within s6:

> A person (P) has a disability if—
>
> (a) P has a physical or mental impairment, and
> (b) the impairment has a substantial and long-term adverse effect on P's ability to carry out normal day-to-day activities.[24]

While someone with a visible difference, without other functional limitations, would be unlikely to satisfy this definition, Schedule 1[25] deems that 'an impairment which consists of a severe disfigurement is to be *treated as* having a substantial adverse effect on the ability to carry out normal day-to-day activities'. This removes the need for the person to demonstrate the functional disadvantage required by the standard definition, but they still have to demonstrate that the impairment is long term (meaning that it has lasted, or is likely to last, for at least twelve months, or for the rest of the life of the person affected).

This idea of deemed disability is confusing; the Act creates one understanding of disability based on functional impairment (what you can't do), but then bolts a category of non-functional impairment onto the end (what you look like). The connection between these two ideas is obscure.

[24] Note also para 5A of sched 1.
[25] Equality Act 2010, sched 1 s3.

To explore this, we must set aside legal definitions for a moment and think about wider concepts of disability.

Traditionally, understandings of disability were based on an analysis of the limitations of an individual resulting from medical impairment – what the person couldn't do. This inward-focused understanding of disability is often referred to as the 'medical model'. The medical model would define the disability of someone in a wheelchair as an inability to climb stairs, and the disability of someone who is deaf as an inability to hear; disability is located within the individual – it is what the person is unable to do. There is no room in a medical model analysis to question why aeroplanes aren't built to be wheelchair accessible, or why children don't learn sign language at school. The medical model sees difference as individual deficiency.

The medical model has been disowned by many within the disability rights movement. One of the main objections is that it places the responsibility on the individual and perpetuates stereotypes of disabled people as helpless. This encourages an approach focused on charity and welfare towards those who are disabled, rather than one based on recognition and rights.[26] It also aims, where possible, to treat disability in medical terms to achieve society's non-disabled norms,[27] often contributing to the removal of individual choice and control from disabled people. By locating the 'problem' within the individual, the medical model approach assumes that, where possible, the person's difference should be treated to achieve sameness; it ignores a role for society in preventing impairment translating into disability.[28]

In 1983, Mike Oliver coined the use of the phrase 'the social model'[29] to describe a different approach emerging from the work of the Union of the Physically Impaired Against Segregation. He described this as 'nothing more or less fundamental than a switch away from focusing on the physical or mental limitations of particular individuals to the way the physical structures, societal systems, culture and social environments impose limitations on certain groups or categories of people'.[30] Arlene

[26] Arlene S Kanter, *The Development of Disability Rights under International Law* (Routledge 2015) 46.

[27] Andrea Broderick, 'The Long and Winding Road to Equality and Inclusion for Persons with Disabilities' (PhD thesis, Maastricht 2015) 22.

[28] Kanter, *The Development of Disability Rights under International Law* (n 26) 46.

[29] Mike Oliver, Bob Sapey and Pam Thomas, *Social Work with Disabled People* (Macmillan 2012) 15.

[30] Ibid.

Kanter explains that, whereas the medical model 'locates the "problem of disability" in the person', the social model 'views disability as part of the diversity of the human experience, placing responsibility on society to remove the physical, environmental, attitudinal, and legal barriers that prevent people with disabilities from exercising their rights to inclusion and participation in society'.[31]

A key aspect of this British social model concept is social oppression; disabled people are seen as a casualty of a society structured around 'the social relations of production and reproduction in modern capitalist societies'.[32] With society focused on materialistic ideals, the perceptions of disabled people as economically hindered leads to exclusion and oppression.[33] Social model understandings therefore engender a political struggle between the (disabled) oppressed and the system which oppresses them.

This social model concept is noted for its rigid distinction between impairment and disability; impairment could be 'lacking all or part of a limb'[34] or 'mechanism of the body'[35] whereas disability is 'the disadvantage or restriction of activity caused by a contemporary social organisation which takes little or no account of people who have physical impairments and thus excludes them from participation in the mainstream of social activities'.[36] As an interaction between an individual's personal factors and environmental factors, disability is context-dependent, so what is accepted as normal or even desirable within one culture can create disability within another.

For many, the social model has provided a life-changing shift in outlook. But it is not without its critics. Some people criticise the social model for its singular fixation on disability which, they argue, ignores the combined disadvantage found at the intersection of disability and other characteristics – such as that experienced by disabled women, for

31 Kanter, *The Development of Disability Rights under International Law* (n 26) 46.

32 Mark Priestley, 'We're All Europeans Now! The Social Model of Disability and European Social Policy' in C Barnes and G Mercer (eds), *The Social Model of Disability: Europe and the Majority World* (The Disability Press 2005) 23.

33 M Berghs, K Atkin and H Graham, 'Implications for Public Health Research of Models and Theories of Disability: A Scoping Study and Evidence Synthesis' (2016) NIHR Journals Library 4.

34 UPIAS and the Disability Alliance, 'Fundamental Principles of Disability' (1975) 14 cited in Mike Oliver, *Understanding Disability* (2nd edn, Palgrave Macmillan 2009) 42.

35 Ibid.

36 Oliver, *Understanding Disability* (n 34) 42.

example.[37] This point has salience in relation to conditions affecting appearance, where research shows that other personal characteristics such as gender and age can sometimes affect someone's lived experience.[38] Others argue that the social model's rigid focus on external barriers denies the reality of living with an impairment[39] and ignores the importance of the body as the medium through which social barriers are encountered. Pain, for example, can be a disabling effect of impairment which cannot be adequately explained by reference to external barriers.[40] Shakespeare and Watson memorably argued that '[m]ost activists concede that behind closed doors they talk about aches and pains and urinary tract infections, even while they deny any relevance of the body while they are out campaigning'.[41]

Visible difference could perhaps be seen as a poster child for a hard social model concept; disfigurement does not necessarily create functional limitation or pain, and this lends itself well on paper to a rigid division between impairment and (socially created) disability. But the lived experience of visible difference can be more nuanced than this. One interviewee, who had experienced a facial paralysis from which they were recovering, expressed an ongoing sensation of difference even after their condition had improved to the point that no one else could see it. They expressed this powerfully as a feeling of 'fall[ing] between the gaps somehow'; a physical sensation of not feeling quite right, and not fitting in, even though their condition was no longer visible to others. At that point of their recovery, the hurdles they were navigating were not necessarily socially created but physically embodied. This observation suggests that a rigid division between impairment and disability can risk silencing part of the lived experience of disfigurement.

Returning to legal definitions, it is models of disability that provide a conceptual link between disfigurement and disability. The definition of

[37] Theresia Degener, 'Disability in a Human Rights Context' (2016) 5 Laws 35, 10.

[38] See Section 4.1.

[39] Dimitris Anastasiou and James M Kauffman, 'The Social Model of Disability: Dichotomy between Impairment and Disability' (2013) 38 Journal of Medicine and Philosophy 441, 449.

[40] Liz Crow, 'Renewing the Social Model of Disability' (*Roaring Girl Productions*, July 1992) <www.roaring-girl.com/work/renewing-the-social-model-of-disability/> accessed 25 June 2019.

[41] Tom Shakespeare and Nicholas Watson, 'The Social Model of Disability: An Outdated Ideology?' in Sharon Barnartt and Barbara Altman (eds), *Exploring Theories and Expanding Methodologies: Where We Are and Where We Need to Go To*, vol 2 (Emerald Group Publishing Limited 2001) 12.

disability in s6 of the Act provides a good example of a medical model approach. The focus is on what activities the person can't do because of impairment. But disfigurement does not fit the traditional medical model mould because it often lacks the functional limits on which this concept of disability is based; the impact is not usually on the individual's ability to carry out activities, but on the perceptions and attitudes of other people. Pursuant to this analysis, a disfigurement may be an impairment, but disablement arises from the expectations and reactions of society which oppress people who are visibly different. It is a social model analysis which explains the siting of disfigurement within disability law; the individual's participation in society can be disabled even when the functions of their body are not. The deeming provision in the Act (which deems someone with a qualifying severe disfigurement to have a disability even though they don't meet the Act's usual test for disability) is therefore an ideological tangle; it bolts a discrete social model provision onto an otherwise medical model definition.

This ideological tangle may have its roots in international law. A closer examination of international law reveals that, while social model principles have been adopted in some instruments and contexts, the medical model still clings firmly to life within others. To illustrate this wider ideological confusion, the discussion below examines the concept of disability in three different international instruments – the Convention on the Rights of Persons with Disabilities ('CRPD'), the EU Employment Equality Framework Directive ('Directive 2000/78') and the European Convention on Human Rights ('ECHR').

2.2.2 Disability in the CRPD

The purpose of the CRPD (which was ratified by the UK in 2009) is to 'promote, protect and ensure the full and equal enjoyment of all human rights and fundamental freedoms by all persons with disabilities, and to promote respect for their inherent dignity'.[42] Although not the first treaty to include measures to combat discrimination, many of its predecessors (including the Universal Declaration of Human Rights[43]) failed to mention disability specifically as a ground of discrimination, hiding it within

[42] UN Convention on the Rights of Persons with Disabilities (12 December 2006) A/RES/61/106, art 1.

[43] Universal Declaration of Human Rights 1948 UN (10 December 1948) General Assembly Resolution 217A (III)).

a provision preventing discrimination on grounds of 'other status'.[44] So, while arguably not creating many new obligations, the CRPD acts as a 'new tool to make the fight against discrimination on the basis of disability more informed and determined'[45] and to set out what human rights mean in the context of disability.

Perhaps one of the most important features of the CRPD is its open recognition of the disabling power of social barriers. Article 1 offers a description (note, not a definition) of disability wide enough to encompass both disfigurement and other types of disability:

> Persons with disabilities include those who have long-term physical, mental, intellectual or sensory impairments which in interaction with various barriers may hinder their full and effective participation in society on an equal basis with others.[46]

This description makes no mention of functional limitation (and the Committee has expressly confirmed that the definition applies to disabilities 'that may or may not come with functional limitations').[47] It also imposes no substantiality or severity requirement; it is the consequence, not the level, of the impairments and their interaction which matters. The drafting of Article 1 (note the word 'include' and the description in the Preamble of disability as an 'evolving concept')[48] is also not fixed or exhaustive, enabling it to sidestep the accusations of rigidity sometimes levelled at the social model. Much of the substance of the CRPD also reflects a social model ideology, with measures targeted at changing society (such as awareness campaigns) sitting alongside those aiming to provide rights to the individual.

Despite the strong social model roots in the CRPD, the guidance which accompanies it refers to a human rights model approach.[49] Theresia Degener argues that the human rights model of disability in the CRPD

[44] Ibid art 2.

[45] United Nations, *The Convention on the Rights of Persons with Disabilities Training Guide* (United Nations 2014) 95.

[46] CRPD (n 42) art 1.

[47] UN Committee on the Rights of Persons with Disabilities, 'General Comment No.3 on Article 6' (2016) CRPD/C/GC/3, para 5.

[48] Wiebke Ringel, 'Non-discrimination, Accommodation, and Intersectionality under the CRPD: New Trends and Challenges for the UN Human Rights System' (2017) 20 Max Planck Yearbook of United Nations Law Online 98, 106.

[49] United Nations, *The Convention on the Rights of Persons with Disabilities Training Guide* (n 45) 10.

builds on social model principles[50] – it still sees disability as socially created rather than a problem within the individual. But while the social model grew from arguments about the structural inequality of disability, the human rights model stems from moral arguments[51] about how all people should be treated. It is therefore about dignity and universal rights which exist both with and without impairment; rights of socio-economic importance as well as non-discrimination.[52] The CRPD, for example, as an embodiment of the human rights model, encompasses positive rights (such as the right to earn a living) as well as negative rights (such as being free from abuse). Degener suggests that the human rights model is also better placed than the social model to acknowledge intersectional identity.[53] A slightly different analysis is found in the work of Anna Lawson and Angharad Beckett, who argue that the human rights model is best conceived not as an extension of the social model, but as complimentary to it. The distinction for them is one of focus: 'the human rights model is a model of disability policy, whereas the social model is a model of disability'.[54] It must be acknowledged that, however conceived, the differences between the social and human rights models are subtle relative to the conceptual gulf between the social and medical models of disability. To maintain a clear focus on this latter contradiction (which has important ramifications for people with visible differences), the nuances between the social and human rights models are not developed further in this book.

Enforcement of the CRPD in Britain is limited. It does not impose obligations directly on private sector bodies, and individuals cannot directly enforce it.[55] In states which signed the Optional Protocol,[56] people can submit allegations of breaches of the Convention to the Committee, who may decide to launch an inquiry into the actions of the relevant state. The UK signed the Optional Protocol. However, the limitations of this as an enforcement mechanism were exemplified when,

[50] Degener, 'Disability in a Human Rights Context' (n 37) 3.
[51] Ibid 4
[52] Ibid 5.
[53] Ibid 10.
[54] Anna Lawson and Angharad E Beckett, 'The Social and Human Rights Models of Disability: Towards a Complementarity Thesis' (2021) 25 The International Journal of Human Rights 348, 369.
[55] *Britlief v Birmingham City Council* [2020] ICR 653 (EAT).
[56] Optional Protocol to the Convention on the Rights of Persons with Disabilities (United Nations, 12 December 2006) A/RES/61/106.

following various complaints, the Committee opened an investigation[57] into changes to the benefits system in the UK under the Welfare Reform Act 2012. The conclusion of the inquiry was that 'grave or systematic violations of the rights of persons with disabilities'[58] were taking place, and recommendations for action were made. However, the government's public, written response was that it disagreed[59] with the findings of the inquiry. The CRPD contains no further legal enforcement mechanism after this point to hold states to account, despite continued public correspondence about it between the parties involved.[60] The perception of the CRPD's lack of legal teeth became very clear during the Parliamentary Joint Committee on Human Rights' session on the Rights of Disabled People to Independent Living (a reporting session required by the CRPD), when the Minister for Disabled People referred to the CRPD on several occasions as 'soft law' which 'does not have legal standing',[61] prompting a seven paragraph correction in the Session report as to its status as 'legally binding' and 'hard law'.[62]

As Great Britain is a dualist state, the CRPD is not incorporated into national law unless Parliament legislates to bring it into force (as, for example, it did by enacting the Human Rights Act 1998 to incorporate the ECHR). This has not happened.[63] So, the UK remains bound by its obligations under the CRPD, and a failure to comply with them constitutes a breach of international law, but lacks domestic enforceability.

Brexit does not withdraw the UK's ratification of the CRPD, but there may be an indirect impact. The EU has itself signed the CRPD, meaning

[57] United Nations Committee on the Rights of Persons with Disabilities, 'Inquiry Concerning the United Kingdom of Great Britain and Northern Ireland Carried Out by the Committee under Article 6 of the Optional Protocol to the Convention Report of the Committee' (2016) CRPD/C/15/R.2/Rev.1.

[58] Ibid 19.

[59] The United Kingdom Government, 'Response to the Report by the United Nations Committee on the Rights of Persons with Disabilities under Article 6 of the Optional Protocol to the Convention' (2017) 3 CRPD/C/17.R.3.

[60] Department for Work and Pensions and Disability Unit, 'UN Committee on the Rights of Persons with Disabilities 2016 Inquiry – UK 2021 Follow-Up Report' (UK Government, 2021).

[61] House of Lords and House of Commons Joint Committee on Human Rights, *Implementation of the Right of Disabled People to Independent Living* (23rd Report of Session 2010–2012, HL257 & HC1074) para 17.

[62] Ibid para 18.

[63] Note a related pledge in the last Labour Party manifesto: see Labour Party, 'Nothing about You, Without You: A Manifesto with and for Disabled People' (2017) <https://labour.org.uk/manifesto/a-more-equal-society/#fifth> accessed 4 July 2018.

that every piece of EU legislation produced, and every decision of the European Court of Justice, should (in theory at least) be upholding the principles and obligations set out in the CRPD. Post-Brexit, CRPD-compliant aspects of new European laws which come into force will not necessarily be reflected in domestic law. The UK's compliance with its obligations under the CRPD are therefore now in sharper focus.

2.2.3 Disability in the Decisions of the ECtHR

A similar approach to defining disability in line with a social model approach is emerging in the decisions of the European Court of Human Rights ('ECtHR'),[64] which domestic courts must 'take into account'.[65] Article 14 of the ECHR provides a right to non-discrimination related to other Convention rights. The ECtHR has held that this right not only encompasses disability but also health status, which it seems willing to apply even where there is no resulting functional limitation (in other words, where the recognised barriers are social, rather than medical). In the case of *I.B. v Greece*,[66] for example, an HIV-positive claimant was found to fall within Article 14 despite the fact that 'the nature of the applicant's job, which did not demand excessive effort, precluded the risk of a reduction in his capacity for work since, during the many years in which a person was merely HIV-positive, his or her working capacity was not substantially reduced'.[67] In the case of *Kiyutin v Russia*,[68] the court noted the historic stigma against and exclusion of people with HIV and afforded states a narrow margin of appreciation as a result. Consistent with the social model of disability, the court recognised the disabling impact of attitudinal barriers. It is submitted that a parallel argument could be made in relation to people with disfigurements who often face stigmatisation and exclusion. Where engaged,[69] the

[64] For a more detailed discussion, see Andrea Broderick, 'A Reflection on Substantive Equality Jurisprudence' (2015) 15 International Journal of Discrimination and the Law 101, 109.

[65] Human Rights Act 1998, s2(1). The obligation on the British parliament to comply with the ECHR is stronger; it must 'abide' by ECHR decisions – see Adam Wagner, 'Can Britain "Ignore Europe on Human Rights?"' (2011) (*UK Human Rights Blog*, 23 October 2011).

[66] *I.B. v Greece* App no 552/10 (ECtHR, 3 October 2013).

[67] Ibid para 86.

[68] *Kiyutin v Russia* (2011) ECHR 439, para 64.

[69] See Sandra Fredman, 'Emerging from the Shadows: Substantive Equality and Article 14 of the European Convention on Human Rights' (2016) 16 Human Rights Law Review 273, 275 for a discussion of the parasitic nature of Article 14.

wider reach of Article 14 may prove to be a useful interpretive tool in respect of shortcomings in domestic disfigurement law.

2.2.4 Disability in EU Law

As the EU is a party to the CRPD, the EU Employment Equality Framework Directive (Directive 2000/78) ('the Directive') 'must, as far as possible, be interpreted in a manner consistent with the Convention'.[70] Prior to Brexit, relevant domestic legislation, including the Act, needed to comply with the Directive, the ECHR and the CRPD, which would seem to have offered a good opportunity for a common approach. However, that opportunity was not seized, and case law on the Directive from the Court of Justice ('ECJ') has not consistently reflected CRPD principles[71] in this respect. While Brexit may offer greater flexibility to depart from this jurisprudence, the continuing influence of EU law (especially as it applied before Brexit) ensures that EU concepts of disability remain relevant.

In the case of *Ring*,[72] the ECJ provided a definition of disability which appeared to embrace the social model. It defined disability for the purposes of the Directive as:

> a limitation which results in particular from physical, mental or psychological impairments which in interaction with various barriers may hinder the full and effective participation of the person concerned in professional life on an equal basis with other workers.[73]

But subsequent applications of this definition were restrictive and have implications for disfigurement.[74] In the case of *Kaltoft*,[75] the court adopted the *Ring* definition but elaborated on the need for a limitation

[70] C-335/11 and C-337/11 *HK Danmark, acting on behalf of Ring v Dansk almennyttigt Boligselskab and HK Danmark, acting on behalf of Lond Skouboe Werge v Dansk Arbejdsgiverforening, acting on behalf of Pro Display A/S (Ring and Skouboe Werge)* [2013] 3 CMLR 21, para 32.

[71] Lisa Waddington, 'Saying All the Right Things and Still Getting It Wrong' (2015) 22 Maastricht Journal of European and Comparative Law 576, 583. See also Gauthier de Beco, 'Is Obesity a Disability? The Definition of Disability by the Court of Justice of the European Union and Its Consequences for the Application of EU Anti-Discrimination Law' (2016) 22 Columbia Journal of European Law 381.

[72] See (n 70).

[73] Ibid para 34.

[74] Waddington, 'Saying All the Right Things and Still Getting It Wrong' (n 71) 588.

[75] Case C-354/13 *FOA v Kommuneres Landsforening (Kaltoft)* [2015] 2 CMLR 19.

resulting from impairment. The case concerned obesity, and the court suggested that 'reduced mobility or the onset, in that person, of medical conditions preventing him from carrying out his work or causing discomfort when carrying out his professional activity'[76] could satisfy this definition. So, the limitation was interpreted as something the individual was physically unable, or less able, to do in professional life as a result of the impairment. As Lisa Waddington argues, 'this seems to render it difficult to interpret the Court's definition of disability as embracing individuals who experience no physical limitation, but who are only hampered by the discriminatory attitudes of others, discriminatory rules or provisions'.[77] This interpretation is strengthened by the reference in the subsequent case of *Daouidi* to a limitation of 'capacity'.[78] It is clear that the required limitation can be a partial hindrance rather than an absolute prevention, but someone who has no physical limitation at all, and is disabled purely by external attitudinal barriers (someone with a pure disfigurement, or someone who is HIV positive[79] but asymptomatic, perhaps), may not be disabled under the Directive.

This interpretation appears to create significant distance between the Directive's concept of disability, and that espoused by Article 1 of the CRPD, despite the latter purportedly being used to interpret the former. It means that Parliament and the courts have been receiving conflicting messages from the wider disability law framework about the scope of disability relating to impairments without functional limitation. This lack of functional consistency risks diluting the strong agenda for reform provided by the social model and the CRPD.

[76] Ibid para 60.

[77] Waddington, 'Saying All the Right Things and Still Getting It Wrong' (n 71) 587. For a more optimistic interpretation of *Kaltoft*, see Tamara Hervey and Philip Rostant, 'All About That Bass? Is Non-Ideal-Weight Discrimination Unlawful in the UK?' (2016) 79 (2) *Modern Law Review* 248–282, 268. But even if the CJEU in *Kaltoft* did intend to embrace the disabling nature of attitudinal barriers (as Hervey and Rostant suggest), this authority would now seem unlikely to assist potential claimants in Britain going forward: s.3 of the Retained EU Law (Revocation and Reform) Act 2023 removed the ability to rely on EU law using the principles of direct and indirect effect, and under s.6 of the EU (Withdrawal) Act 2018 British courts are not always bound by pre-2021 CJEU case law.

[78] Case C-395/15 *Daouidi v Bootes Plus SL* [2017] 2 CMLR 21, para 48. See also Case-C-270/16 *Ruiz Conejero v Ferroser Servicios Auxiliares and Ministero Fiscal* [2018] 2 CMLR 27, para 28.

[79] See Peter McTigue, 'From Navas to Kaltoft' (2015) 15 International Journal of Discrimination and the Law 241 for a discussion of ECJ case law in relation to HIV as a disability.

2.3 Summary

In summary, despite a lack of clarity about the criteria for protection under equality law for any given characteristic, there is a clear case for a legal response to the problem of disfigurement inequality. The legal response in Britain has been to grant rights under equality law to people with impairments which consist of long-term severe disfigurements.

This aspect of the Act was not transposed from EU law and offers a wider interpretation of disability than that adopted by the ECJ. Instead, the severe disfigurement provision seems to follow the approach to disability taken in the CRPD and the ECtHR, implicitly recognising the social barriers faced by people who look different. But this is at odds with the main definition of disability in s6 of the Act, which conceptualises disability as individual, functional deficit. The provisions of the Act are therefore internally inconsistent, perhaps due to similar contradictions in different international legal instruments. This inconsistency and its impact will be a recurring theme throughout the book.

3

Law's Limited Ambitions

This chapter turns its gaze on the specific rights of action which the Act grants under the banner of equality, and the purpose – if any – which they serve.

The Act prohibits discrimination in the workplace against disabled people (including people with qualifying severe disfigurements) in several ways. In brief, it prohibits both less favourable treatment because of a severe disfigurement[1] (direct discrimination) and unjustified unfavourable treatment arising in consequence of severe disfigurement.[2] An obvious example of the latter would be someone dismissed for exceeding sick leave limits related to their disability. Indirect discrimination[3] – where people are unjustifiably disadvantaged by an apparently neutral policy or practice such as a company dress code – is outlawed too, as is harassment.[4] Harassment arises where someone is subjected to unwanted conduct which has the purpose of creating a hostile, intimidating, degrading, humiliating or offensive environment for them, or where it is reasonable for the conduct to have that effect.[5] Victimisation linked with severe disfigurement is also outlawed, to prevent someone from being penalised for asserting (or supporting) rights under the Act in particular ways. Lastly, the Act puts a duty on employers to make reasonable adjustments to avoid a disadvantage caused by certain aspects of work to someone with a severe disfigurement compared with others.[6]

What the Act doesn't do is tell us what these specific rights of action are designed to achieve. Given its title, we might assume that its aim must

1 Equality Act 2010, s13.
2 Ibid s15.
3 Ibid s19.
4 Ibid s26.
5 Ibid s26(4).
6 Ibid s20.

be to ensure that people are treated equally and not disadvantaged because of their disfigurement, race, sex, religion and so on. But equality is an elusive concept. A popular definition of equality might focus on treating everyone the same, regardless of particular characteristics. This is known as formal equality. *Formal equality* means equality which focuses on process not effects; in other words, whether the form of a decision is equal irrespective of its outcome. This is sometimes expressed as 'things that are alike should be treated alike'[7] so that everyone is judged on merit and not according to contextually irrelevant personal traits such as disability or disfigurement. But while this may have the benefit of consistency, it does not guarantee fairness, allowing all groups to be treated equally badly.[8] It also places the focus on individual actions, ignoring underlying structural causes of inequality for which no individual is to blame – such as the social forces which influence educational outcomes for different groups of people.[9] Formal equality is important in relation to appearance discrimination – in theory at least, in that it may prevent someone with a visible difference from being rejected in favour of a less accomplished candidate without a disfigurement – but it leaves very significant gaps.

In contrast, substantive equality recognises that, even with like-for-like treatment, disadvantage often persists. Sometimes asymmetrical treatment (such as action which favours the disadvantaged group) is needed.[10] It stresses that the differences between people, including disfigurement, are worthy of respect, challenging the disadvantage that attaches to difference, not the difference itself.[11]

Like formal equality, substantive equality has been criticised for focusing on measures to accommodate minority group differences, rather than questioning why the appropriate standard should be that of the dominant group.[12] For example, rather than allowing someone with a visible

[7] Ethica Nicomachia Aristotle, V.3.1131a–1131b (W Ross trans. 1925) cited in Peter Westen, 'The Empty Idea of Equality' (1982) 95 Harvard Law Review 537, 543.

[8] Catherine Barnard and Bob Hepple, 'Substantive Equality' (2000) 59 Cambridge Law Journal 562, 563.

[9] Sandra Fredman, 'Substantive Equality Revisited' (2016) 14 International Journal of Constitutional Law 720.

[10] Ibid 728.

[11] Ibid 729.

[12] Oddny Mjoli Arnadottir, *Equality and Non-Discrimination under the European Convention on Human Rights*, Vol 74, International Studies in Human Rights (Martinus Nijhoff 2003) 26.

difference to opt out of having their photograph on the company website as a reasonable adjustment, it might be more appropriate to ask why company websites require staff photos at all, or why the presence of such images online so often leads to abuse. Also problematic is the fact that substantive equality tends to rely on accurate definitions of specific groups in need of additional measures. This can be doubly challenging; not only does it risk wrongly excluding people where group definitions are poorly targeted, but it forces those in the disadvantaged group to accept a group label[13] to bring a claim. It is a paradox that, in asserting rights to full and equal participation in society, minority groups 'must continue to assert their differences'.[14]

Transformative equality seeks to respond to these limitations by building on substantive equality, and targeting the social systems which create the disadvantage. It aims to tackle the causes of disadvantage as well as its effects and put the costs of structural change onto those who can afford to pay it, rather than on the minority group. It moves away from the focus on individual comparisons of sameness and difference, instead addressing institutional and societal causes of disadvantage.[15]

Understandings of equality have developed within a context of other social and legal changes. Theresia Degener suggests that developing notions of equality (from formal, to substantive, to transformative) coincide broadly with policy conceptions of disability.[16] Formal equality links to the medical model of disability: the individual's disfigurement should not influence decisions to ensure like-for-like treatment. Substantive equality links to the social model: impairment needs to be accommodated to prevent disability from being socially constructed. This might include allowing a job applicant with a disability to have a 'camera-off' interview if they wish to avoid negative judgments and increase the comfort of the job applicant. And transformative equality links to a human rights model of disability; for people with a visible difference, this might include action to change the idealised beauty standards in the media and advertising industries.

[13] Tom Shakespeare, *Disability Rights and Wrongs Revisited* (2nd edn, Routledge 2014) 104.

[14] Caroline Gooding, *Disabling Laws, Enabling Acts: Disability Rights in Britain and America* (Pluto Press 1994) 45.

[15] Oddny Mjoll Arnadottir, 'A Future of Multidimensional Disadvantage Equality?' in Oddny Mjoll Arnadottir and Gerard Quinn (eds), *The UN Convention on the Rights of Persons with Disabilities* (Martinus Nijhoff 2009) 54.

[16] Theresia Degener, 'Disability in a Human Rights Context' (2016) 5 Laws 18.

However, while most commentators agree that substantive and transformative equality are needed to move beyond limited principles of formal equality, how to do this is contested. Judging when substantive equality has been achieved is difficult. Should we assess the starting points of different groups or measure the end results, to see when the disadvantaged group is fairly represented in the outcome? Measuring starting points – often referred to as equality of opportunity – has superficial meritocratic appeal; it conjures up the image of a fair contest where illegitimate obstacles are weeded out and talent and merit can win out. But, as Peter Westen notes, recognising and isolating these illegitimate obstacles is a subjective process.[17] He argues that equality of opportunity is an empty concept dependent on the obstacles we choose to prohibit within it.

Sandra Fredman envisages a substantive version of equality of opportunity,[18] which requires positive measures to ensure that everyone can access opportunities equally irrespective of existing patterns of disadvantage. To use a recruitment analogy, this might require levelling up the economic accessibility of educational courses to both candidates, or the availability of appropriate interview clothes, childcare, CV-drafting assistance, or even enough uninterrupted sleep to enable them to perform to the best of their ability. Crucially, though, equality of opportunity does not guarantee an equal outcome[19] and it is difficult to measure without resorting to measuring outcomes;[20] how do we know when the two candidates truly had equality of opportunity without seeing who got the job?

Equality of results may sometimes be easier to measure. It targets outcomes, often through measures such as quotas. But it isn't always easy to tease apart discriminatory and non-discriminatory factors in explaining different outcomes.[21] Nor is it easy to determine the desired outcome; how do intersectional groups (such as women from ethnic minorities with a visible difference) fit within it?[22] A version of equality which focuses exclusively on results could lead to hollow results and even

17 Westen, 'The Empty Idea of Equality' (n 7) 849.

18 Fredman, 'Substantive Equality Revisited' (n 9) 723.

19 Catharine A MacKinnon, 'Substantive Equality Revisited: A Reply to Sandra Fredman' (2016) 14 International Journal of Constitutional Law 739, 740.

20 Mark Bell, *Racism and Equality in the European Union* (Oxford University Press 2008) 37.

21 E Olli and B Kofod Olsen, 'Towards Common Measures for Discrimination: Exploring Possibilities for Combining Existing Data for Measuring Ethnic Discrimination' cited in ibid 38.

22 Fredman, 'Substantive Equality Revisited' (n 9) 721.

increase negative stereotypes. By way of example, a workplace quota on minimum numbers of people with disfigurements may lead to accusations of tokenism and produce a section of the workforce who are unable to fulfil their potential unless attitudinal barriers are dismantled as well. This may partly explain why, in some European countries where workplace disability quotas exist, most employers still choose to pay a fine for not meeting the quotas rather than employing more disabled people.[23]

To reflect the complexity of substantive equality ideals, the UN Committee on the Rights of Persons with Disabilities has adopted a framework of substantive equality (which they term 'inclusive' equality) located in the interaction between four dimensions:[24]

1. 'A fair redistributive dimension'.[25] This means asymmetric treatment, removing the socio-economic disadvantage associated with difference, while acknowledging and respecting difference itself.
2. A 'recognition dimension'.[26] This dimension encapsulates dignity, and the right to be free of a socially imposed identity through stereotyping, stigma, prejudice and violence. It also includes recognition of disability as 'one of several layers of identity',[27] acknowledging the importance of intersectionality.
3. A 'participative dimension'.[28] This is a right to inclusion, recognising the 'social nature of people as members of social groups'.[29] It ensures that minorities have a voice in policy-making processes which might historically have catered exclusively to the majority.
4. An 'accommodating dimension'.[30] This means promoting diversity and changing the social structures which disadvantage people with a particular difference.

[23] International Labour Organisation, *Promoting Employment Opportunities for People with Disabilities: Quota Schemes* (2019) 1, 7 <www.ilo.org/sites/default/files/wcmsp5/groups/public/%40ed_emp/%40ifp_skills/documents/publication/wcms_735531.pdf> accessed 20 December 2024.

[24] UN Committee on the Rights of Persons with Disabilities, 'General Comment No. 6 on Equality and Non-Discrimination' (United Nations 2018) 3. With minor modifications, this framework appears to have very significant parallels with that proposed by Sandra Fredman ('Substantive Equality Revisited' (n 9) 727).

[25] UN Committee on the Rights of Persons with Disabilities, 'General Comment No. 6 on Equality and Non-Discrimination' (n 24) 3.

[26] Ibid.

[27] Ibid.

[28] Ibid.

[29] Ibid.

[30] Ibid.

From a brief reading of the Convention, examples of all four dimensions become immediately apparent. For example, the redistributive dimension is apparent in the Convention's articles directed expressly at women and children with disabilities,[31] as some of the most disadvantaged intersections. Its recognition dimension can be found in its calls for measures to raise awareness and foster respect for disabled people.[32] The Convention's participative dimension is reinforced by its demand for 'full and effective participation and inclusion in society' across contexts,[33] and its insistence on the equal involvement of disabled people within an open, inclusive and accessible labour market.[34] And the accommodating dimension shines through in its cross-cutting principle of accessibility and its calls for specific measures including the employment of disabled people in the public sector,[35] and 'affirmative action programmes, incentives and other measures'[36] in the private sector. In short, the text of the Convention embodies all four dimensions of inclusive equality.

The same cannot be said for the Act. As noted above, the Act creates a series of prohibitions and duties which, when violated, amount to discrimination. But a comparison of the text of the Act with the four dimensions of inclusive equality shows significant lacunas. The Act does not, for example, widely address participation. One minor contribution to ensuring participation and inclusion (found in the proposed consultative element of the duty under s149) was dropped in 2011 with the given rationale of 'reducing red tape'.[37] This suggests that ensuring participation and voice is not a legislative priority.

The accommodating and recognition dimensions are also sparsely represented in the Act's provisions, with two main exceptions relevant to people with visible differences.[38] The first of these exceptions is the

[31] UN Convention on the Rights of Persons with Disabilities (12 December 2006) A/RES/61/106, preamble, paras (17), (18), art 3(7) and art (8).

[32] Ibid art 8.

[33] Ibid art 3.

[34] Ibid art 27.

[35] Ibid art 27(g).

[36] Ibid art 27(h).

[37] Bob Hepple, 'Enforcing Equality Law: Two Steps Forward and Two Steps Backwards for Reflexive Regulation' (2011) 40 Industrial Law Journal 315, 326.

[38] There are some provisions in the Act targeted at social structures in other contexts – such as those relating to accessible public transport for disabled people. In the work context, it is also worth noting s60, which prohibits pre-employment health enquiries in specified circumstances. It aims to alter recruitment processes to prevent inequalities based on

duty on public bodies under s149. This requires public bodies to have due regard to the elimination of discrimination, the advancement of equality of opportunity and the fostering of good relations between people with protected characteristics and others.[39] There are also specific duties to publish equality information[40] and objectives.[41] At first glance, this language seems to promote stigma-reduction initiatives, recognition and dignity, and some examples of positive progress attributed to the implementation of the duty have indeed been identified in scholarship.[42] But the devil of the provision is in the detail – or perhaps the lack of it. Significantly, the duty is just to 'have due regard'.[43] Without more,[44] this basic procedural requirement has been accused of encouraging box-ticking[45] rather than deeper engagement and undermining enforcement avenues.[46] A House of Lords Select Committee highlighted the flaw inherent in the duty's ability to 'make no progress towards the aims of the general duty and yet be judged compliant with it by the courts'.[47] The duty does not apply outside the public sector either, leaving the private sector without a positive equality duty[48] (although some secondary impact may be felt as a result of public procurement and contracting out exercises).[49] In addition, because it applies across protected characteristics, the duty under s149 does not explicitly recognise the differing stereotypes and challenges facing particular groups, allowing the

health. However, many visible differences would already be visibly apparent at interview, so s60 is not addressed in detail here.

39 Equality Act 2010 (n 1), s149(1).

40 Equality Act 2010 (Specific Duties) Regulations 2011 (SI 2260/2011) reg 2.

41 Ibid reg 3. In addition, public authorities in Wales and Scotland have additional specific duties.

42 See, for example, Simonetta Manfredi, Lucy Vickers and Kate Clayton-Hathway, 'The Public Sector Equality Duty: Enforcing Equality Rights Through Second-Generation Regulation' (2018) 47 Industrial Law Journal 365, 379–389.

43 Equality Act 2010 (n 1), s149(1).

44 See Sandra Fredman, 'The Public Sector Equality Duty' (2011) 40 Industrial Law Journal 405, 418–427 for a discussion of the due regard standard and reflexive law.

45 Manfredi and others, 'The Public Sector Equality Duty' (n 42) 386; Fredman, 'The Public Sector Equality Duty' (n 44) 427.

46 Manfredi and others, 'The Public Sector Equality Duty' (n 42) 386; Fredman, 'The Public Sector Equality Duty' (n 44) 420–427.

47 House of Lords Select Committee, *The Equality Act 2010: the Impact on Disabled People* (Session 2015–2016, HL117) 99.

48 Bob Hepple, 'The New Single Equality Act in Britain' (2010) 5 The Equal Rights Review 11, 22; Alysia Blackham, *Reforming Age Discrimination Law: Beyond Individual Enforcement* (Oxford University Press 2022) 283.

49 Fredman, 'The Public Sector Equality Duty' (n 44) 414.

continued neglection of lesser-known types of impairment, such as visible difference. In short, s149 has significant limitations which undermine its ability to promote wider dimensions of inclusive equality.

The second main exception can be found in the positive action provisions in s158 and s159. Positive action involves the use of targeted measures to assist disadvantaged groups, such as outreach programmes under s158, or preferential treatment of equally qualified job candidates under s159. However, these provisions have also been criticised for their narrow approach and the ease with which they can be circumvented or ignored. Positive action is entirely unincentivised in regulatory terms; there is no requirement for employers even to make public their (lack of) efforts in this regard. Compounding this, the provisions are complex, creating a concern that employers may get it wrong, exposing themselves to claims.[50] It is perhaps not surprising, then, that research has identified a reluctance among many employers to use the provisions to the maximum extent permitted.[51] In summary, therefore, neither the duty on public bodies under s149 nor the positive action provisions under s158 and s159 provide a credible reason to doubt that the Act is intentionally narrower in scope than the CRPD and its multi-dimensional concept of inclusive equality.

Narrowly targeted legislative ambitions are not necessarily a bad thing; as Chapter 8 will explore, the belief that law alone can solve complex societal problems is difficult to sustain against the empirical evidence. Law is, at best, one part of a social armoury, and being realistic about its potential contribution may help to target laws where they can make at least *some* impact. But how do we make sense of what the Act *might* realistically look to contribute to equality ideals?

3.1 Constructing an Evaluative Framework

A different approach is to take our cue from the law itself. While statutory preambles tend to be both vague and quixotic, the scope of the Act's provisions offer the clearest indication of its purpose. The Act's provisions are predominantly individualistic: they look to penalise

[50] Lizzie Barmes, 'Equality Law and Experimentation: The Positive Action Challenge' (2009) 68 *The Cambridge Law Journal* 623, 628.

[51] Chantal Davies and others, 'Bridging the Gap' (2016) 16 International Journal of Discrimination and the Law 83, 96; Barmes, 'Equality Law and Experimentation' (n 50) 643.

individual people and companies whose behaviour falls foul of the very specific standards set out in the Act to the detriment of a particular person. The primary focus is therefore on interpersonal relationships, not on wider structural factors. By way of example, negative portrayals of people with disfigurements in the film industry[52] may have a significant impact on beliefs and norms relating to appearance but fall outside the scope of the Act. Similarly, internalised stigma may help to maintain the disadvantage of looking different – perhaps through self-moderated decisions not to apply for jobs in high profile industries. But the Act does not engage with this either.

From the Act's narrow, interpersonal focus, we can infer five possible equality contributions. The first – and most far-reaching – is attitudinal change. In theory, introducing a law against disfigurement discrimination raises awareness about the problem of bias against people who look different, and sends a symbolic expression that this behaviour is wrong. Although most people don't keep track of statutory amendments, any media coverage which results from a change in the law may help to spread the message. One potential outcome of the Act could therefore be to assimilate these messages, changing the way we as individuals think and feel about people who look different. The attitudes of people with visible differences may themselves be altered too; the creation of such a law could foster resistance against ill-treatment, with individuals embracing the stance of rights-holders rather than victims.

The second potential equality outcome is changes in perceived social norms. For these purposes, perceived social norms are 'impressions of what opinions or behaviours are common among, or considered desirable by, a group of people'.[53] So, a (fictional) perceived social norm might be phrased as 'I think most British people are in favour of equality for people with disfigurements' whereas a corresponding individual attitude might be 'I am in favour of equality for people with disfigurements'.[54] Without always relying on sanctions, law may sometimes have the power to reinforce or bend both perceived and actual social norms,[55] creating a

[52] See Section 9.1.1.

[53] Robert Cialdini and Noah Goldstein, 'Social Influence: Compliance and Conformity' (2004) 55 Annual Review of Psychology 591, 597.

[54] On the same concept, see Margaret E Tankard and Elizabeth Levy Paluck, 'The Effect of a Supreme Court Decision Regarding Gay Marriage on Social Norms and Personal Attitudes' (2017) 28 Psychological Science 1334, 1334.

[55] Ibid. See also Richard H McAdams, *The Expressive Powers of Law: Theories and Limits* (1st edn, Harvard University Press 2015) chap 5; Emanuela Carbonara, 'Law and Social

symbolic statement about other people's values and 'what society expects from its members'.[56] This expressive influence is more likely where the legal norm created by statute does not openly clash with an existing social meaning or norm,[57] and where the subject matter is seen to be an appropriate focus for regulation.[58] Perceived social norms may guide individual behaviours,[59] because most people want to avoid the social rejection which could follow from openly transgressing what they perceive as the 'done thing'. So, perceived social norms might be able to motivate behavioural change, even where problematic individual attitudes remain untouched.

The third potential outcome in the framework is direct behavioural change flowing from the law. In other words, even if our attitudes towards people who look different remain negative, we are motivated not to act on them. This might be for reasons of classic punishment deterrence – because we don't want to face paying a financial penalty for breaking the law. Or it could be because we see the law as a legitimate source of authority which should be obeyed.[60] Or perhaps because we want to avoid the social stigma of being seen to break the law.[61] In these examples, law causes us to change our behaviours.

The fourth possible outcome is indirect behavioural change resulting from reduced opportunities to discriminate. Imagine that Company A needs to hire new customer service staff. Company A's interviewing manager prefers good-looking sales staff and thinks clients won't like staff who look different. He is not afraid of refusing jobs on that basis because he is confident that he can put forward a plausible alternative reason to explain his decision. But Company A, mindful of the new law in this area, has changed their recruitment processes. They have

Norms' in Francesco Parisi (ed), *The Oxford Handbook of Law and Economics* (Oxford University Press 2017) 466–482.

56 Carbonara, 'Law and Social Norms' (n 55) 472.

57 Ibid 477.

58 Janice Nadler, 'Expressive Law, Social Norms, and Social Groups' (2017) 42 Law & Social Inquiry 60, 68.

59 Carbonara, 'Law and Social Norms' (n 55) 476; McAdams, *The Expressive Powers of Law* (n 55) 137. For a different perspective, see Frederick Schauer, *The Force of Law* (Harvard University Press 2015).

60 Tom R Tyler, *Why People Obey the Law* (Princeton University Press 2021) 3.

61 Cass R Sunstein, 'On the Expressive Function of Law' (1996) 144 University of Pennsylvania Law Review 2021, 2032; McAdams, *The Expressive Powers of Law* (n 55) 137.

introduced first round camera-off interviews so the interviewing manager doesn't know what the candidates look like until further into the process. The interviewing manager is also no longer allowed to interview alone, to ensure a breadth of experience and views in the recruitment process. And the panel (who have all undergone extensive equality training) uses pre-prepared skills-based questions which leave no room for subjective lines of questioning and make it harder to justify ratings on anything other than job skills. In essence, indirect behavioural change is about the development of best practice techniques which narrow opportunities for discrimination.

Taken together, these first four possible outcomes *should* all contribute to increased workplace integration, changing the behaviours, attitudes and perceptions that have kept people with visible differences out of jobs, in lower paid work, or without fair treatment. The fifth possible contribution of the Act is not to change attitudes or behaviours, but simply to ensure that victims of discrimination can be financially compensated for the discrimination they suffer. It aims to create an effective mechanism where victims can challenge discrimination to punish the people who have discriminated against them. An important question here is whether *actual* enforcement is required to meet this potential objective. In other words, does law's potential for an effective remedial mechanism hinge on high levels of enforcement, so that most victims of discrimination *are* compensated? Or it is sufficient that law creates a mechanism which *can* be used effectively should the victims so choose, whether or not this happens in practice? If widespread systematic enforcement were intended, law could promote this by making claims easier to bring: offering investigatory and enforcement support by dedicated agencies, reducing the technical formalities of the law and the Tribunal process, offering increased financial support for claimants, and so on. Instead, the picture in recent years has been quite different, with many changes having the purpose or effect of reducing the number of claims. Examples include the introduction of Employment Tribunal fees[62] (which were later ruled unlawful),[63] the undermining of the discrimination questionnaire process (which makes it harder for potential

[62] For a discussion of the given reasons for this change, see Matthew R Smith, 'A Comparative Analysis of the Criminal and Civil Justice Systems in England and Wales' (1 edn, Manchester University Press 2017) 95.

[63] *R. (on the application of UNISON) (Appellant) v Lord Chancellor (Respondent)* [2017] UKSC 51 (SC).

claimants to gather information),[64] and the introduction of a mandatory Advisory, Conciliation and Arbitration Service (ACAS) conciliation opportunity before a claim can be issued.[65] Against this background, it would be hard to sustain an argument that law intended every act of discrimination to be challenged and compensated. So, in evaluating whether the Act has created an effective remedial mechanism, effectiveness will be evaluated according to the potential for enforcement, not numbers of claims.

These five impacts, inferred from the scope of the Act itself, provide a spectrum of statutory purposes which will guide the analysis in subsequent chapters. For clarity, the claim is not to have uncovered the subjective intent of the parliamentary draftsmen of the Act. But instead that what the Act says – and perhaps more importantly what it doesn't say – allows us to narrow down a wide range of potential equality objectives to these five.

3.2 Methodological Implications of the Framework

This spectrum of inferred purposes provides a theoretical benchmark against which to evaluate the effectiveness of the Act. However, the reality of that evaluation is far from simple. Lawrence Friedman argues that, in order to evaluate how well a law is working, we must first establish what its impacts are, and then ask whether those impacts further the presumed goals of the law.[66] Impact (which Friedman defines as 'changes that take place after, and because of, some activity within the legal system')[67] can be hard to pin down.[68] Using the example of the severe disfigurement provision, we might look to assess impact by searching for changes in the employment rate of people with visible differences. But, even if those statistics were available (and sadly they aren't) we wouldn't necessarily know whether other factors, such as the cost-of-living crisis, could have contributed to individual decisions to go back to work. Indirect impact is also possible but even harder to trace. If more people with visible differences were able to find work as a result

64 Enterprise and Regulatory Reform Act 2013, s66.

65 Employment Tribunals Act 1996, s18A.

66 Lawrence Friedman, *Impact: How Law Affects Behavior* (Harvard University Press 2017) 45.

67 Ibid 44.

68 Ibid 63.

of this law, the government would receive a boost in income tax, and perhaps a reduction in jobseekers' allowance costs. If the government chose to spend that extra money improving the quality of public green spaces, this might boost mental health – this would be an indirect impact of the law on disfigurement equality, even though we could never prove it. Although this is a far-fetched example, it illustrates the challenge of attributing societal changes to the impact of a particular law.

Assessing impact is even harder when it comes to less tangible measures such as changes in attitudes. The empirical research in this book does not attempt to measure prejudice (attitudes), social norms or instances of discrimination (behaviours) towards people with disfigurements. The law on severe disfigurement was first passed many years ago in 1995;[69] as an under-researched field of study, data isn't available to conduct a 'before the law' and 'after the law' comparison. Even if it were, the social world has changed significantly in the interim so attributing changes to law would be difficult. Any attempt to measure attitudes as a one-off snapshot only would tell us little about the law's impact, beyond confirming that some level of problem still exists, which is probably to be expected of even the most impactful equality laws. We would have much to learn from longitudinal study in this area, tracking changes in social norms, personal attitudes and enacted prejudice in respect to specific interventions.

In the interim, however, this book collates and connects the evidence that we do have from different sources. Those sources include qualitative data from my interviews with affected people and employers, studies in the social sciences, evidence from other countries, data collected by charities working in this area, the few official statistics which have partial relevance and factual accounts in case law. Drawing on these different sources, all with their strengths and limitations, allows us to identify key themes and propose likely inferences, without making claims which are bolder than the data from this relatively new field of study can sustain.

3.3 Summary

This chapter has argued that, although the drafting of the CRPD reflects a multi-layered concept of equality, the provisions in the Act are, overall,

[69] For 'before and after' comparisons of other legal changes, see Silvia Luis and Jose Palma-Oliveira, 'Public Policy and Social Norms: The Case of a Nationwide Smoking Ban among College Students' (2016) 22 Psychology, Public Policy, and Law 22; Tankard and Paluck, 'The Effect of a Supreme Court Decision Regarding Gay Marriage on Social Norms and Personal Attitudes' (n 54).

much narrower in scope. Implicitly, the Act's intended equality contribution is more limited. For example, the Act's provisions are mainly individual; aimed at compensating particular instances of interpersonal discrimination, not at creating wider structural change or at making up for the effects of internalised stigma. Focused legislative ambitions may have merit; as later chapters will explore, the relationship between law and social change is not straightforward, so narrowly targeted laws may sometimes be justified. But making sense of the Act's intended outcomes is difficult.

With this in mind, the chapter uses the Act's chosen scope to build a framework of five potential outcomes. These concern prejudice reduction, alterations to perceived social norms, behavioural change, developing good practice among employers and effective paths to enforcement. These potential outcomes are used in subsequent chapters to evaluate the Act's impact. Chapters 4 and 5 seek empirical evidence of these outcomes through the experiences of those living with disfigurement and of employers. And Chapters 6, 7 and 8 use doctrinal analysis to assess the extent to which law has achieved, or is capable of achieving, these outcomes.

Establishing the impact of a law in the real world is challenging given the interaction between numerous social factors. It is particularly difficult here, given a lack of reliable longitudinal data. For this reason, the book collates information and evidence from a range of sources to establish what we know so far about the problem of visible difference inequality. But it also embraces the need for further work in this area going forward.

4

The Lived Experience of Visible Difference

Does having a disfigurement affect our encounters with others? Does it impact how we feel or choose to live our lives? Is the experience of disfigurement consistent among people with different types of visible difference, or life contexts or ages? And how do those of us with a visible difference feel about using the law to challenge negative behaviours? In this chapter, the reality of the lived experience of disfigurement is examined.

The evidence presented here concerns both the psychological and the social experience of visible difference (or the 'view from the inside' as well as the 'view from the outside').[1] But these ideas are permeable to a degree because our experiences in society may sometimes affect the way we feel about ourselves, and vice versa. This chapter is intended to be read with that fluidity in mind.

4.1 Psychological Impact

The impact of visible difference on mental health is frequently noted, with individuals reporting experiences such as social anxiety, low self-confidence and self-esteem, negative self-image and depression.[2] One interviewee, who acquired a sudden visible difference as an adult, told me that:

> You're a different person when you've got something that's very obviously recognisable as a difference. So the person I am today is not the person

1 Andrew Thompson and Gerry Kent, 'Adjusting to Disfigurement: Processes Involved in Dealing with Being Visibly Different' (2001) 21 Clinical Psychology Review 663, 664.

2 Sandra Jowett and Terence Ryan, 'Skin Disease and Handicap: An Analysis of the Impact of Skin Conditions' (1985) 20 Social Science & Medicine 425, 427; R Newell and I Marks, 'Phobic Nature of Social Difficulty in Facially Disfigured People' (2000) 176 The British Journal of Psychiatry: The Journal of Mental Science 177, 177; Nichola Rumsey and Diana Harcourt, 'Body Image and Disfigurement: Issues and Interventions' (2004) 1 Body Image 83, 103; David B Sarwer and others, 'The Psychosocial Burden of Visible Disfigurement Following Traumatic Injury' (2022) 13 Frontiers in Psychology 979574.

> I was then, 20 years ago, because I was confident before that. Then it takes away your confidence. So you don't actually fight back. You don't defend yourself, because you feel it's indefensible.

However, not everyone feels the same way, and reported experiences vary.[3] It is sometimes suggested that the level of psychological distress likely to be experienced depends on the nature of the disfigurement. This kind of 'disfigurement-based' explanation seems logical at first glance but, in fact, it is largely unsupported by the evidence. Severity is a case in point. It may seem rational that the worse the disfigurement, the worse the psychological impact, but studies do not tend to support this.[4] Some researchers have even argued that having an objectively mild disfigurement can be more distressing than more severe differences, because sporadic reactions from others increase uncertainty and fear.[5] This unreliable relationship between objective severity and distress can also be found in individual accounts. One interviewee told me that going out in public was hardest when her visible difference was at its most severe. But another gave a compelling account of psychological discomfort despite self-rating the severity of her visible difference as 'mild'.

The visibility of a disfigurement does not reliably determine levels of distress either. Assumptions that disfigurements of the face, hands and neck will cause more distress due to their visible locations are not always correct. The added stress of waiting for a hidden disfigurement to be discovered by others proves extremely difficult for some people.[6]

[3] Katie Egan, Diana Harcourt and Nichola Rumsey, 'A Qualitative Study of the Experiences of People who Identify Themselves as Having Adjusted Positively to a Visible Difference' (2011) 16 Journal of Health Psychology 739, 742; IK Carlsson, LB Dahlin and HE Rosberg, 'Congenital Thumb Anomalies and the Consequences for Daily Life: Patients' Long-Term Experience after Corrective Surgery. A Qualitative Study' (2018) 40 Disability and Rehabilitation 69, 71. See also William Eiserman, 'Unique Outcomes and Positive Contributions Associated with Facial Difference: Expanding Research and Practice' (2001) 38 The Cleft Palate-Craniofacial Journal 236, 241.

[4] For a summary see Timothy P Moss and Ben Rosser, 'Adult Psychosocial Adjustment to Visible Differences: Physical and Psychological Predictors of Variation' in Nicola Rumsey and Nicola Harcourt (eds), *Oxford Handbook of the Psychology of Appearance* (Oxford University Press 2012) 274.

[5] Frances Cooke Macgregor, 'Facial Disfigurement: Problems and Management of Social Interaction and Implications for Mental Health' (1990) 14 Official Journal of the International Society of Plastic Surgery 249, 252; Moss and Rosser, 'Adult Psychosocial Adjustment to Visible Differences' (n 4) 275.

[6] Sue Cahners, 'Young Women with Breast Burns: A Self-Help "Group by Mail"' (1992) 13 Journal of Burn Care and Rehabilitation 44, 44; Moss and Rosser, 'Adult Psychosocial Adjustment to Visible Differences' (n 4) 276; Nicholas D Sharratt and others, 'Becoming

Other explanations for variable levels of distress focus on the characteristics of the person. There is some evidence that people who are adept at using coping mechanisms are less likely to experience extreme distress from looking different.[7] Among the people I interviewed, one of the central coping mechanisms was to explain one's condition.[8] But sometimes explaining is felt not to be a choice but a necessity[9] – perhaps because of a need to take sick leave or have treatment, or to deal with unwanted questions from colleagues:

> the person at work who went 'am I going to catch it?' I was just like . . . I said you're not going to catch it, [. . .] and I just tried to explain it. This person wasn't convinced[. . .] It just becomes in built, it becomes like a reflex that you know you need to do, to get through the situation.

And on occasion some people resent being put in a position where they feel *expected* to explain, with the privacy invasion this involves. In the words of one interviewee:

> Quite often, if some people have just come out with a flyaway question or comment, you know, 'Have you been to the dentist?' or, 'Have you had a stroke?' These days, I'm more likely to just say, 'Did you miss your manners education?' you know? [. . .] And just, sort of, pull them up on their bad manners as a deflection or they just get a short, 'No,' and a stare. That's pretty much it, really. I'm sure there are ways of coping, but it's like – you feel like, 'Oh, why do I have to be the person who teaches this person a lesson?'

Sometimes coping strategies focus on self-protection. Avoiding photographs and videos can provide relief by preventing close scrutiny of a difference but this can narrow opportunities at work and in social settings. People can also be deterred from types of jobs where they anticipate that appearance will be important. One interviewee recalled realising that they would be unable to pursue their dream career in the theatre or on screen, because 'those jobs, you have to look good, don't

Known: Disclosure and Exposure of (In)Visible Difference' (2020) 5 Stigma and Health 413.

7 Egan and others, 'A Qualitative Study of the Experiences of People Who Identify Themselves as Having Adjusted Positively to a Visible Difference' (n 3) 743.

8 A correlation between open disclosure of facial difference and positive psychosocial outcomes was also noted by Kathleen R Bogart, Brooke A Bryson and Diana Harcourt, 'Disclosing the Obvious: Psychosocial Implications of (Not) Explaining Facial Differences' (2023) 46 Body Image 91–102.

9 Ibid 99.

you? That's the perception that you have, it's all to do with how you look if you're put on camera or on stage'.

For some, humour can provide extra resilience in coping with looking different.[10] But although humour may help people manage, it is sometimes a double-edged sword, serving to mask distress rather than to prevent it. As one participant remarked:

> I come across as very confident, very gobby, chatty, you know [. . .] quirky, and therefore I think people don't ever consider how, I'm going to swear, fucking hard it is for me just to walk out the door sometimes. So I guess it's my own bloody fault for being so good at hiding it.

Lived experiences can also be affected by other personal characteristics, such as gender and age.[11] People commonly assume that disfigurement will be harder for some groups of people to live with – especially women and young people. But research on body image shows that both older people[12] and men[13] can experience significant appearance dissatisfaction too, and, of course, experiences are not always uniform within groups. So, while personal context can sometimes play a part, assumptions about disfigurement only 'mattering' if you are young and female are definitely best avoided.

In summary, living with a disfigurement can have a profound psychological impact on some people. But there is variability, and it is hard to predict who will experience most distress, or how their experience might change over time.

4.2 Meeting Others

Studies have shown that people living with disfigurements often worry more about social interaction, avoiding social situations as a result.[14]

10 Marion D Meyerson, 'Resiliency and Success in Adults with Moebius Syndrome' (2001) 38 The Cleft Palate-Craniofacial Journal 231, 233.

11 There is perhaps less evidence on the intersection between disfigurement and race, but see Jennifer Hughes and others, 'South Asian Community Views about Individuals with a Disfigurement' (2009) 6 Diversity and Equality in Health Care 241; Habib Naqvi and Saul Krysia, 'Culture and Ethnicity' in Nicola Rumsey and Diana Harcourt (eds), *The Oxford Handbook of the Psychology of Appearance* (Oxford University Press 2012).

12 Lucie Baker and Eyal Gringart, 'Appearance in Later Life' in Diana Harcourt and Nichola Rumsey (eds), *The Oxford Handbook of the Psychology of Appearance* (Oxford University Press 2012) 160.

13 Helen Fawkner, 'Gender' in Diana Harcourt and Nichola Rumsey (eds), *The Oxford Handbook of the Psychology of Appearance* (Oxford University Press 2012) 176.

14 Thompson and Kent, 'Adjusting to Disfigurement' (n 1) 666.

Many people with a visible difference report awkwardness such as 'the guarded references, the common everyday words suddenly made taboo, the fixed stare elsewhere, the artificial levity, the compulsive loquaciousness, the awkward solemnity'.[15] Explicit negative reactions are reported too; surveys and personal accounts confirm experiences of teasing, name-calling, staring and unsolicited comments, questions and even hate-crime.[16] One individual with a visible difference recounted an experience of being out one night as a teenager with friends:

> There were some guys behind me and they kept, like, you know, touching my bum and that. So, in the end, I turned around and said, 'What are you doing?' and the guy just ripped into me, 'Look at the state of you, you're not fucking speaking to me,' and he just absolutely ripped into me and tore shreds off me.

The late Sir James Partridge, founder of the charity Changing Faces, who had a burns injury himself, used the acronym SCARED to describe common reactions of others:[17] staring, curiosity, anguish, recoil, embarrassment, dread. Sometimes negative reactions can prevent the individual from going about their daily life; one study reported that 19 per cent of participants had been rejected by a restaurant, swimming pool or other public place because of the appearance of a particular skin condition.[18]

Friendship and romance can also be affected by looking different.[19] This may be exacerbated by social media which, while opening lines of communication and support for many people, can expose users to abuse. Changing Faces found that 92 per cent of survey respondents with a visible difference who had used a dating app had received negative comments about their appearance from other users.[20]

[15] Fred Davis, 'Deviance Disavowal: The Management of Strained Interaction by the Visibly Handicapped' (1961) 9 Social Problems 120, 123.

[16] Changing Faces, 'Disfigurement in the UK' (Changing Faces 2017) 20.

[17] James Partridge, *Changing Faces: The Challenge of Facial Disfigurement* (Penguin Books 1990) 65.

[18] Iona Ginsburg and Bruce Link, 'Psychosocial Consequences of Rejection and Stigma in Patients with Psoriasis' (1993) 32 International Journal of Dermatology 587, 587.

[19] Emma Robinson, 'Psychological Research on Visible Differences in Adults' in Richard Lansdown and others (eds), *Visibly Different* (Butterworth-Heinemann 1997) 103; Nicholas David Sharratt and others, 'Understandings and Experiences of Visible Difference and Romantic Relationships: A Qualitative Exploration' (2018) 27 Body Image 32, 35.

[20] Changing Faces, 'Disfigurement in the UK' (n 16) 28.

4.2.1 At Work

Negative reactions to appearance when looking for a job are commonly reported. One participant said:

> As soon as you do a health disclosure ... I have even tested it. I've put everything down and not got an interview. Then I've put nothing down and have got an interview. [...] I think it's looked at and it's like, 'Oh no. You know, you're going to be a liability. You're not going to turn up for work, so we won't bother with you ...'

They recalled one memorable interview where their facial difference was pointed out by the interviewer, who then remarked 'well, this is a front of house job ...'. Another interviewee, looking to move to a new role within the organisation, recollected being told by a senior colleague that, despite performing well, the key to career progression would be to 'go on a sunbed' and 'get rid of that wonky face'. And sometimes an inability to smile (which can result from various types of visible difference) is thought to have been misinterpreted by job interviewers as a lack of enthusiasm for the role.

Once in a job, some feel that visible difference has prevented them from fitting in. In line with this, research has suggested that facial disfigurement makes coworkers more uncomfortable than many other types of disability.[21] One participant, for example, recalled noticing that colleagues were talking about them behind their back, and hearing from a friend that colleagues had given them a secret nickname which made fun of their visible condition. It should be said, though, that this feeling of social exclusion was not universal; some people that I spoke to had enjoyed happy working lives and never suspected that their appearance had held back their career.

Sometimes people express a tension between what is good for their health, and what is required for their jobs. One participant felt unable to take time off for NHS surgery on their visible difference because 'you often are in a team of people where you would feel like you were letting them down. But people are really open about just being annoyed with someone being off sick.[...]'. For them, this would have meant waiting for medical treatment until the summer when the workload impact on their colleagues would have eased. And work stress can sometimes

[21] Gwen Jones and Dianna Stone, 'Perceived Discomfort Associated with Working with Persons with Varying Disabilities' (1995) 81 Perceptual and Motor Skills 911, 915. Facial disfigurement was ranked 7/20 for perceived discomfort.

aggravate health conditions underlying visible differences. This prompted one to 'get a job that's more tick along and manageable, for my own health and for the hours, so that I can manage the rest of my life, so that actually I can keep surviving. And that felt, kind of, very restricting'.

Some people that I spoke to felt the need to overcome extra hurdles to prove themselves as fit to work. These hurdles were steps such as passing a referral to occupational health, disclosing personal medical details and overcoming potential workplace risks caused by strong prescribed medication. Hurdles also occurred in the operation of sick leave procedures; several participants perceived unfairness in the operation of absence policies, with concerns that long-term medical conditions should not always be treated the same as the sort of unconnected short-term absences which everyone has from time to time. Overcoming these various hurdles was not always straightforward and the relationship with Occupational Health departments was not a positive one for some participants. The Occupational Health function is intended to provide a bridge in the relationship between health and work, supporting both employers and workers in dealing with medical issues with the potential to affect the workplace. Yet for some participants, the relationship was unsupportive and lacked proper understanding of their condition:

> And . . . it also mentioned 'when [name] gets better . . . these adjustments can be taken away'. I questioned that – I actually rang the company that does the occupational health – but got told only a manager could speak to them. It's about the report that you sent, 'when [name] gets better' – I said 'I'm not going to get better.' [. . .] 'I will deteriorate.'

This lack of understanding of their medical circumstances sometimes extended to primary healthcare too, with some having to battle for treatment because their condition is seen as cosmetic and given low priority for care. For a couple of participants, this process had gone beyond one of active management and turned into a battle for treatment lasting, in one case, for several years, until the participant decided that 'you know what, I don't have the physical or mental ability to do this anymore'. And one participant worried that people at work would doubt the veracity of a condition which did not qualify for NHS medical treatment.

For some, career opportunities may be impacted by earlier experiences at school. For one participant, the sudden acquisition of a facial difference as a child meant that they went 'quite literally from being a straight

A student to being like a D and an E student because I just didn't have the information [...] the school were told I might be contagious so not to come near me'. And for another, bullying at school led to low confidence, meaning that they couldn't face going to university in a different city and meeting new people again. This educational impact is one with the potential to influence career options throughout life.

Much of the research in this area is relatively small-scale. Assessing the wider extent of workplace disfigurement inequality is challenging, because there are no accurate statistics available detailing the numbers of people with disfigurements, let alone their work-related experiences. But the Annual Population Survey ('APS') data collected by the Office for National Statistics[22] is helpful in part. The APS collects household data on employment, including details about the number of disabled people who are economically active. Within that, there is a category for people with 'severe disfigurements, skin conditions and allergies'. The statistics show that in 2020/21, an estimated 77 per cent[23] of people within this category were economically active relative to 84 per cent of people[24] without a disability – a gap of 7 per cent. This gap is smaller than for many other given categories of impairment, and over recent years the statistics seem to have been moving in the right direction; in the eight years before 2021 the figures broadly show an 8 per cent increase in the number of people in the UK with skin conditions, severe disfigurements and allergies who were economically active.[25]

However, although potentially encouraging, these figures raise many more questions than they answer. They don't tell us what the position is for people with severe disfigurements disaggregated from skin conditions and allergies, even though one might expect the job market barriers facing these groups to be very different. They also don't tell us how these figures translate into detailed work types and pay rates, to ensure that the

22 Annual Population Survey, 'Disability and Employment, UK, 2021 Edition' (*Office for National Statistics – Annual Population Survey*, 2021) <https://bit.ly/3Pm8Ibq> accessed 23 January 24.

23 Ibid Table 6.

24 This figure relates to England specifically. See ibid Table 9.

25 Annual variations are present. In addition to (n 23), see Annual Population Survey, 'Disability and Employment, UK, 2020 Edition' (*Office for National Statistics – Annual Population Survey*, 2020) Table 4 <https://bit.ly/3Pm8Ibq> accessed 23 January 2024 and Annual Population Survey, 'Disability and Employment, UK, 2019 Edition' (*Office for National Statistics – Annual Population Survey*, 2019) Table 3 <https://bit.ly/3Pm8Ibq> accessed 23 January 2024.

increase is not largely lower paid and casual (there is evidence that people who look different often earn less than their contemporaries).[26] We don't know whether Covid, Brexit or the current labour shortage have impacted the figures over this period, nor whether a greater focus on equality inspired by Black Lives Matter and #MeToo could have played a part. We do know, though, that the survey data is at odds to some degree with data collected by the charity Changing Faces. Their 2021 survey[27] (which polled just over 1,000 people with a visible difference) showed some downward trends in the previous two years, including a 7 per cent deterioration in the number of people who felt employers took them seriously during recruitment.

Given these uncertainties, it is difficult to make quantifiable claims about both the scale of this problem, and about how it has changed over time. But the weight of evidence points to looking different still being a significant source of unjust inequality in the labour market.

4.3 All in Your Head?

Given the number of studies and surveys reporting negative social reactions to visible difference, the sceptics reading this might be wondering how reliable those reports are. Isn't it possible that people who look different could just be overly sensitive, imagining negativity towards them where none exists?

An early study by Robert Kleck and Angelo Strenta[28] is sometimes used to justify this line of thinking.[29] In that study, participants without a disfigurement had make-up applied to simulate a disfigurement. They believed that their role was to attend a social event and report on how people reacted to their altered appearance. They were shown the disfigurement in a mirror, before being told that it now needed to be fixed in position. Believing themselves still to be wearing the simulated disfigurement, they were then introduced to other people, looking to report others' reactions to the disfigurement. Afterwards, the participants

[26] Daniel S Hamermesh, *Beauty Pays* (Princeton University Press 2011) 39; Changing Faces, 'Disfigurement in the UK' (n 16) 18.

[27] Changing Faces, 'Strategy Survey' (Changing Faces 2021) 13.

[28] Robert E Kleck and Angelo Strenta, 'Perceptions of the Impact of Negatively Valued Physical Characteristics on Social Interaction' (1980) 39 Journal of Personality and Social Psychology 861, 864.

[29] See, for example, Short Reads Today, 'The Dartmouth Scar Experiment: Revealing the Power of "Victim Mindset"' medium.com <https://bit.ly/3Tlwplq> accessed 8 February 2024.

reported negative reactions – particularly staring – from other people. In fact, however, the fixing of the make-up had removed it, so any reactions were to their normal appearance without any disfigurement. As with much research in this area, the study acknowledged several limitations. For one, the relatively small sample of participants were exclusively female undergraduates in the US, so it was unrepresentative in terms of both gender[30] and, presumably, age. In addition, the research design was far removed from real world social interaction; participants were required to pay close attention to the reactions of the other person in test conditions, despite the authors noting that 'gaze behaviour appears to be an aspect of the behaviour of others that we do not consciously attend to in most situations and, therefore, have little awareness as to what would constitute a normal level and style of looking'.[31] Notwithstanding these limitations, this study is sometimes cited as evidence of a 'victim mindset'[32] among people with facial disfigurements – the implication being that reports of negative reactions from other people can be solved by the person with a visible difference simply changing their attitude.

However, this reductive interpretation conveniently ignores a body of evidence in which researchers have sought to measure some of the social consequences of looking different *objectively*, rather than subjectively. For example, studies have shown that the general public tend to avoid interaction with people with disfigurements where possible. In 1982, researchers conducted an experiment on a busy pedestrian crossing. When an actor wearing a simulated disfigurement used the crossing, the general public stood further away from the actor than they did from other strangers without disfigurements.[33] A similar experiment found that the general public were less likely to sit next to someone with a disfigurement on a train.[34] And again a charity collector with a simulated disfigurement was less likely to receive donations than a collector without

[30] The authors suggest that women are more responsive to gaze behaviour during an interaction than men: Kleck and Strenta, 'Perceptions of the Impact of Negatively Valued Physical Characteristics on Social Interaction' (n 28) 871.

[31] Ibid.

[32] Short Reads Today, 'The Dartmouth Scar Experiment' (n 29).

[33] Nicola Rumsey, Ray Bull and Denis Gahagan, 'The Effect of Facial Disfigurement on the Proxemic Behaviour of the General Public' (1982) 12 Journal of Applied Social Psychology 137, 146.

[34] Vicky Houston and Ray Bull, 'Do People Avoid Sitting Next to Someone Who Is Facially Disfigured?' (1994) 24 European Journal of Social Psychology 279, 279.

a disfigurement.[35] (It is perhaps worth mentioning that the disfigurement in these studies was simulated with make-up. This requires us to take on trust that the simulation was not apparent to the general public in some way.)

Reported fears of workplace discrimination also appear to be well-founded. Stevenage & McKay[36] conducted a mock recruitment study to ascertain the effect of facial disfigurement on hiring decisions. Based on participants reviewing mock job applications, they identified a significant negative perception of the applicant with a facial disfigurement (a port wine stain), as against both a non-disabled applicant and an applicant in a wheelchair. An applicant with both a physical disability *and* a disfigurement fared worst of all. Interestingly, although hiring decisions differed, the personality and job skill judgments made by HR professionals and college students were the same, which may suggest that HR training does little to reduce underlying bias against visibly different people. The increased disadvantage of the visibly different applicant in the wheelchair also suggests that complex disfiguring conditions – which include some type of functional impairment as well as an aesthetic impact – are likely to be a point of compound disadvantage.

While this was a mock study lacking the real-life validity of decisions with consequences,[37] a similar result was established by Stone and Wright in their real-world job application study. In Stone and Wright's study, applications were submitted in response to job advertisements which fitted specific parameters. The applications were different but validated as equal in calibre and appropriateness to the relevant job. For each job, three applications were submitted – one for a wheelchair user, one for someone with a congenital disfigurement and one with no apparent disability. The applications contained a worded statement describing the relevant condition (if any), not a photograph. Stone and Wright found discrimination against people with a facial disfigurement where the role applied for entailed high levels of customer contact

35 Ray Bull and Julia Stevens, 'The Effects of Facial Disfigurement on Helping Behaviour' (1981) 8 Italian Journal of Psychology 25, 25.

36 Sarah V Stevenage and Yolanda McKay, 'Model Applicants: The Effect of Facial Appearance on Recruitment Decisions' (1999) 90 British Journal of Psychology 221.

37 Some studies have suggested that in a simulated setting, results may differ from real world decisions with consequences, e.g. Anna Stone and Toby Wright, 'When Your Face Doesn't Fit: Employment Discrimination against People with Facial Disfigurements' (2013) 43 Journal of Applied Social Psychology 515, 516.

(a theme consistent with other studies too).[38] Discrimination against the wheelchair user was consistent – the authors speculated that this may be due to concern about the cost of adjustments for a mobility-impaired applicant. The authors also mooted a possible explanation for the focus on customer contact in disfigurement discrimination; employers might be concerned about reactions of customers and a knock-on effect on their business.

The study stopped (for ethical reasons) at the shortlisting stage, so one cannot disregard the potential for bias influencing the interview process, even for behind-the-scenes roles. Research has shown that interviewers tend to recall less of what a visibly different job applicant has said during interview, and often score them lower than other candidates.[39] So, while individual accounts of discrimination during recruitment are difficult to verify, there is some objective evidence which backs up the tenor of those accounts.

In summary, while there is likely to be some interplay between psychological and social factors, negative reactions and discrimination are certainly not simply imagined by those who look different.

4.3.1 Seeing You, Knowing You

A particularly striking research discovery in this field is the correlation between appearance and perceptions of personality. Individuals tend to form assumptions about someone's character based on how they look, often linking physical attractiveness with positive personality traits. This phenomenon is succinctly captured by Dion et al. in the iconic phrase 'what is beautiful is good'.[40]

[38] William Drew Gouvier and others, 'Employment Discrimination against Handicapped Job Candidates: An Analog Study of the Effects of Neurological Causation, Visibility of Handicap, and Public Contact' (1991) 36 Rehabilitation Psychology 121, 125; Alexander Tartaglia and others, 'Workplace Discrimination and Disfigurement: The National EEOC ADA Research Project' (2005) 25 Work 57, 63.

[39] Juan M Madera and Michelle R Hebl, 'Discrimination against Facially Stigmatized Applicants in Interviews: An Eye-Tracking and Face-to-Face Investigation' (2012) 97 The Journal of Applied Psychology 317.

[40] Karen Dion, Ellen Berscheid and Elaine Walster, 'What Is Beautiful Is Good' (1972) 24 Journal of Personality and Social Psychology 285. The veracity of this has also been tested with mixed results – see Judith H Langlois, 'Maxims or Myths of Beauty? A Meta-analytic and Theoretical Review' (2000) 126(3) Psychological Bulletin 390, 402.

Studies on disfigurement specifically produce similar conclusions.[41] A US study by Rankin and Borah[42] used a two-group comparative research design of photographs of people with disfigurements and 'normal' faces, which were then rated by adult volunteer evaluators. In this study, photographs of real disfigurements were used and then digitally retouched to create a 'normal' image, seemingly reversing the possibility of simulated scars negatively impacting results. Even so, the study found that most of the photographs displaying real disfigurements were rated significantly lower in terms of perceived honesty, employability, trustworthiness, optimism, effectiveness, capability, intelligence, popularity and attractiveness than the same photographs after digital removal of the disfigurement.[43] This is consistent with research by Bull et al.[44] which found that, from the age of 12, people associate pictures of people with disfigurements with negative character traits. A 'disfigured is bad' bias has also been proven using medical technology, with MRI scans identifying this active subconscious bias when participants were shown photographs of visibly different people.[45]

Some have suggested that appearance bias has a biological element, as an evolutionary response to perceptions of potential disease.[46] But recent research has cast doubt on this idea, suggesting that the bias against visible difference is culturally learned, not innate.[47] When photographs of faces, some with scarring and some without, were shown to groups of people in Tanzania who had had very little engagement with other cultures, the negative moral associations of visibly different faces did not exist. This suggests that there may be a big role to play for the media, and other cultural forces, in removing the negative associations with visibly different faces.

41 See, for example, Anja Jamrozik and others, 'More Than Skin Deep: Judgments of Individuals with Facial Disfigurement' (2017) Psychology of Aesthetics, Creativity, and the Arts 124.

42 Marlene Rankin and Gregory Borah, 'Perceived Functional Impact of Abnormal Facial Appearance' (2002) 111 Plastic & Reconstructive Surgery 2140.

43 Ibid.

44 Ray Bull, 'The General Public's Reactions to Facial Disfigurement' in Jean Ann Graham and Albert M Kligman (eds), *The Psychology of Cosmetic Treatments* (Praeger 1985) 188.

45 Franziska Hartung and others, 'Behavioural and Neural Responses to Facial Disfigurement' (2019) 9 Scientific Reports 8021, 10.

46 Gillian Rhodes, 'The Evolutionary Psychology of Facial Beauty' (2006) 57 Annual Review of Psychology 199, 211.

47 Clifford I Workman and others, 'Evidence against the "Anomalous-Is-Bad" Stereotype in Hadza Hunter Gatherers' (2022) 12 Scientific Reports 8693.

4.3.2 Factors Affecting the Social Consequences of Disfigurement

Just as the psychological impact of disfigurement varies from person to person, the social experience can too. While some people report very negative social consequences, for others the experience is much less marked. This has led researchers to ask why.

One possibility which is often mooted is that someone's social experience will be worse if their disfigurement is somewhere very visible on their body. This is logical to an extent, but visibility is not a static concept. Few people are able (or choose) to keep covered from neck to toe all year round, and reports are frequent about the difficulties experienced when a usually covered disfigurement is exposed, such as when required to wear shorts,[48] or when removing a cardigan in hot weather.[49] One person with acne quoted in the All Party Parliamentary Group on Skin report explained:

> Any activities that need uncovering myself at all, (I live covered from neck to toe, and with makeup on my face) are a no-no as I get stares and people cat calling or moving away from me, thinking I have something catching. This particularly includes swimming, dancing, gym, going to the beach or being out in the sun.[50]

Kent and Keohane, in a study of psoriasis patients, found that the extent of visibility only impacted quality of life in those patients who also demonstrated high social anxiety.[51] Again, this neatly illustrates the difficulties in drawing firm conclusions where a variety of factors (internal and external, clinical and personal) interact.

Researchers have also considered the extent to which the cause of the disfigurement (or, more accurately, society's perception of the cause of the disfigurement) affects the stigma attaching to it. People are stigmatised more where they are seen as personally responsible for their

[48] Jowett and Ryan, 'Skin Disease and Handicap' (n 2) 428.

[49] Gerry Kent and Steve Keohane, 'Social Anxiety and Disfigurement: The Moderating Effects of Fear of Negative Evaluation and Past Experience' (2001) 40 British Journal of Clinical Psychology 23, 31.

[50] All Party Parliamentary Group on Skin, *The Psychological and Social Impact of Skin Diseases on People's Lives* (2013) 18.

[51] Kent and Keohane, 'Social Anxiety and Disfigurement' (n 49) 27. See also John Lawrence and others, 'Visible vs Hidden Scars and Their Relation to Body Esteem' (2004) 25 Journal of Burn Care and Rehabilitation 25, 30, which found a low-to-moderate association between burn scar visibility and self-appraisals of appearance.

problems.[52] An obvious example is the widespread lack of media sympathy for Daniella Westbrook's nasal disfigurement, which she has admitted resulted from drug use.[53] Some aetiologies (such as car accidents or war injuries) may be seen as more socially acceptable than others.[54] Yet the cause of a disfigurement is not always clear to an observer, and research has also noted that some types of disfigurement (such as burns scars) may be better understood, and consequently accepted, by society[55] than others. Applying this, while some causes of visible difference may help reduce social awkwardness once explained, this is unlikely to alleviate initial reactions of strangers, and public ignorance of less well-known conditions may lead to increased stigmatisation.

4.3.3 Real Life and the Law

The evidence summarised in this chapter shows that looking different can cause considerable disadvantage. Yet, as the introductory chapter sets out, the part of the law which provides a remedy for some of this disadvantage has seen little enforcement by individuals in the Employment Tribunals. To understand this mismatch between disadvantage and enforcement, we need to understand how people with a visible difference make sense of their experiences and relate these to the law.

In broad terms, the way in which real people 'experience, understand, and act in relation to law'[56] in their daily lives can be termed their 'legal consciousness'. Merry defined legal consciousness as '[t]he ways people understand and use law' and 'the way people conceive of the "natural" and normal way of doing things, their habitual patterns of talk and

[52] Eugene Stone, Diana Stone and Robert Dipboye, 'Stigmas in Organizations: Race, Handicaps and Physical Unattractiveness' in Kathryn Kelley (ed), *Organizational Psychology* (North-Holland 1992) 433.

[53] Geraldine Bedell, 'Girl, Interrupted' *The Guardian* (London, 5 May 2002) Culture <www.theguardian.com/theobserver/2002/may/05/features.review27> accessed 15 August 2019.

[54] Macgregor, 'Facial Disfigurement' (n 5) 251. See also Zali O'Dea and Jane Southcott, 'My Mummy Has a Hole in Her Face: Living with Facial Eye Disfigurement' (2023) 28 Qualitative Report 1, 3006.

[55] Ornella Masnari and others, 'Self- and Parent-Perceived Stigmatisation in Children and Adolescents with Congenital or Acquired Facial Differences' (2012) 65 Journal of Plastic, Reconstructive & Aesthetic Surgery 1664, 1669.

[56] Lynette J Chua and David M Engel, 'Legal Consciousness Reconsidered' (2019) 15 Annual Review of Law and Social Science 335, 336.

action, and their commonsense understanding of the world'.[57] Legal consciousness acts as an interpretive filter, influencing actions, inactions, perceptions and assumptions.

Dave Cowan has argued that legal consciousness has developed into 'the study of society, rather than the study of law per se',[58] focused on the subjective experiences of individuals rather than on the impact of law on people. But many studies, like Cowan's and like this one, start with an aim which is inherently 'law first',[59] only to find themselves drawn into wider discussions about meanings, understandings and identities. In my case, my original aim was to understand why claims under the severe disfigurement provision were not being brought. For this reason, what follows is presented not as a legal consciousness study per se, but an exploration of possible connections between the experiences of some people with a visible difference and the wider legal consciousness literature.

Among the people with lived experience that I interviewed, challenging discrimination – by bringing a claim in the Employment Tribunal if needed – was often seen as an exercise in solidarity. This was described in terms closely akin to a moral duty. One participant, for example, described feeling that they would be letting themself and their children down if they didn't challenge their employer's behaviour. They wanted to show their children that they are prepared to stand up for themself against something that isn't right. This sense of solidarity was also exhibited by another in wanting to 'make things better for other people' by using legal rights to challenge bad behaviour.

This idea of using law to stand up for oneself as a form of moral solidarity can be found in some of the wider literature too. Anna Kirkland's exploration of the fat acceptance movement in America, for example, delineates the practice of 'moral instruction'[60] as 'a didactic comeuppance to someone who has discriminated against her or otherwise rebuked her in the past'.[61] This included a participant who regretted that she 'should have done something about' a past instance of

[57] Sally Engle Merry, *Getting Justice and Getting Even: Legal Consciousness Among Working-Class Americans / Sally Engle Merry* (University of Chicago Press 1990) 5.

[58] Dave Cowan, 'Legal Consciousness: Some Observations' (2004) 67 Modern Law Review 928, 929.

[59] Ibid 933.

[60] Anna Kirkland, 'Think of the Hippopotamus: Rights Consciousness in the Fat Acceptance Movement' (2008) 42 Law & Society Review 397, 408.

[61] Ibid.

discrimination to 'bring it out in the open'.[62] And Hirsch and Louie's study with plaintiffs in discrimination claims in the US identified 'a desire to produce a public good by ensuring that others did not suffer the same kind of wrongdoing in the workplace'.[63]

Among the people I interviewed, the feeling of solidarity was, for many, countered by a strong wariness about what they saw as the likely reality of using rights under equality law. This kind of tension – between feeling that you should do something and being wary of doing it – is perhaps not unusual; in their seminal work, Ewick and Silbey describe legal consciousness as often 'multifaceted and possibly contradictory',[64] recognising that layers of meaning do not always fall neatly into one clear category. For my participants, this wariness about using law was found in three different areas.

The first iteration of wariness concerned the link in the law between disability and disfigurement. Many did not self-identify as disabled and frequently this was due to wariness about being labelled or categorised. One participant commented that 'I try to avoid the term disability and the definition and things like that' because of the stigma attaching to it.

This wariness of a disabled identity is also found among people with other conditions,[65] so is probably not surprising. But there is an additional complication where visible difference is the health condition at issue; the reluctance often links to disability being seen as an exclusively *functional* concept. One person interviewed, for example, told me that they did not think of themself as disabled because their condition did not stop them from going to the supermarket, cleaning their house, driving to work and so on, but they felt conscious of people staring and judging while they did this. Another participant's decision not to self-define as disabled was explained by the fact that their cleft did not impact their speech or hearing, which it can do for some people. This rejection of a

62 Ibid 409.

63 C Elizabeth Hirsh and Patricia Louie, 'Legal Consciousness, Mobilization, and Discrimination Disputes at Work' in *The Oxford Handbook of Workplace Discrimination* (Oxford University Press 2018) 273.

64 Patricia Ewick and Susan Silbey, *The Common Place of Law: Stories from Everyday Life* (University of Chicago Press 1998) 50.

65 Nick Watson, 'Well, I Know This Is Going to Sound Very Strange to You, but I Don't See Myself as a Disabled Person: Identity and Disability' (2002) 17 Disability & Society 509; J Hurstfield and others, *Monitoring the Disability Discrimination Act (DDA) 1995: Phase 3* (Disability Rights Commission, Department for Work and Pensions and the Equality Commission (Northern Ireland) 2004) 12. See also Kirkland, 'Think of the Hippopotamus' (n 60) 420 for a discussion of identity, rights and weight.

disabled identity may explain why some people used the terminology of 'difference' or 'chronic health condition', not disability.

In my interviews with people with visible differences, some felt trapped in the middle between the categories of disabled and not-disabled, neither of which felt like quite the right fit to them:

> I don't want to put myself in a box where I'm classified as kind of in that category of disabled, because there's all that stigma attached to it, and all those preconceptions, and all those things that are attached to being disabled. And there's nothing, something like, 'Oh, I've got this condition but it doesn't affect me', or someone who maybe, 'Oh, I've got depression, but I don't consider myself . . .,' there's no – kind of – I just find it frustrating. It almost feels like it's an equality tick box.

This perception of disability as something that affects what you can do, not what you look like, mirrors the medical model of disability and its heavy reliance on functional impairment. Given that the Act categorises qualifying severe disfigurements as a type of disability, the wariness of the word 'disability' reveals an obvious clash between the construction of individual self-identities and the structure of the law.

Wariness about the label and concept of disability sometimes had very practical implications for people – like when job applicants were faced with 'disability' tick boxes on application forms ('Do you have a disability? Tick yes or no'). This caused anxiety and uncertainty for some, because they were not sure whether their condition counted as a disability, or whether it would be a good idea to disclose it. One person that I spoke to worried about being accused of dishonesty if they disclosed a disability. They decided not to tick that disability box because 'if you make any false declaration on your application form, then that gives them grounds really, doesn't it, to not give you the job if they think you're lying'. The application of law here is seen as a powerful, oppressive threat in the background,[66] impacting the individual's ability to be the expert on her own life.

The second iteration of wariness about law concerned the process of bringing a discrimination claim. From the perceived cost of the process to the stress of it, and from the hurdle of proving what happened to the indignity of having to listen to other people talking about your appearance, many participants expressed worries about the practical implications of using law. For some people, these worries about practical factors

[66] On this point, see Ewick and Silbey, *The Common Place of Law* (n 64) 165–220.

may be grounded in fact. A small number of the people that I spoke to had had some involvement – even if indirectly – with legal claims before, and so may have witnessed these well-documented practical problems[67] in the past.

But many had had no experiences of this kind, so for them these barriers were purely anticipated. There are parallels here with Bumiller's research on the legal consciousness of potential discrimination claimants in the US. While acknowledging that the anticipation of practical factors – such as cost – might play a role in the decision-making of her participants, Bumiller notes that 'these persons were not rejected by unresponsive agencies, deterred by the cost and availability of lawyers, or barred from pursuing legal claims by technicalities'.[68] Instead, she argues, 'they did not take action primarily because they legitimized their own defeat'.[69] In other words, Bumiller argues that the anticipation of practical difficulties can mask a more deep-rooted and generalised feeling that using legal rights is not an option.[70] Instead, the reluctance to mobilise laws forms part of an 'ethic of survival'[71] borne from a belief that discrimination is inevitable. This deep-rooted reluctance suggests that, even if rights could be made easier to use – perhaps by providing more free legal advice centres and guidance to remove legislative uncertainty – enforcement may remain low. Many people may still prefer to walk away and consider themselves to be 'better off out of it' rather than rely on the law to challenge an unfair situation.

The third iteration of wariness towards laws is found in the context of the duty to make reasonable adjustments. This legal duty requires employers to make changes in some contexts to avoid a disabled member of staff from being placed at a disadvantage. Some participants could identify aspects of their jobs which they found hard due to visible difference. For one interviewee, for example, the need to attend external

[67] In relation to legal consciousness of people seeking to challenge unfairness at work through legal means, see Eleanor Joanne Kirk and Nicole Busby, 'Led Up the Tribunal Path? Employment Disputes, Legal Consciousness and Trust in the Protection of Law' (2017) 7 Onati Socio-Legal Series 1397, 1407.

[68] Kristin Bumiller, *The Civil Rights Society: The Social Construction of Victims / Kristin Bumiller* (Johns Hopkins University Press 1988) 29.

[69] Ibid 29. See also Kirk and Busby, 'Led Up the Tribunal Path?' (n 67) 1410.

[70] See also Beth A Quinn, 'The Paradox of Complaining: Law, Humor, and Harassment in the Everyday Work World' (2000) 25 Law & Social Inquiry 1151, 1172.

[71] Bumiller, *The Civil Rights Society* (n 68) 88.

conferences was difficult, because it involved meeting so many new people at once.

But often people were wary about requesting small changes at work. Sometimes this was because they didn't think the duty would apply to aesthetic, rather than functional, differences. As one participant said, 'You can't make adjustments for looking different'. Others were wary that having adjustments made would single them out and make them look less capable. And sometimes they were worried about the process of talking to their employer about personal issues. One person was reluctant to request adjustments to their role because of a previous experience; their request to have the air conditioning on in the summer had been turned down by a manager who did not understand that they wanted to cover up their visible difference with long clothing.

For a minority of people in my study, having their employer raise the issue of adjustments with them individually would have been very intrusive. One participant would have found their employer starting this discussion 'too much. I think I'd be too sensitive about it and be thinking "Oh God, is that the first thing you thought about for me, then?"'. And although most participants were open to their employer raising the topic in principle, they were wary about how this would work in reality. Some feared that, if they asked for support, their employer would somehow manage to make things worse – either by intruding on their privacy, making assumptions or pushing for poorly thought-out changes. Inclusivity training was one example of this; some participants envisaged that poorly run appearance-inclusivity training for staff would create awkwardness and resentment towards them because 'everyone knows what it's about'. There is a sense here that individual dignity might be at risk from employers handling poorly the process of reasonable adjustment. This exposes a tricky dilemma for employers about whether – and how – to discuss support with a member of staff with a visible difference. Should employers prioritise the possibility of support or the desire to avoid potential awkwardness or offence?[72]

In summary, despite feeling that legal rights 'should' be used, the evidence suggests that people with a visible difference are often wary about doing so. The lived experience of visible difference can, at times and for some people, be both psychologically and socially difficult. Yet there is friction between the terminology, structure and perceived process

[72] See further Chapter 5.

of the law and the reality of what it is like to live with a visible difference. Equality law is often seen not as a solution but as a risk, with the potential to make things worse.

4.4 Summary

The evidence in this chapter suggests that significant bias against people with disfigurements does exist, and can permeate through different aspects of life, including the workplace. This bias is complex in nature, extending beyond aesthetic judgments into perceived associations about morality, personality and capability. The attitudes of other people towards someone who looks different have the power not just to isolate socially but to prevent participation in certain activities, compromise personal security and privacy and reduce the ability to support oneself financially. As noted in the framework of statutory equality outcomes identified in Chapter 3, the research discussed here indicates that problematic attitudes and behaviours towards people who look different are still common, even though over twenty-five years have passed since the severe disfigurement equality provision was first brought into law. Although the limited data available makes it difficult to trace any changes to these attitudes and behaviours over the years, there is little evidence to suggest that the law has resulted in a significant reduction of prejudice. *If* any positive changes have occurred, they do not appear to have gone far enough.

The evidence in this chapter provides some basic parameters which a law with lived experience at its heart would need to respect. First, it would need to move beyond basic assumptions of 'more clinical severity equals more discrimination' and 'disfigurements aren't a problem if they can be hidden'. These common assumptions are not supported by the evidence. A law which has these assumptions at its heart will grant rights of action to some people and not others even though they all share experiences of social disadvantage and resulting distress.

Second, this is a three-dimensional problem. It is not 'just' about looks; it is also about grappling with unconscious assumptions which erroneously link looks with attributes salient to the workplace, such as someone's abilities, character and chances of success. So even when looks aren't perceived to 'matter' for a particular job – perhaps because it is not customer-facing – someone's looks can still count against them in other ways.

Third, if individual enforcement of the law by individuals is needed – whether in bringing a discrimination claim or having the confidence to request reasonable adjustments at work – this has to *feel* like a genuine, viable option in real life.

Perhaps most importantly, in the social understandings of some people with lived experience of disfigurements, we see inconsistent meanings about the word 'disability' coming to the fore again, just as they did in the legal framework summarised earlier in the book. Many people in this group did not self-identify as disabled because disability was seen as something that affects your ability to perform certain functions, not what you look like. This mirrors the conceptual confusion that exists within the international legal framework and in the provisions of the Act and influences the identities of many people with visible differences.[73] This can deter the willingness to claim ownership of rights under the heading of disability, both in the workplace and the Employment Tribunal.

[73] The rejection of a disabled identity has been acknowledged by charities working in this area too. See Face Equality International, 'Face Equality Is a Human Right' (*Face Equality International*, 2022) <https://faceequalityinternational.org/wp-content/uploads/2022/05/Face-Equality-is-a-Human-Right-Report.pdf> accessed 7 November 2023.

5

Disfigurement Equality at Work

Employer Perspectives

How can employers create inclusive workplaces for people with visible differences? Are there ways to ensure that job applicants who look different are not disadvantaged? What reasonable adjustments might be made to support staff with aesthetic differences? And how should employers go about having those very personal conversations? This chapter examines employer perspectives on disfigurement in the workplace. It includes evidence drawn from thirteen semi-structured interviews with employer representatives who are working, or have previously worked, in human resources or equality and diversity roles in Britain.

Despite considerable organisational diversity among the participants,[1] many expressed the sense that, in HR circles, the problem of disfigurement inequality 'isn't particularly out there, unfortunately. It's not something that we're talking about'. Consistent with this, awareness of the severe disfigurement provision was also low among the employers in this study. During interviews, only around 25 per cent demonstrated an understanding that people with severe disfigurements may be protected as disabled people under the Act without needing to satisfy a test of functional impairment. Participants often presumed that people with disfigurements would be treated as disabled people in the law but then described an understanding of disability based on functional impairment. One interviewee noted the illogicality of this when asked what they could remember about the law on disfigurement:

> It's something that would affect someone for more than 12 months, so a long-term condition, which would affect their ability to do things on a day-to-day basis. So, well yes, would it be covered, facial disfigurement? I don't know now. [. . .] Because why would it affect your ability to do something? It shouldn't do, should it? No.

[1] The organisations varied in size, location and spanned a number of different industries and sectors.

Many of the participants also found it challenging to identify what good practice might be in this area. They commonly anticipated that relations with colleagues would be a significant challenge facing someone with a visible difference, particularly when new to the workplace or meeting people for the first time. And there was a shared belief among some that existing staff might need to learn how to interact with someone who looks different. This was often interpreted as well-intentioned awkwardness, rather than bias. For example, one HR professional who had supported someone with a disfigurement into the business before, said:

> So the conversation and building a rapport was the challenge for team members. So we often had people coming to us saying 'I feel really guilty. I don't know how or where to look or what to say. How can I say things?' So it was people feeling awkward, wanting to do the right thing.

Some employers also recognised, however, that relations with others could be impacted by bias and discrimination – from managers, colleagues and third parties such as customers in public-facing roles. In the words of one HR participant:

> we have some great managers, but we will also have what I'm going to call a few dinosaurs. [. . .] they could get a great manager. They could get a dinosaur. And that would be my concern. My concern is that all that dinosaur would see is the disfigurement. They wouldn't actually see the person. They wouldn't see the skill set. You know, they wouldn't actually see what that person has to offer. They would just be focusing in on that disfigurement, and then would make their decision based on that disfigurement.

Suggested ways of dealing with these anticipated difficulties varied, and often revealed competing tensions which participants felt the need to balance. These tensions were most apparent at times of change and transition – particularly when recruiting new staff, and when discussing support measures, as set out below.

5.1 Recruitment

Recruitment was a key transition point when participants tended to feel conflicted. When discussing hiring procedures, there was often an underlying tension between the need for consistency and the desire for flexibility. Many of the employers felt that consistency – in terms of applying the same process to all – was vital during recruitment, to ensure fair comparisons between candidates. But at the same time, there was often a recognition that a 'one size fits all' approach could favour some candidates over others, putting minority groups at a disadvantage. This conflict mirrors a wider tension between formal and substantive equality. Formal equality equates to consistency – treating everyone the same and being blind to difference. Whereas substantive equality implies the flexibility to treat groups differently to provide genuine equality of opportunity which can alleviate disadvantage. Just as the law has yet to resolve this tension – with its lacklustre commitment to substantive equality through positive action, for example – so some employers are struggling to balance the two opposing imperatives in their daily interactions.

One example of this 'consistency versus flexibility' tension is found when planning interview processes. Most recruitment methods tend to be visual, in that the candidate is seen as well as heard – but this doesn't have to be the case. Interviewing by telephone, in a camera-off remote interview, or even behind a screen (as in orchestral auditions) reduces the opportunity for appearance bias to operate. Although some physical characteristics might be perceptible from someone's voice,[2] many visible differences would not be apparent from a non-visual interview. However, the idea of non-visual interviews received a very mixed reaction from employer participants. Some HR staff anticipated pushback from management to the idea, or problems assessing interpersonal skills. Giving the candidate a flavour of the work environment was also felt to be a challenge in a non-visual context, as it would preclude an office tour. And there were concerns – including from some employers who had used telephone interviews before – about how blind recruitment could impact wider recruitment fairness goals, such as the need to be accessible for people with hearing impairments who may want to lip-read, or to recruit people from less privileged economic backgrounds who may not be as confident presenting themselves orally.[3]

Concerns about non-visual interviews were mirrored by some people with a visible difference. Ideally, they wanted choice – the freedom to select a non-visual or visual interview to suit them. The idea of choice is empowering and aligns with what we know already: the lived experience of visible difference is different for different people and can change over time. As one focus group participant with a visible difference said:

> there was a period in my life when I couldn't look at myself on zoom. I couldn't even look at myself in a mirror. I'll be honest, I'm doing this,

[2] Cleft palate, for example, can affect intonation.

[3] In contrast, another participant who had used telephone interviews chose to do so because they believed it *increased* the socio-economic diversity of successful candidates, as neither environment nor clothing was evident to the interviewer.

> looking at you [. . .] on gallery view but everyone is on a different journey so we've got to include everyone regardless of where they are in their journey, not just try and make it from, this is how we used to work, to this is now the one size fits all protocol. Facial difference is not a one size fits all scenario.

But the idea of giving candidates a choice of a visual or non-visual interview was met with concern by some employers because it creates inconsistent assessment conditions. Some felt that opting for a non-visual interview would disadvantage a candidate in an otherwise 'visual' process; interviewers would be suspicious of a candidate's reasons for turning off their camera or might find it harder to form a personal connection with a candidate that they haven't actually seen. One participant in an EDI role suggested that:

> if you give the flexibility, maybe bias might creep in more when you're looking at someone that you've had a really good video interview with, you've really connected, they had great body language, great eye contact, all this kind of stuff, compared with someone who wrote a really good article about themselves or someone that answered some questions on the telephone, but you didn't see them, you didn't kind of get a sense of who they were from that. So I'd be worried about offering too much flexibility because again . . . it just . . . it could allow inclusion or diverse candidates to again fail subject to the stronger, kind of more prepped, white affluent male coming through, because they're able to do things that people from a more diverse background feel less comfortable doing.

This tension between consistency and flexibility creates a difficult dilemma: a consistently visual recruitment process could be tainted by bias against visibly different candidates, and a uniformly non-visual process might be impractical and disadvantage some other groups of candidates. But a flexible process which offers a range of different mediums risks disadvantaging any candidate who opts for a non-standard process.

Setting non-visual interviews to one side, some employer participants felt that measures could be taken to reduce the risk of biased outcomes from visual job interview processes. Using structured questioning techniques was suggested by some. This means 'asking a predefined set of questions, in the same order, to all candidates' in order to 'minimise bias and ensure there is a level playing field for candidates from marginalised groups'.[4] Interviewing in teams was a technique adopted by others, as a

[4] CIPD, 'Inclusive Recruitment: Guide for Employers' (*CIPD*, 2022) <www.cipd.org/uk/knowledge/guides/inclusive-employers/#role-design-and-the-job-advert> accessed 24 October 2023.

way of mitigating the bias of any particular interviewer and ensuring a range of views. Some HR participants also welcomed the idea of training for interviewers about appearance bias, to encourage them to question their own assumptions. And if a visibly different candidate chose to send in a photo or brief familiarisation video of themself before interview, many HR staff indicated that they would have shown it to interviewers in advance, to prevent awkward reactions on the day. The caveat here, of course, is that submitting a video or photo in advance to reduce difficult reactions is a personal choice and should not be expected by employers. The social model of disability places the responsibility on society to break down barriers, not on the individual to anticipate and navigate them.

Another tension which was apparent in discussions about recruitment was the need to balance efficiency against inclusion. Participants often spoke forcefully about the time and budget pressures they were under, and the difficulties of keeping up with fast-changing demands for inclusion and different treatment from so many different groups. Standard hiring processes tend to be perceived as easier to manage, and therefore more efficient. One participant used pre-recorded video interviews to increase efficiency, because they were quicker to review than live interviews. Although systems vary, often automated video interviews require the candidates to log onto a remote system and answer a series of questions while the system videos their responses. The organisation which used these did note that many people asked to complete an automated interview dropped out of the process before doing so and speculated that the people who drop out 'don't feel comfortable answering questions into a computer, I guess'. This is concerning, especially if organisations never find out why the candidate chose not to take part, as it may deter certain groups of candidates to a greater degree. Some other HR participants were reluctant to use artificial intelligence or technology applications in recruitment; in one HR participant's view, recruitment is 'a very human process' for which computers are not best suited.[5] Another participant had previously worked for an organisation where the computer system itself would shortlist or reject applications, creating perceived unfairness in some cases which HR staff were powerless to remedy.

[5] See Section 9.1.5.

5.2 Support and Adjustments

Another area of tension occurred in the context of support and reasonable adjustments for people with visible differences. The duty to make reasonable adjustments under the Act[6] applies where:

1. a provision criterion or practice ('PCP') puts a disabled person at a substantial disadvantage in relation to a relevant matter in comparison with persons who are not disabled.
2. a physical feature (of premises) puts a disabled person at a substantial disadvantage in relation to a relevant matter in comparison with persons who are not disabled.
3. a disabled person would, but for the provision of an auxiliary aid, be put at a substantial disadvantage in relation to a relevant matter in comparison with persons who are not disabled.

The requirement is to take such steps as are reasonable to avoid the disadvantage (in the case of the first and second requirements) or provide the auxiliary aid (for the third requirement).

The application of the duty to people with disfigurements may not initially be obvious in the way that it would be for a disability with a clear functional consequence. While a ramp may provide a straightforward solution to the disadvantage of an office entrance step for someone in a wheelchair, the mechanics of adjustment may be more obscure where the impairment is a disfigurement. This lack of clarity came across when interviewing employers: many HR and EDI participants struggled to identify a range of adjustments which could be made in respect of visible difference. When discussing adjustments, the participants frequently tended to focus their answers on adjustments for any functional impairments related to visible difference:

INTERVIEWER: What kind of support might you think somebody might require, subject to consultation?

HR PARTICIPANT: Well, I mean it depends. Because if they had a disfigurement that affected their eating, for instance – it could be eating, it could be eyesight, you know. There could be things that they need – computer help for eyes it could be. Or if they can't speak properly because they've had an operation or something, then it may be that the computer –

[6] Equality Act 2010, s20.

> you turn on the type text at the bottom. It could be a variety of things. So we'd have to look at what we've got available, and also what is available out there, new technology to help people.

This perception of reasonable adjustment as a response to purely functional deficit is strongly influenced by the medical model of disability. In other words, disability is seen as negatively affecting the individual's ability to perform certain activities, and adjustments are made to remedy this disadvantage. This may partly explain why – in the experiences of both the participants with lived experience and the employer participants – there was sparse evidence that discussions about adjustments for staff with visible differences are commonly taking place in response to the social barriers of disfigurement.

Despite this very functional interpretation of the reasonable adjustment duty, some participants did suggest a few possible adjustments which might be relevant for some people with visible differences. This included allowing cameras to be off during video meetings and permitting new joiners to bring photos from home rather than having one taken in the workplace (or to avoid submitting a photo at all). Changes to working hours or home working were also suggested, as well as the provision of well-being support. Adjustments to dress codes were also mooted; rigid enforcement of a dress code may place employees with a severe disfigurement at a substantial disadvantage.[7] For example, one interviewee with a visible skin condition on their arms struggled with being asked to wear a short-sleeved polo shirt. Another found the dark-coloured uniform difficult because it highlighted flakes of peeling skin. And a third faced a dilemma about whether to wear make-up with a facial palsy on one side of their face.

I would venture a couple of other possible adjustments relevant in some work contexts. The first relates to the rules on performance evaluation, which can prove problematic given the subconscious tendency to associate negative character traits with visibly different people. Policies which involve making judgments about staff may need to be adjusted to reduce the possibility of hidden bias. A particular area of concern is soft skills such as 'teamworking ability', 'attitude' or 'ambition' which are

[7] See, for example, *Riam Dean v Abercrombie and Fitch* [2009] (August 2009, unreported, ET); *Hutchison 3G Ltd v Edwards* [2014] UKEAT/0467/13/DM (4 August 2017, unreported, EAT).

almost invariably subjective and could easily be influenced by unfounded assumptions of how popular, employable or capable someone is likely to be. Evaluation scoring systems may need to be altered so that they are linked to objectively verifiable criteria and avoid ratings based heavily on perceptions (such as customer feedback ratings in store surveys).

Second, adjustments might be required in respect of the role itself. Returning to the psychological consequences identified earlier, some people with a visible difference report feeling particularly uncomfortable meeting new people.[8] A role requirement to give external presentations, for example, could put a visibly different employee at a substantial disadvantage compared with someone who is not disabled. One participant with a visible difference explained that, when asked to give presentations, their face became 'like a big neon light' in their head, taking away their confidence and making them conscious of people looking. Even where the employer is aware of the disfigurement, though, the employee may need to expressly explain the nature of this disadvantage in order to trigger the duty to make reasonable adjustments as, unlike the 'wheelchair and office step' scenario envisaged earlier, it may not be reasonable for an employer to investigate this without knowledge of the likely impact on the employee.

Many HR participants would also want to mediate awkward relationships with colleagues.[9] Although not often expressed in formal terms as an adjustment, HR teams would often look to resolve team awkwardness with informal discussions, reassurance, mentoring and even training about allyship with colleagues who look different. There was, however, occasionally an expectation that this kind of mentoring and training would not be necessary for people in professional roles, who would be expected to have enough common sense to ignore visible differences and not let any surprise show outwardly. For one employer participant, it would be 'more the support staff that would find it more uncomfortable, if they hadn't had training [. . .] on how to deal with someone. You know, do you make eye contact? Do you not make . . . you know, all those kinds of things, that's where it's important for us to do'. This may miss an opportunity to embed good practice throughout the organisation.

8 See Sections 4.1 and 4.2.

9 For an example of a case involving bullying by colleagues, see *Smith v HM Prison Service* [2004] ET/2406059/03 (10 August 2004, unreported, ET) discussed in IDS Diversity at Work 9 (March 2005).

Whether – and when – to raise the topic of support with someone with a visible difference was a particularly vexing issue for many HR participants. There was a concern that raising the topic might cause offence or might be seen as jumping to unjustified assumptions. While most would feel comfortable talking to a visibly different member of staff who raised the topic first, many were unsure whether it would be appropriate to initiate a discussion about adjustments for visible difference. This tension between offering support and respecting someone's privacy involved a delicate balancing act. One employer participant expressed this as an interest in finding out 'where the lines are, because I wouldn't want to offend someone. I'd want to make someone feel comfortable in their workplace. But obviously they do look different and they are going to attract attention. So yes, it's a bit of an unknown for me, I suppose, in the work setting'. Interestingly, the awkwardness expressed by employers was also anticipated by many people with lived experience; while most interviewees with a visible difference would have welcomed their employer initiating a discussion about support if handled in the right way, there was considerable concern that many employers would handle the conversation poorly and risk making things worse.

Some employers choose to have a discussion with *every* worker, irrespective of impairment, to ask whether they want to request any adjustments. This avoids the possibility of causing offence by singling out some people because of their appearance. However, other employers choose not to open the idea of adjustment beyond the legal requirements (which only require an employer to make reasonable adjustments once they know – or ought reasonably to know – that a disabled person is likely to be placed at a substantial disadvantage).[10] Current guidance from the EHRC about when to raise the topic of reasonable adjustments with disabled employees is vague. It says:

> The employer must, however, do all they can reasonably be expected to do to find out [whether the employee has a disability and is being, or is likely to be, placed at a substantial disadvantage]. What is reasonable will depend on the circumstances. This is an objective assessment. When making enquiries about disability, employers should consider issues of dignity and privacy and ensure that personal information is dealt with confidentially. (EHRC, 2011)[11]

[10] Equality Act 2010, sched 8 para 20.

[11] Equality and Human Rights Commission, *Employment: Statutory Code of Practice* (The Stationery Office Limited, 2011) para 6.19.

This guidance is particularly difficult to apply in the visible difference context – where an impairment will often be visible but its effects (if any) on the individual more likely to be psychological than functional, and where managers (sometimes correctly) perceive the potential to cause offence. Given this lack of clarity, it is understandable that some HR staff simply don't know when to raise the issue, and when to respect the individual's privacy. In that context, saying nothing may feel safer, but risks missing an opportunity to ensure that the member of staff is fully supported. This presents a difficult conundrum.

A possible solution to this dilemma (which was suggested by some of the employer participants) is to wait for a 'trigger' to have an individual discussion about support. The trigger could, for example, be noticing that the employee was experiencing awkwardness with colleagues, hearing that they had been asked intrusive questions by a customer or observing that they were nervous about public speaking or having their camera on in remote meetings. This ensures that actual problems are not ignored, while not jumping to unjustified assumptions.

Once a decision has been made about the need for that conversation, helping managers to find ways to do so appropriately is still a concern for some HR participants. Due to organisational structures, often it is line managers, not HR, who need to have these conversations, and the HR participants perceived that many are scared of doing so, or less skilled at doing it sensitively. Terminology was highlighted as a particular hurdle in asking managers to have conversations about appearance. As one EDI participant put it:

> Language is important. I still think that disfigurement is a . . . such a negative term in itself. It's such a negative term. It's so charged with 'you are less than', 'you are other' all that sort of stuff, so that's the last phrase I would want to use with somebody with a disfigurement. What I would want to say is 'so what happened is you have a birthmark, yes' or, you know, if there was something congenital, 'you still have the marks from your cleft lip and palate operation' or something like that 'and you're very self conscious about it'. So actually the issue is not labelling it as a disfigurement but actually creating an environment where you can normalise the conversation without it being so powerfully negative.

A major challenge for HR departments, then, is how to ensure that good HR practice can be translated into the conversations which happen on the ground. For this reason, the model of good practice at Appendix 1 includes a brief guide to having conversations about support related to visible difference, which could be used as part of a training programme for managers.

5.3 HR Practice and the Law

As a qualitative study, the sample of employers interviewed was small. But the lack of awareness of disfigurement inequality at work among these participants is borne out by a lack of debate about this topic in the professional press and on HR forums. Despite the severe disfigurement provision in the Act, little evidence was found of any community of good practice or debate among employers about creating appearance-inclusive workplaces. To understand this lack of impact, the literature on law in action is informative. Ruth Dukes and Eleanor Kirk's work on the legal consciousness of HR management identifies a difficult duality of role within HR departments – sometimes badged as employee champions and sometimes as business partners. They argue that:

> HR managers work within a context that is riven with contradictions. At the same time as the profession strives to maintain a reputation as an employee champion, it also presents itself as a partner of business. In recent years, such contradictions have become ever more apparent, to the extent that the profession now faces a profound crisis of social legitimacy.[12]

In their view, it is the business-partner side of HR which increasingly wins the day,[13] with HR teams' main duty being, ultimately, to promote organisational priorities: 'flexibility, profit-making, maximisation of shareholder value'.[14] This is demonstrated, Kirk argues, by the HR profession's selective embrace of workplace rights issues with the power to enhance corporate interests – such as race and sex equality – at the expense of other issues – such as the insecure position of casual workers.[15] The declining influence of trade unions within the workplace exacerbates the contradictions found within the functions of HR departments,[16] as it removes an extra employee champion from the mix.

Many of the employer participants' reflections supported this contradiction. Their actions are under considerable pressure – in terms of time, budget, ever-changing HR priorities and achieving corporate goals. Although some spoke passionately about their organisation's belief in

[12] Ruth Dukes and Eleanor Kirk, 'Law, Economy and Legal Consciousness at Work' (2022) 72 Northern Ireland Legal Quarterly 741, 764.

[13] Ibid 765.

[14] Eleanor Kirk, 'Law and Legalities at Work: HR Practitioners as Quasi-Legal Professionals' (2021) 50 Industrial Law Journal 583, 587.

[15] Ibid 586.

[16] Ibid 588.

equality, others identified commercial drivers for people initiatives, such as the need to show inclusion initiatives to attract the best talent in a difficult labour market. Or the need to 'do something to get them through the process' of winning a government contract, even though it's not a priority within the industry. There was sometimes a sense that it's not enough to do EDI; you need to be *seen* to be doing EDI externally.

The conflicted position of HR functions in many organisations means, perhaps, that whatever the individual values of the people working within HR (including the thirteen who very generously gave up their time to speak to me for no personal gain), communities of good practice are perhaps more likely to develop if they align with a commercial priority of some kind. In other words, if championing visible-difference equality aligns with the company's commercial interests – perhaps responding to changing public feeling or creating an opportunity to increase profits – HR departments will be better able to justify working towards it. But the almost total invisibility of both the problem of disfigurement inequality and the law in this area perhaps indicate that communities of good practice will be low down the priority list of many organisations unless something changes.

Another issue which might be limiting attempts to develop best practice in this area is the need for HR functions to take into account the differing needs of so many groups. There was a sense of frustration in the accounts given by some employer participants about the scale of the challenge that this represented:

> I struggle to put my hand around every type of community network or group of individuals that need extra help in some way, because it is so vast. So sometimes by targeting different groups to either raise awareness or inclusivity, it becomes overwhelming to try and get managers' heads around that. So if there is generic crossovers, if there is ways and solutions that can be put in place that work for more than one particular group, or that can be replicated with a small tweak for other people, then I think that's the winner. You know, you've got to get people to listen in business, we've got to make it easy for them. Which is wrong, I know that. You know, everyone has got to put effort in. But if I go to someone and say 'You've got five different things to think about in your team. You know, you've got a single mum, you have an elderly woman, you've got someone with a disfigurement' they're going to be like 'well how am I ever going to do my business?' But if I can go to them and say 'Look, you've got a diverse group of people, this is how you organise a team meeting to service everybody, this is how you run a performance process to service everybody' that message is really, really different. (HR participant)

While an issue-specific approach to good practice might be helpful in identifying adjustments for a particular member of staff, for reasons of perceived practicality, processes affecting multiple people – such as recruitment – are most likely to be used if they work for a majority of people. Strategically, therefore, smaller identity groups – such as people with visible differences – may create greater traction by seeking commonalities with other groups.

5.4 Summary

In summary, the capacity of employers to create appearance-inclusive workplaces – where people with a visible difference are not disadvantaged in any way – is hindered in several respects.

First, the evidence suggests a lack of awareness about this issue. And even where awareness is raised, there is a lack of practical guidance about how to achieve this. Concerns about causing offence, and invading people's privacy risk leading employers to ignore the issue. The model of good practice at Appendix 1 is a small step towards supporting employers with this.

Second, progress towards appearance-inclusive workplaces may be hindered by tension between the aims of consistency and flexibility. In other words, employers often feel torn between treating everyone the same to ensure consistency and creating flexible processes to enable diverse groups of people. This tension echoes the same unease found in the law between the concepts of formal and substantive equality and suggests that employers are struggling to understand how to balance these competing imperatives. The strain is heightened by the practical difficulties of being flexible; with so many different disadvantaged groups, identities and inclusion needs, employers sometimes grapple with the risk of taking steps to support one group which incidentally exclude another.

Inclusion efforts are sometimes hindered by commercial drivers too. With HR departments increasingly occupying a conflicted middle ground between championing employees and supporting business priorities, the need to progress business objectives (especially efficiency and profitability) is pressing for many. Accordingly, equality initiatives may gain greater traction with HR departments if they are aligned with business priorities, not just ethical values. Chapter 9 considers ways to tap into commercial imperatives as a way of pushing appearance-inclusive workplaces to the top of their priority list.

Third, progress is hindered, once again, by conceptual confusion about the meaning of the word 'disability'. When asked about rights under equality law for people with disfigurements, most of the employer participants provided a description of disability based on functional impairment. Although it is evidentially difficult to trace social meanings back to law, many of the HR participants used partial quotes taken from the Act's definition of disability (such as 'day-to-day activities'). This suggests that the law has at least played a part in the manifestation of the medical model concept of disability encapsulated in their responses. More worrying still, this conceptual confusion filtered through to their discussions about daily HR practice. When asked about possible reasonable adjustments for someone with a visible difference, some HR participants struggled to answer, and often resorted to discussing adjustments for functional impairments which might accompany a visible difference – such as hearing loss. Although wider research would be beneficial, this suggests that, in many workplaces, there may be little understanding of the social barriers of visible difference and how to dismantle them.

6

Defining Disfigurement

This chapter[1] takes a closer look at the severe disfigurement provision, which was introduced earlier in the book. To recap, Chapter 2 concluded that the social model of disability underlies the inclusion of people with severe disfigurements within the disability provisions of the Act, because society's reactions to someone who looks different can be disabling. However, despite this underlying logic, the Act doesn't attempt to protect everyone who experiences social barriers because they look different. It includes only those with severe disfigurements which meet certain criteria. Understanding what a severe disfigurement is – and isn't – is crucial to understanding the Act's boundaries. This is the task undertaken in this chapter and in Chapter 7, which scrutinise the concepts of disfigurement and severity respectively.

6.1 Disfigurement: An Appearance Disability

Discrimination against people with visible differences is, at least to some extent, prohibited by disability provisions in the Act. Schedule 1[2] says that:

> An impairment which consists of a severe disfigurement is to be treated as having a substantial adverse effect on the ability of the person concerned to carry out normal day-to-day activities.

The meaning of the word 'disfigurement' is crucial, but elusive. Given the much-debated definition of disability, it is strange that there is no equivalent definition of disfigurement in the Act. EU law yields no

[1] Much of this chapter (and part of Chapter 9) is reproduced and amended from: Hannah Saunders, 'Difficult Distinctions in Anti-discrimination Law: Disfigurement, Appearance and Disability' (2020) 20 International Journal of Discrimination and the Law 21–44. Copyright © [2020] (The author). DOI: 10.1177/1358229120927917.

[2] Equality Act 2010, sched 1 s3.

definition either; the disfigurement provision in the Act does not stem from EU law expressly. The CRPD equally provides no definition, although its wide description of disability as a social construct would include those with a visible difference.

There is a partial explanation of the concept of severe disfigurement in the guidance which accompanies the Act.[3] This provides:

> Examples of disfigurements include scars, birthmarks, limb or postural deformation (including restricted bodily development), or diseases of the skin. Assessing severity will be mainly a matter of the degree of the disfigurement which may involve taking into account factors such as the nature, size, and prominence of the disfigurement. However, it may be necessary to take account of where the disfigurement in question is (e.g. on the back as opposed to the face).[4]

The guidance is not comprehensive; the types of disfigurement listed are examples only. Scars and birthmarks are perhaps the most commonly envisaged type of disfigurement which (provided they meet the severity threshold) fall readily within the scope of the provision, as do some skin conditions, such as psoriasis.[5] The other examples given, however, are a more curious choice. Without question, limb deformation (to use the terminology of the Guidance) can affect others' perceptions of someone's appearance. In 2009, for example, the BBC received numerous complaints from viewers about the appearance of a children's TV presenter whose arm stopped at the elbow.[6] But the inclusion of limb deformation as one of only five listed examples of severe disfigurement is surprising because most limb deformities will also produce functional effects on what the affected person can do; a deformation of the hand will often impact on tasks involving manual dexterity, while a deformation of the leg or foot may impair mobility.

The same argument can be made for many postural deformities; people with these conditions unable to demonstrate a substantial adverse effect on their ability to carry out normal day-to-day activities may be in a minority of people with similar conditions. By way of example, in

[3] Office for Disability Issues, *Equality Act 2010: Guidance on Matters to be Taken into Account in Determining Questions Relating to the Definition of Disability* (HM Government 2011).

[4] Ibid para B25.

[5] *Cosgrove v Northern Ireland Ambulance Service* [2007] IRLR 397 (NICA).

[6] ITV News, Ex-CBeebies presenter: 'Parents Criticised My Decision Not to Wear Prosthetic Arm' (2017) <www.itv.com/news/2017-05-04/ex-cbeebies-presenter-cerrie-burnell-parents-rang-up-complaining-about-my-arm/> accessed 31 January 2019.

Hutchison 3G UK Ltd,[7] the EAT upheld the Tribunal's finding that the claimant's chest deformity caused by Poland syndrome was both a severe disfigurement *and* a physical impairment which had a substantial and long-term effect on the claimant's ability to carry out normal day-to-day activities.

So, without doubting that limb and postural deformations conditions merit rights under equality law as disabilities, their express inclusion in the guidance on severe disfigurement in place of many other disfiguring conditions misses an opportunity to expressly extend, rather than overlap with, the scope of protection provided by the standard definition of disability in s6.

There have been relatively few reported cases under the severe disfigurement provision, but those reported have not really moved much beyond the examples given in the Guidance. For example, *Hutchison* concerned a postural deformity of the chest cavity; *Cosgrove*,[8] *Blyth*,[9] *Leighton*[10] and *Whyte*[11] concerned skin conditions (psoriasis, acne and folliculitis); *Johansson*[12] and *Hand*[13] (both decisions of the Northern Ireland Industrial Tribunals applying similar severe disfigurement wording)[14] and *Griffiths*[15] all concerned facial scarring.

Principles of statutory interpretation could shed some light on the scope of the severe disfigurement provision in Schedule 1 of the Act. In the case of *Goodwin v Patent Office*, the EAT stated (of the Disability Discrimination Act 1995, which preceded the Act) that 'with social legislation of this kind, a purposive approach to construction should be adopted. The language should be construed in a way which gives effect to the stated or presumed intention of Parliament, but with due regard to

7 *Hutchison 3G Ltd v Edwards* [2014] UKEAT/0467/13/DM (4 August 2017, unreported, EAT).

8 *Cosgrove* (n 5).

9 *Blyth v Historic Scotland* [2001] ET/S/4000514/00 (14 February 2001, unreported, ET).

10 *Leighton v VR Music Limited and others* [2020] 2301546/2018 (17 April 2020, unreported, ET).

11 *Whyte v First Capital East Limited* [2005] UKEAT/0686/04/DM (22 March 2005, unreported EAT).

12 *Johansson v Fountain Street Community Development Association* [2005] NIIT 311_03 (4 July 2005, unreported, NIIT).

13 *Hand v The Police Authority for Northern Ireland* [2002] NIIT 1691/01 (2 August 2002, unreported, NIIT).

14 Disability Discrimination Act 1995, sched 1 s3.

15 *Griffiths v Lancashire County Council* [2009] (17 April 2009, unreported, ET).

the ordinary and natural meaning of the words in question'.[16] The EAT specifically urged Tribunals to consider the relevant code of practice and guidance. In this instance, however, neither document[17] is instructive on the meaning of the word 'disfigurement', beyond the loose parameters in the guidance quoted above.

The extent to which wider Parliamentary records can be relied on in the search for Parliament's intended meaning is debatable.[18] However, that debate need not trouble us here, as extensive searches of Hansard have not revealed any detailed debates about the meaning of disfigurement itself, beyond oft-cited examples of scars and birthmarks. Ironically, one MP remarked during a standing committee debate that 'there are many types of severe disfigurement and we can all imagine what they might be'.[19] The debates do, however, reveal a concern that the severe disfigurement provision should be 'comprehensive',[20] and not unjustifiably watered down (perhaps by excluding from protection purportedly 'blameworthy' disfigurements such as burns resulting from solvent abuse, or scars from self-harm). A purposive analysis of Parliamentary records therefore perhaps brings with it a small glimmer of optimism, if not clarity, as to the intended comprehensiveness of the severe disfigurement provision.

A literal interpretation, on the other hand, involves assessing the natural and ordinary meaning of the Act: what the words of the statute actually mean. The Oxford dictionary defines disfigurement as 'something that spoils the appearance of someone or something; a blemish',[21] whereas Black's legal dictionary defines it as 'the result of an accident or an injury that impairs the beauty, symmetry and appearance'.[22] The

[16] *Goodwin v Patent Office* [1999] IRLR 4 (EAT) para 2.

[17] See Office for Disability Issues, *Equality Act 2010* (n 3); Equality and Human Rights Commission, *Employment: Statutory Code of Practice* (The Stationery Office Limited 2011).

[18] In *Pepper v Hart* [1992] 3 WLR 1032 (HL), the House of Lords appeared to relax the rules about using explanations from parliamentary records in statutory interpretation. However, also see Johan Steyn, 'Pepper v Hart: A Re-examination' (2001) 21 Oxford Journal of Legal Studies 59.

[19] HC deb, 7 February 1995, standing committee E, per David Hanson.

[20] Ibid.

[21] See Oxford Dictionaries online <https://en.oxforddictionaries.com/definition/disfigurement> accessed 29 April 2019.

[22] Henry Campbell Black, *Black's Legal Dictionary Online* (2019) <thelawdictionary.org.uk> accessed 18 March 2024. A similar focus can be found in some US case law; in *Superior Min. Co. v Industrial Commission* (1923) 309 Ill. 339, 141 N.E. 165 the court defined disfigurement as 'that which impairs or injures the beauty, symmetry, or

focus on accidents and injuries in the Blacks definition perhaps arises because disfigurement in legal terms usually occurs in a personal injury context, where someone or something is to blame. The case law under the Act is not constrained in this way, however; disfigurements present from birth and arising through natural causes are recognised as well as those acquired later. Setting this causation aspect aside, however, both dictionary definitions have at their core the idea of impaired appearance.

The idea of 'impaired appearance' is interesting because it is a semantic hybrid of two concepts: disability (through the concept of impairment) and appearance. In theoretical terms, disfigurement can be thought of as occupying a middle position between the concepts of appearance and disability, as illustrated in the diagram below.

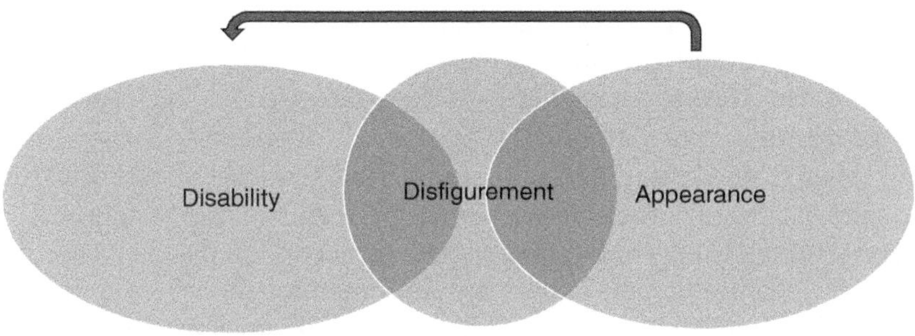

In legal terms, being able to differentiate these three concepts is vital because they have different legal consequences; people with a disability or a severe disfigurement (represented by the darker overlap between disability and disfigurement) are granted rights under equality law. People who have an imperfection of appearance, or a moderate disfigurement, are not. Understanding the relationship between these concepts is therefore key to defining where disfigurement (and disability) stop, and appearance begins.

6.2 The Relationship between Disfigurement and Disability

The relationship between disability and disfigurement stems from two related factors; first, models of disability, and second, legislation.

appearance of a person or thing; that which renders unsightly, misshapen, or imperfect, or deforms in some manner'.

Turning first to models of disability, many people with a visible difference would not be disabled under medical model principles, because disfigurements often don't hinder the individual's ability to do particular activities. However, they are hindered by social attitudes towards people who look different. This simple distinction encapsulates the essence of the medical / social model distinction. The social model explains the overlapping conceptual relationship between disability and disfigurement: attitudes facing someone who looks different can be disabling.

This conceptual overlap is reinforced in the law. The Act deems severe disfigurement to be a disability. Its definition of disability in s6 is functional; the disadvantage which it seeks to capture and respond to is rooted in a medical model analysis. The severe disfigurement provision, on the other hand, seeks to capture another type of disadvantage. Appearance-related disadvantage seems to be its target, rooted in a social model analysis and the attitudes of society towards people who look different. (It is worth clarifying here that the 'disadvantage' referred to should perhaps more accurately be termed 'difference'. Some writers have argued powerfully against assumptions that any departure from physical 'normality' should necessarily be seen as disadvantageous or inferior rather than simply different.[23] Concepts of disadvantage are, however, intricately bound up in the Act's medical-model-led definition of disability, with its focus not on difference but 'adverse' effects, which explains the use of the term 'disadvantage' here.)

The need for the relevant type of disadvantage to result from impairment applies to both the definition of disability in s6 and the severe disfigurement provision. This means that those who are placed at serious functional disadvantage, perhaps by having a lower-than-average IQ or a personality trait of shyness or low self-confidence, do not fall, without more, within the protection of the Act. Similarly, the Act does not protect pure differences of appearance (without impairment) even where these produce severe disadvantage. This is so despite evidence showing that people can face attitudinal barriers because of the way they look *without* having an impairment. Appearance and disfigurement are part of a spectrum and, as Chapter 4 set out, physically beautiful people have a better chance at leading beautiful lives.[24] They are likely to be perceived

[23] Ron Amundson, 'Biological Normality and the ADA' in Leslie Pickering Francis and Anita Silvers (eds), *Americans with Disabilities* (Routledge 2000) 103.

[24] For a discussion, see Judith H Langlois, 'Maxims or Myths of Beauty?: A Meta-Analytic and Theoretical Review' (2000) 126(3) Psychological Bulletin 403.

by others not just as more attractive, but also more socially adept, and more successful.[25] The implicit corollary of this is that we, less-than-beautiful people – who don't have a disfigurement but are prone to a few spots, whose ears stick out more than we'd like, or who are carrying an extra stone in weight – are relatively disadvantaged by our appearances. Impairment acts as a filter, separating the 'unlucky' disadvantage of appearance and function from the *actionable* disadvantage of appearance and function resulting from impairment.

It could be argued that the scope of the law is wrong; that disadvantage should be the sole determinant of rights under equality law, and that extra 'filters' such as impairment are unwarranted. That argument is embraced in Chapter 10 when considering whether equality law should extend its reach to appearance more generally to protect those of us without impairments who are still disadvantaged by the way we look. But in this chapter, I will address an even more basic question: whether the Act's current drafting *achieves* its underlying choices. In other words, are all people who experience severe, long-term appearance-related disadvantage resulting from impairment granted rights under the Act?

6.3 The Relationship between Disfigurement and Appearance

As noted above, disfigurement and appearance are part of a spectrum but equality law engages with one part of that spectrum only: an impairment which consists of a severe disfigurement. Impairment is therefore key to understanding how law distinguishes disfigurement from appearance.

The term 'impairment' is included in the Act's provisions on both functional and appearance-related disadvantage (disability and severe disfigurement respectively). Impairment is not defined in the Act but case law determines that a physical impairment means 'something wrong with them physically',[26] and it is an undemanding threshold which is to be given its 'ordinary and natural meaning'.[27]

The Guidance is clear that, in determining whether an impairment exists, tribunals do not need to identify its cause.[28] In most situations, this benefits claimants, who are relieved from the obligation of proving

[25] Karen Dion, Ellen Berscheid and Elaine Walster, 'What Is Beautiful Is Good' (1972) 24 Journal of Personality and Social Psychology 288.

[26] *Rugamer v Sony Music Entertainment UK Limited* [2001] IRLR 644 (EAT) para 34.

[27] *McNicol v Balfour Beatty* [2002] IRLR 711 (CA) para 17.

[28] Equality and Human Rights Commission, *Employment* (n 17) appendix 1, para 7.

why they have a particular impairment – they simply have to prove that they have it, which can often be helped by considering the effects of the alleged impairment on the ability to perform day-to-day activities. Sometimes tribunals have adopted a 'back to front' approach by identifying the effects on day-to-day activities first, and assuming that 'as a matter of common-sense inference'[29] any effects found must point to the presence of an impairment producing them. Accordingly, someone can still be disabled even when doctors cannot identify a cause for the problem they are experiencing. Although this sounds simple, closer examination of the legal concept of impairment reveals fault lines beneath the surface.

The first fault line is that a binary distinction between impairment and non-impairment (i.e. physical norms) is often too simplistic. Numerous degrees of human functioning exist, making an assessment of what is 'normal' or 'impaired' tricky. Mary Crossley argues that 'the immense variety found in human bodies makes it quite difficult to draw a bright line between those bodily characteristics that are considered impairments and those that are not'.[30] A second, related, fault line appears where an issue falls close to the dividing line between appearance and disfigurement. The binary distinction between impairment and physical 'normality' is joined by a third category: imperfections of appearance. These are both undefined and unprotected. So how does the law differentiate what is 'wrong' (i.e. impairment), both from what is 'normal' (i.e. unimpaired) and from what is unimpaired but looks different?

The challenge of separating appearance from impairment sometimes encourages tribunals to default back to the physiological cause underlying a condition.[31] Although this sits uncomfortably with the Guidance which, as outlined above, places the emphasis on the effect of an impairment rather than its cause, a focus on biomedical causation is clearly identifiable in case law under the Act. In *Hussain v Sky In-Home Services Ltd*,[32] a male claimant who was 4′8″ (without a proven, relied-on, medical cause) was held not to have a physical impairment. Yet someone

[29] *J v DLA Piper LLP* [2010] ICR 1052 (EAT) para 38.

[30] Mary Crossley, 'Impairment and Embodiment' in Leslie Pickering Francis and Anita Silvers (eds), *Americans with Disabilities* (Routledge 2000) 112.

[31] See also David Wasserman, 'Stigma without Impairment' in Leslie Pickering Francis and Anita Silvers (eds), *Americans with Disabilities* (Routledge 2000) 149 on this point.

[32] *Hussain v Sky In-Home Services Ltd ET/2300908/16* [2017] (10 January 2017, unreported, ET).

of a similar height due to restricted bodily development[33] appears likely to qualify for protection given the express inclusion of this condition in the Guidance on the meaning of 'severe disfigurement'.[34] Indeed, the Employment Tribunal made a particular point of noting that the claimant's short stature had not been expressly argued as resulting from a hormone deficiency, despite a suggestion of this in a doctor's letter.[35] The physiological cause of a characteristic *is* therefore sometimes relevant to its status as an impairment – even though it shouldn't be.

Judging impairment according to biomedical causation is not always clear cut, however. As the boundaries of medical knowledge expand, we are increasingly able to identify underlying physiological reasons for aspects of the way we look and age, as well as for conditions more traditionally viewed as impairments. Physiological causation can't always delineate the two concepts. The issue of hair loss illustrates this. In the Scottish case of *Campbell v Falkirk Council*,[36] the claimant (a 61-year-old man) complained of unfair dismissal and disability discrimination. His disability claim relied on the fact that he was balding. Mr Campbell's claim was made under the standard definition of disability rather than the severe disfigurement provision, but this made little difference as both require the presence of an impairment, which the Tribunal found was not satisfied. The Tribunal commented that 'if baldness was to be regarded as an impairment then perhaps a physical feature such as a big nose, big ears or being smaller than average height might of themselves be regarded as an impairment under the DDA'.[37]

The judgment does not specify the cause of the claimant's hair loss in this case, but male pattern baldness (also known as androgenetic alopecia) commonly occurs as a part of the ageing process. Statistics suggest that up to 50 per cent of men aged over fifty experience male pattern baldness,[38] and on that basis, the Tribunal's finding that hair loss was not an impairment (and therefore a matter of appearance but not disability

[33] Restricted bodily development is generally interpreted as a final adult height of 4′10″ or less; see Restricted Growth Association, 'About Restricted Growth' (undated, RGA) <https://rgauk.org/about-restricted-growth> accessed 29 April 2019.

[34] Office for Disability Issues, *Equality Act 2010* (n 3) para B25.

[35] See (n 32) para 31.

[36] *Campbell v Falkirk Council* [2008] S/136261/07 (9 April 2008, unreported, ETS).

[37] Ibid para 15.

[38] William Cranwell, Rodney Sinclair and Leila Asfour, 'Male Androgenetic Alopecia' (*Endotext*, 2023) <www.ncbi.nlm.nih.gov/books/NBK278957/> accessed 9 February 2024.

or disfigurement) is unremarkable. Yet there is an identified physiological cause for male pattern baldness: both genetic and hormonal factors tend to play a part, inducing the hair follicles to shrink permanently, making them unable to support hair growth.[39] So, a focus on biomedical causation doesn't always explain which aesthetic characteristics are found to be impairments, and which are not. (It is worth mentioning here that, although the case law on disability does not offer much hope to those treated badly as a result of hair loss, recent developments in sex discrimination law may offer greater hope for at least some of those affected.)[40]

The distinction in *Campbell* becomes more complex still when we consider other causes of baldness. Alopecia areata, for example, affects only 2 in 1,000 people and can cause partial or total hair loss of the head and body at any stage of life, but predominantly in those under thirty.[41] It is believed to result from an autoimmune condition and, unlike male pattern baldness, it tends not to occur gradually over years but suddenly, repeatedly and in clumps.[42] Alopecia areata is often connected with stress and can be very traumatic for those affected, as well as very visible to other people. Should these different types of hair loss should be treated differently by the law? Clarity is urgently needed about how to determine aesthetic (rather than functional) impairment, to ensure that the boundaries of protection are properly drawn.

So, the presence of a physiological cause underpinning a particular condition doesn't always offer a reliable way of sifting impairment from imperfections of appearance. But an additional filter is implicit: prevalence. Male pattern baldness was (at least within Mr Campbell's demographic) extremely common. The prevalence of a condition does not necessarily reduce the social barriers or stigma that it engenders; the continuing stigma faced by people with a high BMI is a case in point. But prevalence often leads to distributive arguments about 'opening the floodgates'[43] with unmanageable numbers of claims. And prevalence perhaps becomes an even greater obstacle when it comes to conditions

[39] Alopecia UK, 'Types of Alopecia' (Alopecia UK, undated) <www.alopecia.org.uk/Pages/FAQs/Category/types-of-alopecia> accessed 30 January 2019.

[40] See Section 6.5.

[41] Anonymous, 'Hair Loss Reversed in Alopecia Areata Sufferers' (BBC, 18 August 2014) <www.bbc.co.uk/news/health-28834058> accessed 30 January 2019.

[42] British Association of Dermatologists, 'Alopecia Areata' (BAD, July 2020) <www.bad.org.uk/shared/get-file.ashx?id¼68&itemtype¼document> accessed 9 February 2024.

[43] See for example *Taylor v Ladbrokes Betting and Gaming Limited* [2017] IRLR 312 (EAT) para 9.

which only impact appearance; it is harder to argue that an aesthetic characteristic is a physical 'wrong' (i.e. an impairment) when it is shared with a significant proportion of the relevant population. In other words, prevalence blurs with appearance normality, making it harder to prove impairment, and less likely to fall within the Act's scope.

Case law suggests that prevalence is being used as a blunt tool. In *Hussain*, for example, the Employment Tribunal, as part of its reasoning for finding that the (adult male) claimant's short stature was not an impairment, relied on the fact that women and children are often short too.[44] The implicit logic appears to be that a man is not impaired on the basis of short stature because being short is prevalent among a lot of other people – including children. But clearly a normal height range for a man is different from a normal height range for a child, and to a lesser degree, for a woman. The Tribunal's blunt comparison fails to take into account the relative nature of appearance which surely must be salient when differentiating appearance from impairment.

In a similar vein, consider again the issue of hair loss. Despite placing particular importance on facial disfigurements due to their visibility, the Guidance[45] is silent about (often very visible) hair conditions. Remembering *Campbell*,[46] the decision (that baldness – presumably male pattern baldness – was not an impairment) implies a keenness to distinguish (unprotected) issues of appearance from (protected) issues of disability and disfigurement. The comparative examples cited by the Tribunal (a big nose, big ears or being smaller than average) are common physical appearance traits. But while male pattern baldness may be a common feature of appearance for men of Mr Campbell's age, it is much less common in young women. An 18-year-old woman with severe male pattern baldness (despite the name, it can happen to women too) would stand out to a much greater degree from her peers for this reason. Yet, neither the Act nor the Guidance expressly situate the threshold of impairment or severe disfigurement within the context of the personal characteristics of the person affected.

Hair loss is not the only example of a condition which can fall on either side of the cusp of impairment according to personal context. Consider, for example, a man with enlarged breast tissue, which would

44 See (n 32) para 32.

45 Office for Disability Issues, *Equality Act 2010* (n 3).

46 See (n 36).

be considered aesthetically typical for women,[47] or wrinkled skin[48] or varicose veins on an adolescent, which may be a prevalent appearance trait in older people. Just as disability is individually determined (by assessing the effects of an impairment on that specific person's ability to carry out normal day-to-day activities, rather than the typical impact of that condition on people generally),[49] so potential disfigurements should be assessed individually relative to *that* person's appearance. Disfigurement (and impairment as one aspect of the legal test) should not be viewed as a universal standard irrespective of context, but as a measure of the extent to which that person's appearance is impaired by 'something wrong with them physically'.[50] This personal context allows the law to recognise that a condition which may be relatively commonplace within a particular demographic (such as baldness in men over 60) can be a physical 'wrong' and have a much greater negative aesthetic impact on the appearance of someone with different personal characteristics.

It is worth clarifying that the contextual approach presented here is not based on misplaced assumptions about appearance 'mattering more' to certain groups of people. The law has, until recently, been shaped by such an assumption in relation to personal injury, with the JC Guidance prior to 2017[51] providing that damages for a woman who sustained a facial disfigurement should be greater than those for a man sustaining a similar injury. This appears to have been based on an erroneous assumption that the extent to which appearance matters to someone will be affected by their gender (an assumption which has been challenged by a considerable body of research in the social sciences).[52] Instead, the proposition argued here is that a characteristic which is a commonplace appearance characteristic for a person of one demographic (such as thinning hair for an older man, or acne for a teenager) may be an

[47] Gynecomastia is swelling of the breast tissue in men due to hormonal imbalance.

[48] Genetic and Rare Diseases Information Center, 'Wrinkly Skin Syndrome' (*National Center for Advancing Translational Sciences*, 2016) <https://rarediseases.info.nih.gov/diseases/273/wrinkly-skin-syndrome> accessed 1 February 2019.

[49] *Paterson v The Commissioner of the Police of the Metropolis* [2007] IRLR 763 (EAT) para 39.

[50] *Rugamer* (n 26) para 34.

[51] Judicial College, *Guidelines for the Assessment of General Damages in Personal Injury Cases*, vol 14 (Oxford University Press 2017) 81.

[52] See, for example, Andrew Thompson and Gerry Kent, 'Adjusting to Disfigurement: Processes Involved in Dealing with Being Visibly Different' (2001) 21 Clinical Psychology Review 668.

impairment for another. This contextual argument was implicitly accepted in *Leighton*,[53] where the claimant's acne was found not to amount to a severe disfigurement because the Tribunal factored in its 'own knowledge that acne, or a tendency to spots developing on the face, is not uncommon among young people including those of the claimant's age'.

It is regrettable that, so far, the little case law about the impact of personal context is inconsistent. In the two reported cases found where personal context was explicitly taken into account in determining the issue of aesthetic impairment or severe disfigurement, the logic employed by the two Tribunals was antithetical; in *Hussain*, the rarity of the trait in the claimant's demographic was ignored, whereas in *Leighton*, the prevalence of the trait among the claimant's demographic was taken into account. What unites these cases is that this contradictory logic was used to find against the claimant in both claims.

To sum up, in assessing whether the law achieves its aim of protecting all people who experience severe, long-term appearance-related disadvantage resulting from impairment, the concept of impairment comes under particular strain. The concept of impairment, as it applies to non-functional limitations, is in urgent need of review.

Setting the issue of impairment aside, the meaning of 'disfigurement' is also problematic. The apparent logic behind the severe disfigurement provision is, as identified above, one of appearance-related disadvantage. Yet the Act doesn't use the word 'appearance', but 'disfigurement'. The two concepts are connected but it is arguable that common usage of the word 'disfigurement' creates a narrower subset of appearance-related disadvantage than 'appearance'. Whereas the noun of (severe) disfigurement suggests that there is a static, self-contained 'thing' (such as a scar, a birthmark or similar) to be judged, the logic of appearance-disadvantage seems to be wider and could include an impairment which has a *disfiguring effect*, without the condition itself *being* a disfigurement.

Involuntary facial movement impairments illustrate this point. An involuntary facial movement impairment is any condition which causes the face to move in unexpected or unintentional ways. Tourette syndrome, for example, can cause involuntary facial tics and fleeting contortions of the face. While some sufferers also experience other symptoms such as vocal tics (which would be likely to meet the usual

[53] *Leighton* (n 10) para 75.

definition of disability because of the impact on speech), for others the disruption of facial expressions is the defining feature of the condition.[54] Similarly, synkinesis can cause involuntary grimaces to be trigged by voluntary movements, such as smiling.

There are strong arguments suggesting that the law should not treat involuntary facial movement impairments differently from other types of visible difference. First, involuntary facial movement impairments may visibly hinder stable facial expressions. Second, they often create intermittent facial asymmetry, which is strongly correlated with judgments about appearance.[55] Third, involuntary facial movement impairments are not easy to disguise with make-up, and very likely to be visible at a distance. All three of these factors have been considered by Tribunals applying the severe disfigurement wording to different kinds of visible differences,[56] suggesting a degree of commonality between involuntary facial movement disorders and other types of disfigurement. Yet, despite this commonality, instinctively involuntary facial movement impairments feel like an awkward fit with the severe disfigurement provision as it is currently drafted.[57] When preparing this argument, not one person who was consulted informally on the issue[58] instinctively aligned conditions such as Tourette syndrome and synkinesis with the concept of severe disfigurement.

I suggest that the reason for this disconnect is linguistic. The phrase 'which consists of a severe disfigurement' in the Act implies an unchanging state – such as a permanent facial palsy, for example, or a scar. This doesn't lend itself easily to conditions which can alter from one moment to the next. This is reinforced by the examples given in the Guidance of which almost all (apart from a small proportion of skin conditions) would usually be permanent and unchanging. We might tend to describe

[54] In *Vatcher v Kelly Services (UK) Ltd* [1999] UKEAT 595/99/0510 (5 October 1999, unreported, EAT), the claimant had facial tics of Tourette's syndrome which did not meet the standard definition of disability. For procedural reasons, the EAT refused to hear his contention that this amounted to a severe disfigurement.

[55] See Domagoj Svegar, 'What Does Facial Symmetry Reveal about Health and Personality?' (2016) 47 Polish Psychological Bulletin 356.

[56] See, for example *Johansson* (n 12) relating to facial expressions; *Hand* (n 13) relating to asymmetry and visibility.

[57] Facial movement impairments which prevent facial movement – such as facial palsy – are an easier fit within the implicitly static concept of disfigurement.

[58] No suggestion is made that these informal consultations were academically rigorous, but simply informal discussions with colleagues and a practising lawyer on the general principles.

a scar as a disfigurement but a condition which causes involuntary additional facial movements as a *disfiguring condition*; the latter description focuses more on the appearance-altering power of the condition rather than the appearance of the condition itself. A definition which allowed greater focus on disfiguring *effects*, rather than *disfigurement*, may resolve this disconnect. This focus may benefit people with conditions beyond facial movement disorders too; the severe dandruff-like skin flakes in the eyebrows and scalp produced by seborrheic dermatitis, or the visual impact of excessive facial perspiration are examples of conditions which are a difficult fit within the word *disfigurement* because of their processual, ongoing nature, but which surely produce a disfiguring effect and appearance-related disadvantage.

In summary, common usage of the word ‘disfigurement’ highlights a narrow subset of appearance-related impairments, which risks making other appearance-related impairments (such as involuntary facial movement disorders, and conditions which can produce varying degrees of disadvantage according to the personal characteristics of the person concerned) legally invisible.

6.4 The Relationship between Disability and Appearance

One might not expect significant overlap between the areas of disability and appearance without the engagement of disfigurement too. However, obesity is one area where this overlap occurs. Some obese people will experience functional effects from their size, such as restricted mobility or joint pain. If sufficiently substantial and long term, these functional effects would bring them within the reach of disability law. But some people are obese without it affecting what they can do.

As touched on briefly in Chapter 2, this was alleged to be the case in the ECJ decision of *Kaltoft*,[59] where the claimant argued that he had been dismissed from his job because he was obese, but that his size did not prevent him from fulfilling his role.[60] His case was that he was discriminated against because he was fat, not because his weight impacted on his activities. On this point, there is strong evidence that people who are

[59] Case C-354/13 *FOA v Kommuneres Landsforening (Kaltoft)* [2015] 2 CMLR 19.

[60] Bruno Waterfield and Justin Huggler, ‘“I Don’t Feel My Weight Is a Big Problem,” Says Dane in EU Obesity Ruling’ *The Telegraph* (24 May 2019) <https://bit.ly/48Y2Xrt> accessed 24 May 2019.

overweight are stigmatised because of it.[61] This can take different forms; from stereotypes of laziness and low self-control to health-policy-induced stigma designed to encourage people to lose weight. Under a social model analysis, there clearly are barriers hindering overweight people even when their ability to carry out day-to-day activities is not affected. Research from the US suggests that those who feel stigmatised because of their weight are more at risk of a variety of adverse psychological and physical health consequences, including further increases in obesity levels.[62] Weight stigmatisation therefore seems to have a complex interaction with disability.

In *Kaltoft*, the ECJ considered when obesity could be a disability. They began by reaffirming a definition of disability from the earlier case of *Ring*, which partially reflects a social model understanding of disability:

> a limitation which results in particular from long-term physical, mental or psychological impairments which in interaction with various barriers may hinder the full and effective participation of the person concerned in professional life on an equal basis with other workers.[63]

This definition locates disability in the interaction between impairment and external barriers (which could presumably include attitudinal barriers and stigmatisation). However, the ECJ then progressed to narrow its analysis by suggesting that this definition would be fulfilled only in cases of functional limitation, such as 'reduced mobility or the onset, in that person, of medical conditions preventing him from carrying out his work or causing discomfort when carrying out his professional activity'.[64] The examples given appear to suggest that the ECJ's interpretation of a 'limitation' is a functional one such that obesity will only be a disability if it produces functional limits or hindrances on what the person can do, such as walking upstairs, or performing daily work tasks without getting out of breath. If this was their intent, the decision appears to take a significant step back from the social model of disability, as it fails to

[61] World Health Organisation, 'Weight Bias and Obesity Stigma: Considerations for the WHO European Region' (undated) <www.euro.who.int/__data/assets/pdf_file/0017/351026/WeightBias.pdf> accessed 24 May 2019.

[62] Rebecca M Puhl and Chelsea A Heuer, 'Obesity Stigma: Important Considerations for Public Health' (2010) 100 The American Journal of Public Health 1019.

[63] C-335/11 and C-337/11 *HK Danmark, acting on behalf of Ring v Dansk almennyttigt Boligselskab and HK Danmark, acting on behalf of Lond Skouboe Werge v Dansk Arbejdsgiverforening, acting on behalf of Pro Display A/S (Ring and Skouboe Werge)* [2013] 3 CMLR 21, para 53.

[64] Ibid para 60.

recognise the stigma barriers faced by Mr Kaltoft on account of his size. A similar approach can be found within domestic case law.[65]

Despite apparently strong reasons for recognising non-functional obesity as a disability,[66] it is possible that one complication in doing so, as touched on earlier, is the issue of prevalence. Obesity is very common; it is estimated that over 25 per cent of the UK adult population is obese, and around 3 per cent of us are morbidly obese with a BMI over 40.[67] Indeed, some studies predict that severe obesity levels in the UK are set to almost double over the next twenty years.[68] Extending rights under equality law to people with all degrees of obesity would represent a significant expansion of the numbers (on paper, at least) of disabled people. This could give rise to (possibly ill-founded)[69] policy concerns about opening the floodgates, both in terms of numbers of potential claims and other duties on employers such as the need to make reasonable adjustments. Although not expressly mentioned in *Kaltoft*, the prevalence of (non-functional) obesity does perhaps makes it more likely to be viewed by some as an issue of appearance rather than impairment.

There is already a considerable body of scholarship which considers whether, and how, obesity should trigger rights under equality law, but the legal relationship between disfigurement and obesity merits further exploration. *Kaltoft* was not a British case so the claimant would not have been able to invoke the severe disfigurement provision in the Act. However, regardless of the jurisdictional aspect, this probably would not have helped him in any event; to suggest that obesity could be a severe disfigurement seems to stretch the statutory wording beyond breaking point linguistically. It is also extremely doubtful whether many

[65] See *Walker v Sita Information Networking Computing Limited* UKEAT/009/12 (8 February 2013, unreported, EAT). For a post-Kaltoft example, see the Northern Irish case of *Bickerstaff v Butcher* (2015) IT92/14 (3 February 2015, unreported, NIIT).

[66] For example, research conducted by *The Economist* identified a very significant obesity pay gap of up to 19 per cent for women with graduate degrees and 14 per cent for men with graduate degrees. See Anonymous, 'The Obesity Pay Gap Is Worse than Previously Thought' (2023) <https://econ.st/3TkkkwJ> accessed 2 January 2024. See also Zofia Bajorek and Stephen Bevan, *Obesity Stigma at Work: Improving Inclusion and Productivity* (PURPOSE 2020).

[67] Carl Baker, 'House of Commons Briefing Paper No. 3336' (20 March 2018).

[68] Andrew Gregory, 'More than 42m UK Adults "Will Be Overweight by 2040"' *The Guardian* <www.theguardian.com/society/2022/may/19/more-than-42m-uk-adults-will-be-overweight-by-2040> accessed 28 March 2023.

[69] Wasserman, 'Stigma without Impairment' (n 31) 154.

people who are overweight would self-identify as having a severe disfigurement.

But the ongoing tussle over rights under equality law for people who are obese has an important ramification for disfigurement law; if obesity is not recognised, this creates inconsistency with some other conditions which may be more likely to fall under the severe disfigurement provision. Conditions such as lipoedema, lymphedema and elephantiasis, for example, all cause bodily swelling, usually just in the legs and ankles (and, for lipoedema, the arms). These conditions are not caused by overeating[70] and they can all affect people irrespective of their prior BMI. Like obesity, sometimes they limit what the person can do. They can be painful and can reduce mobility, but not in all cases. They are much less common than obesity among the population; both elephantiasis and primary lymphedema are rare, and lipoedema is thought to affect up to one in nine women,[71] of whom only a smaller percentage would be severe cases potentially qualifying as a severe disfigurement, which helps to avoid suggestions that these conditions are common matters of appearance only, rather than impairments. Yet observers – and sometimes even medical professionals – often mistake conditions such as lipoedema for obesity,[72] which suggests that the experiences and social barriers faced by all groups are likely to be similar. One Love Island contestant publicly admitted that she had faced years of trolling about having fat legs and 'cankles' before appearing on TV led her to a lipoedema diagnosis.[73]

A further inconsistency could arise in respect of formerly obese people who, having lost weight, may be left with excess skin. Despite a lack of case law on this point, it is arguable that this excess skin could be viewed as a type of skin condition resulting in (severe) disfigurement. This would lead to the illogical conclusion that, while obesity is not treated as a disability in the absence of functional consequences, the visible effects of

[70] Lipoedema is thought to be hereditary fat cell deposit problem affecting women, primary lymphedema is caused by a genetic problem in the lymphatic drainage system, and elephantiasis is a reaction to mosquito bites.

[71] Donald W Buck and Karen L Herbst, 'Lipedema: A Relatively Common Disease with Extremely Common Misconceptions' (2016) Plastic Reconstructive Surgery Global Open 1043, 1043.

[72] Ibid.

[73] Yasmin Harisha, 'I Felt Like the Fat Girl on Love Island and Was Killing Myself Doing Workouts to Slim My Legs, Says Shaughna Phillips' *The Sun* <www.thesun.co.uk/fabulous/13500351/shaughna-phillips-lipoedema-battle/> accessed 28 March 2023.

former obesity may be. Failing to give rights under equality law to obese people could therefore create inconsistencies or exclusions which are hard to justify.

Returning to the question posed earlier, it is clear that large numbers of people who experience severe, long-term appearance-related disadvantage resulting from impairment do not receive rights under equality law under the Act. For some, this is because the threshold of impairment is applied in an inconsistent and opaque way. For others, it may be because the law ignores the personal context which can profoundly impact on the way that some appearance traits are perceived. Or because the nature of their condition is an uncomfortable fit linguistically with the narrowness of the word 'disfigurement'. And sometimes – as in the case of obesity – it is because courts still have their ideological roots firmly planted in medical model soil. These gaps show us that the scope of the severe disfigurement provision is falling well short of the logic which underlies it.

6.5 Can Other Protected Characteristics Fill the Gaps?

Appearance overlaps to some degree with existing protected characteristics.[74] To what extent can these other protected characteristics be employed to fill some of the unprotected gaps in relation to appearance traits such as hair loss, weight and height?

Someone dismissed from a job for displaying henna designs on their hands to celebrate the Hindu festival of Diwali may be able to argue discrimination on the ground of religious belief.[75] And someone demoted because of their greying hair may have an age discrimination claim. Both examples are in some way appearance-related but fall logically within the scope of another protected characteristic. But this logic can easily be turned on its head with a tweak of the facts. For example, someone with a tattoo for non-religious reasons would have no claim. And age discrimination would not help someone harassed because their hair was any colour other than grey.

[74] This section is adapted from a blogpost and reproduced with the permission of UK Labour Law blog: Hannah Saunders, *Appearance, Harassment and the Equality Act 2010* (UCL UK Labour Law Blog, 2022).

[75] For guidance on the law on dress codes and religion at work, see EHRC, 'Religion or Belief: Dress Codes and Religious Symbols' (2018) <www.equalityhumanrights.com/guidance/religion-or-belief-workplace/religion-or-belief-dress-codes-and-religious-symbols> accessed 21 March 2024.

So, other protected characteristics are sometimes useful in addressing appearance overlaps, but usually only where the appearance aspect is secondary to another characteristic. We could expect both of the examples listed to be easily recognisable as such by the general public. One real case example of this 'secondary' appearance aspect can be found in the Tribunal decision of *Primmer v Mayflower Kebabs Ltd*,[76] where a female employee reported being subjected to months of verbal insults and sexual innuendo about her red hair. Given the sexual nature of some of the insinuations, the Tribunal's finding of sexual harassment is perhaps not surprising.

In the recent case of *Finn v British Bung Manufacturing Company Ltd*,[77] however, the Tribunal showed a willingness to move beyond these obvious links, engaging other characteristics where an appearance trait seemed to be the primary behaviour complained of. In that case, an older male worker insulted by a male colleague who called him a 'bald cunt' was found to have been subjected to harassment related to sex.

The decision in *Finn* was assisted by the fact that conduct 'related to' a protected characteristic provides a deliberately wide threshold which does not require a test of causation.[78] It includes not only treatment because of a protected characteristic, but also treatment which is related to the protected characteristic by the form it takes (such as discriminatory jokes or banter), even if not so motivated.[79] The conduct need only have a 'connection or association'[80] with the protected characteristic. This low threshold made it possible for the claimant to argue that certain aspects of physical appearance may be 'related to' sex or other protected characteristics.

In *Finn*, the Tribunal drew an analogy with the earlier case of *Insitu Cleaning v Heads*.[81] In that case, the comment 'hiya big tits' (made by a male manager to a female member of staff) was found to be sex discrimination. The link drawn by the Tribunal in *Finn* was that:

> It is much more likely that a person on the receiving end of a comment such as that which was made in the Insitu case would be female. So too, it

[76] Sam Middlemiss, 'Protection against Discrimination on the Ground of Looks? Primmer v Mayflower Kebabs Ltd', Employment Law, Issue 80, October 2007.

[77] *Finn v British Bung Manufacturing Company Ltd* [2022] ET/1803764/2021 (11 May 2022, unreported, ET). The decision on harassment related to sex was upheld by the Employment Appeal Tribunal: *British Bung Manufacturing Company Ltd and another v Finn* [2023] EAT 165.

[78] *EOC v Secretary of State for Trade and Industry* [2007] ICR 1234 (QBD).

[79] *Hartley v Foreign and Commonwealth Office Services* [2016] ICR D17 (EAT).

[80] See (n 78) para 6.

[81] *Insitu Cleaning v Heads* [1995] IRLR, 4 (EAT).

> is much more likely that a person on the receiving end of a remark such as that made by [the claimant's colleague] would be male. [The claimant's colleague] made the remark with a view to hurting the claimant by commenting on his appearance which is often found amongst men.[82]

Following that logic, sufficient prevalence of any trait within a protected group (in that case men) seems to be enough to show that it is 'related' to that characteristic. The implications of this extend far beyond baldness because there are lots of physical traits which would be much more prevalent within one protected group than another. Think of facial hair or prominent Adam's apples – both of which are much more common in men than women. Or lipoedema which is usually only found in women. But traits which may be equally at risk of harassment – such as having big ears or a double chin – would seem not to relate to any particular group in terms of prevalence and therefore remain unprotected. This sort of trait-specific distinction may be hard to justify when it excludes some immutable, stigmatised physical traits but includes others purely on the basis of the likely distribution between groups.

Baldness itself offers a good example of this potential unfairness. In *Finn* it is not clear from the judgment what type of baldness the Tribunal was referring to in its comments about prevalence, but statistically this is likely to be male pattern baldness. While most people experiencing male pattern baldness are indeed men, the same cannot be said of other hair loss conditions such as alopecia areata. Would the Tribunal's logic mean that harassment about male pattern baldness engages rights under the Act, but harassment about alopecia areata would not? It would be very difficult to justify that distinction; not enough is known about the relative experiences of people with the two types of hair loss. The limited research available on this point has reached varying conclusions and, most recently, research conducted at the Centre for Appearance Research at the University of the West of England suggests that the experiences of the two groups can be similar.[83] There appears to be insufficient empirical justification for including people with pattern baldness within the scope of the Act but not other types of hair loss.

[82] See (n 77) para 238. The Employment Appeal Tribunal (2023, n77) later confirmed that, in order to be 'related to' sex, the trait at issue does not need to be found exclusively in people of a particular sex: "the context of a remark said to constitute harassment within the meaning of section 26(1) of the EqA encompasses the prevalence amongst persons having the relevant protected characteristic of the feature to which that remark alludes and the absence of any other factor or circumstances said to explain the remark" (para 26).

[83] Fabio Zucchelli and others, 'Men's Experiences of Alopecia Areata: A Qualitative Study' (2022) 9 Health Psychology Open 2.

The illogicality of relying on group prevalence to allocate rights under equality law is amplified when we consider that some personal styling choices can presumably also be 'related to' sex following this logic. To give an extreme example, wearing tights – or having long hair – is much more common among women than men; given the low threshold for 'related to' claims, illustrated in *Finn*, should these traits attract the protection of the discriminatory harassment provisions even though so many other immutable traits do not?

Another difficulty with the Tribunal's application of the law in *Finn* is that it's not clear what impact – if any – the claimant's own sex has on the decision. Given the importance which the Tribunal places on prevalence, where does this leave someone in a 'non-prevalent' group? In other words, would a woman harassed in the same way as Mr Finn still be able to argue that the harassment was 'related to sex'? It is well-established that harassment under the Act does not need to relate to the claimant's own sex, so female claimants with the same condition *should* also be able to argue that their treatment was related to sex even though relatively few women suffer from male pattern baldness. But the logic of the woman's claim would seemingly be the opposite of that adopted in *Finn*; in other words, it is related to sex because baldness is atypical for women, so not conforming to typical gendered stereotypes of appearance. This is important, because one might expect the social barriers facing someone with an 'unusual' trait for their sex to be greater, deserving of more protection from the law, not less. But that 'social barriers' approach seems to be the exact opposite of the focus on prevalence adopted in *Finn*. Clarity on this point is needed.

Finally, another uncertainty created by the Tribunal's approach in *Finn* is that it is not clear how prevalence for these purposes should be measured and evidenced. No statistics are provided in the judgment to back up the finding of prevalence of baldness among the male population. Instead a 'social-facts' approach appears to have been adopted, with the (all-male) Tribunal commenting that 'as all three members of the Tribunal will vouchsafe, baldness is much more prevalent in men than women'.[84] Tribunals do sometimes take notice of facts which are 'so well-established to the knowledge of the court that they may be accepted without further enquiry'.[85] So the Tribunal's approach on the issue of prevalence and sex is probably uncontentious as a standalone point. But

[84] *Finn* (n 77) para 235.

[85] Phipson on Evidence, 19th edition (Sweet and Maxwell, 2017) and exemplified in *London Underground v Edwards (No2)* [1988] IRLR 364 (CA).

they then found – again without disclosing any empirical basis – that baldness is not related to age, because hair loss can affect men of any age. While this is certainly true to some degree, baldness does become significantly more common with advancing years. (Studies have found that around 16 per cent of men aged 18–29 and 53 per cent of men aged 40–49 will notice the first signs of balding, with percentages continuing to increase with age).[86] These statistics certainly show a strong correlation between age and hair loss – but the Tribunal's assessment of the link was that it was not strong enough to demonstrate that baldness was 'related to' age. Given the apparently narrow margins at issue here, it is not clear which traits will be found to be 'related' to a particular group, nor what empirical evidence (if any) is required to prove this, creating uncertainty. Regrettably, the EAT did not hear an appeal on the age discrimination claim so this issue was not fully considered.

In summary, using other protected characteristics to address appearance discrimination, as illustrated in *Finn*, may provide a remedy for some claimants. But it does not provide the basis for a fair or consistent solution to the wider problem of appearance harassment. It is, at best, an additional route in a minority of cases of appearance disadvantage falling outside the severe disfigurement provision. And there is perhaps a risk that protecting appearance discrimination through the back door in this way will backfire in the long term. A link between baldness and sex is not one which is readily comprehensible for many people. While discussing *Finn* on LBC radio,[87] the barrister Daniel Barnett of Outer Temple chambers, commented that:

> I do think these sorts of cases give discrimination law a bad name, because it's just counter- intuitive. It's not the sort of thing you instinctively think should be sex discrimination.

His interviewer replied:

> I'm afraid, I've got to be honest with you sport, it sounds utter nuts.

As Chapter 8 will demonstrate, laws which are commonly perceived to be illogical are less likely to be adhered to. So this lack of understanding is problematic, and perhaps risks a backlash against the law relating to sex harassment more widely. Using the vehicle of harassment 'related to'

[86] T Rhodes and others, 'Prevalence of Male Pattern Hair Loss in 18–49 Year Old Men' (1998) 24 Dermatologic Surgery 1330.

[87] Sam Sholli, 'Daniel Barnett Reacts to "Bizarre" Tribunal Ruling that Calling Man Bald Is Sex Harassment' (*LBC*, 2022) <https://bit.ly/4cdsGih> accessed 9 February 2024.

another protected characteristic may sometimes create more problems than it solves.

6.6 Summary

The previous two chapters noted that the inclusion of people with severe disfigurements in the Act has not succeeded in promoting understandings of disability based on the social model in the real world. On the contrary, both people with lived experience of visible difference and employers tend to conceptualise disability in functional terms, influencing their self-identities and HR practices respectively.

The analysis in this chapter suggests that the failure of the social model to translate into real-world understandings is unsurprising. Although the severe disfigurement provision implicitly has its roots in the social model of disability, the narrowness and uncertainty of its scope creates so many inconsistencies that any wider messages about the link between disability and social barriers are lost. The words 'impairment' and 'disfigurement' include only a small subset of people experiencing social barriers because of the way they look. This creates illogical distinctions with other conditions and individual personal contexts. This undermines the severe disfigurement provision's potential for impact. Wider case law about the links between disability and appearance – particularly relating to obesity – again fails to grasp the social model mantle, returning instead to the familiar criterion of functional deficit.

The gaps left by the severe disfigurement provision cannot always be filled by enlisting other protected characteristics; here again the law ends up embracing some people within scope (such as men with male pattern baldness) but perhaps not others (women with male pattern baldness or men with alopecia) in a hit-and-miss fashion.

Given the Act's failure to send a clear message about the disabling power of impairments of appearance, expecting significant attitudinal, normative or behavioural change to result from it may be unrealistic. The Act does not provide a symbolic statement about the importance of appearance equality. Moreover, uncertainty over the Act's scope impacts the ability to create an effective remedial mechanism. Although this uncertainty could be addressed by the courts, this places a heavy burden of the victims of discrimination to seek clarification of the law.

7

Severity and Complexity

This chapter[1] turns to the meaning and function of the severity threshold in the severe disfigurement provision. It explores how severity is determined, whether this threshold can be justified and whether the concept of perceptive discrimination can mitigate any resultant harshness. This chapter also probes the Act's treatment of conditions which include both disfigurement and functional impairment, to assess whether the law is capable of addressing the holistic lived experience of complex conditions.

7.1 Determining Severity

There is no definition within the Act on what makes a disfigurement severe, but the Guidance provides that:

> Assessing severity will be mainly a matter of the degree of the disfigurement which may involve taking into account factors such as the nature, size, and prominence of the disfigurement. However, it may be necessary to take account of where the disfigurement in question is (e.g. on the back as opposed to the face).[2]

The Act makes no distinction between congenital or acquired conditions, though tattoos which have not been removed and piercings are expressly excluded.[3]

The open scope of the severity threshold has, to some extent, been addressed in case law. In *Johansson v Fountain Street Community*

[1] Much of the content of this chapter (and parts of Chapters 2, 5 and 9) are reproduced from Hannah Saunders, 'The Invisible Law of Visible Difference: Disfigurement in the Workplace' (2019) 48 Industrial Law Journal (London) 487 by permission of Oxford University Press on behalf of Industrial Law Society. Copyright © 2018 (The author) 2019.

[2] Office for Disability Issues, *Equality Act 2010: Guidance on Matters to Be Taken into Account in Determining Questions relating to the Definition of Disability* (HM Government 2011) para B25.

[3] Equality Act 2010 (Disability) Regulations 2010, SI 2010/2128, reg 5.

Development Association [2005] NIIT 311/03,[4] for example, a lack of prominence seems to have contributed to the finding that the claimant's disfigurement was not severe. The Tribunal relied on expert evidence that, although the scarring was visible at conversational distances, there was no distortion of the Claimant's facial features and her facial expressions were unaffected. So it appears that the visibility of a disfigurement from a distance, and any impact on facial expressions, can sometimes be relevant in determining severity. The Claimant's own evidence that her appearance had never been a problem at work over a twenty-year period also contributed to the conclusion that she did not have a severe disfigurement. (It is worth noting, however, that in this case, the Tribunal also commented that 'there was nothing in [the claimant's] appearance which could be considered repellent', which seems to represent an interpretation of the severity threshold which is both overly demanding and inappropriate.) *Johansson* can be contrasted with *Hand v The Police Authority for Northern Ireland*,[5] which also concerned facial scarring, resulting from a cleft lip and palate. Unlike in *Johansson*, the contours of the Claimant's profile were impacted, the scarring was visible from a distance as well as close-up, and the Tribunal noted the Claimant's self-consciousness about the scarring. The Tribunal also placed emphasis on the location of the scarring in the central portion of the face. The test of severity was satisfied.

Case law has also addressed the delicate topic of proving severity. In *Hutchison 3G UK Ltd v Edwards*,[6] the claimant had Poland syndrome which caused a significant asymmetry of his chest cavity. He felt that this would have been obvious when wearing the mandated company polo shirt. His condition also made some movements (e.g. pushing/pulling) more difficult. The first instance Tribunal decided that Mr Edwards had a severe disfigurement, but this was appealed, with the respondent arguing that the Tribunal did not have enough evidence in front of it on which to reach this conclusion. The Employment Appeal Tribunal ('EAT') expressed discomfort about being asked to make visual judgments on

4 *Johansson v Fountain Street Community Development Association* [2005] NIIT 311_03 (4 July 2005, unreported, NIIT) was a decision of the Northern Ireland Industrial Tribunal applying similar wording.

5 *Hand v The Police Authority for Northern Ireland* [2002] NIIT 1691/01 (2 August 2002, unreported, NIIT) was a decision of the Northern Ireland Industrial Tribunal applying similar wording.

6 *Hutchison 3G Ltd v Edwards* [2014] UKEAT/0467/13/DM (4 August 2017, unreported, EAT).

the extent of a disfigurement evidenced photographically or in person, recognising that 'the protection is afforded to those for whom issues of appearance are likely to be particularly sensitive'.[7] The EAT concluded instead that it was entitled to take into account 'the impact of the disfigurement on the claimant'[8] in assessing the severity of a disfigurement – in other words, the claimant's perception of, and behavioural response to, it. By promoting 'a degree of sensitivity'[9] in the evidential requirements for establishing severe disfigurement, the EAT introduced both flexibility for claimants[10] and uncertainty for respondents, accepting that different forms of evidence may suffice in different cases. The EAT did, however, conclude that the test for severe disfigurement could not be wholly subjective; 'not simply what the claimant believed to be the case'.[11]

Prima facie, Tribunal willingness to take account of the impact of a disfigurement on the individual in assessing severity should benefit claimants, allowing more people to meet the evidential threshold and balancing the Act's requirements of process with 'respect for inherent dignity'[12] of the claimant. However, there is a risk that this could disadvantage claimants whose disfigurements are borderline in their severity but who have not allowed their life choices to be inhibited. Tribunals must guard against this, as it threatens to remove access to justice for those who have exercised a 'full and effective participation in society';[13] the antithesis of what disability law policy, enshrined in the principles of the CRPD, seeks to achieve.

7.1.1 The Bodily Location of Disfigurement

Returning to the Guidance,[14] the bodily location of the disfigurement is another factor to be taken into account in deciding whether the severe

7 Ibid para 56.

8 Ibid para 55.

9 Ibid para 57.

10 For a case in which this flexibility was tested, see *Leighton v VR Music Limited and others* [2020] 2301546/2018 (17 April 2020, unreported, ET) para 70 in which the Tribunal was unwilling to accept the findings of a medical report which had been produced based solely on the Claimant's own description of her symptoms and some black and white photographs, without a physical examination.

11 *Hutchison* (n 6) para 60.

12 UN Convention on the Rights of Persons with Disabilities (12 December 2006) A/RES/61/106, art 3(a).

13 Ibid art 1.

14 Office for Disability Issues, *Equality Act 2010* (n 2).

disfigurement threshold test is met. In *Blyth v Historic Scotland*,[15] for example, the Tribunal noted that the claimant's psoriasis was mainly on her torso and legs – parts of her body which she covered up. The Tribunal found her not to have a severe disfigurement. In *Whyte v First Capital East Ltd*,[16] again the EAT found that the claimant's folliculitis on his back was not a severe disfigurement, commenting that 'location is important as it affects ordinary people's judgment about its severity . . . protection against discrimination . . . is more necessary when it is visible on the face than when it is invisible on the backside' [sic].[17] And in *Dhillon v Leeds Teaching Hospital NHS Trust*,[18] a cyst in the genital area was not a severe disfigurement due to its location.

This focus on invisibility suggests that the rationale for the guidance lies at least partly in how likely the disfigurement is, given its location, to be seen by others. On one level, this seems both logical and in line with the social model of disability, reflecting the frequency with which attitudinal barriers would be expected to be encountered. But, while recognising that facial disfigurements can be particularly challenging for those affected, on closer analysis the possibility that this guidance will be used to exclude non-facial disfigurements from equality protection is troubling in two respects.

First, it creates an expectation that a disfigurement which *can be* covered, *should* be covered; or, at least, that legal redress may be limited where it *could have been* covered. While the Guidance which accompanies the Act provides that:

> [a]ccount should be taken of how far a person can reasonably be expected to modify his or her behaviour, for example by use of a coping or avoidance strategy, to prevent or reduce the effects of an impairment on normal day-to-day activities.[19]

the emphasis of these coping mechanisms is on small, practical activity choices, such as avoiding skiing, but not shopping, to alleviate back pain. The issue of coping mechanisms is not directly relevant to severe disfigurements which, as discussed above, do not need to satisfy the substantial

[15] *Blyth v Historic Scotland* [2001] ET/S/4000514/00 (14 February 2001, unreported, ET).

[16] *Whyte v First Capital East Limited* [2005] UKEAT/0686/04/DM (22 March 2005, unreported EAT).

[17] Ibid para 34.

[18] *Dhillon v Leeds Teaching Hospital NHS Trust* [2019] ET/1800222/19 (18 December 2019, unreported, ET) para 16.

[19] Office for Disability Issues, *Equality Act 2010* (n 2) para B7.

adverse effect test. But linking the bodily location of a disfigurement with its severity imports a similar expectation; that a person will 'cope' by hiding their difference. Far from being a small, practical activity choice, this goes to the root of the individual's self-identity and body image. The respect for difference and human diversity[20] emphasised in the CRPD reflects a move away from the 'care or cure' approach to disability, embodied in the medical model, towards an approach which values disability not as 'a "mistake" of society but an element of its diversity'.[21] Restricting access to justice in situations where diversity can be covered up – perhaps with clothing, facial hair[22] or cosmetics – is a retrograde step which shifts the focus away from the employer's alleged discriminatory behaviour back to the specifics of individual impairment.

The second concern with the focus on the visibility of the bodily location stems from the risk of conflating visibility and knowledge. While a disfigurement in a visible place, such as the face, is very likely to become known to others, the converse is not necessarily true; disfigurements in places of the body often covered by clothes can also become 'known'. They could, for example, be disclosed voluntarily, gleaned from a sick note or visible in hot weather. So, while facial disfigurements are likely to be noticed and at risk of stigmatisation, thus meriting legal redress, it isn't the case that disfigurements on the torso are immune from such stigma or undeserving of legal remedy if they do give rise to discrimination.

It is submitted that, instead of using the likelihood of a disfigurement being noticed to exclude some people from the definition of disability, the better approach (and one which reinforces the CRPD's focus on hindered participation) is for the employer's actual knowledge and conduct to be assessed on the facts of each case in determining whether discrimination has taken place.

7.1.2 Progressive Conditions

Although the Act makes provision for progressive conditions generally[23] (the Act provides that a person with a progressive condition is protected

[20] CRPD (n 12) art 3(4).

[21] United Nations, *The Convention on the Rights of Persons with Disabilities Training Guide* (United Nations 2014) 10.

[22] See, for example, *Griffiths v Lancashire County Council* [2009] (17 April 2009, unreported, ET).

[23] Equality Act 2010, sched 1 pt 1 s8.

as a disabled person from the first time when his impairment has some adverse effect, provided that the adverse effect is likely to become substantial in the future), similar protection has not been afforded to people with progressively disfiguring conditions, such as neurofibromatosis type 1[24] or vitiligo,[25] which are likely to lead to severe disfigurement over time.

The progressive condition provision under the Act was introduced to combat stigma before the condition reached a stage where the substantial adverse effects test was satisfied; it recognises the potential for social barriers to pre-empt functional barriers. HIV, multiple sclerosis and cancer are expressly included as disabilities,[26] rather than being left to fall under the progressive conditions provision, because they were identified as conditions which could be diagnosed and lead to stigmatisation while the affected person was asymptomatic, thereby also failing the progressive condition test. There is an obvious parallel here with progressively disfiguring conditions, which may *never* produce an adverse effect on day-to-day activities, but which can lead to stigmatisation from an early stage.

The CRPD does not discuss progressive conditions, because it does not need to; its concept of disability is not limited to a given level of impairment. Someone with a progressively disfiguring condition would be covered by the CRPD from the moment that the condition, in interaction with various barriers, has the potential to hinder full participation in society. The failure to extend the progressive condition protection to disfigurement is therefore out of step with the CRPD. It is arguable that, if this point were tested in court, this gap could be easily filled without sacrificing the integrity of the Act's existing provisions. However, the lack of clarity may discourage these claims from being brought in the first place.

The discussion in this section so far has raised several concerns which are, directly or indirectly, related to one thing: the threshold test of severity. The real question is therefore not how severity should be determined, but whether the severity threshold should exist at all.

[24] Neurofibromatosis Type 1 is a genetic condition which can cause (usually benign) tumours to grow over time along the nerves, both inside the body and on the skin. In some people, it also causes other symptoms such as scoliosis, high blood pressure and learning difficulties.

[25] Vitiligo causes patches of skin to lose pigmentation, often progressively.

[26] Equality Act 2010 (n 23) sched 1 pt 1 s6(1).

7.2 Why Have a Severity Threshold?

When the severity threshold for disfigurement was first introduced (in the Disability Discrimination Act 1995 ('DDA'), which preceded the Act), Parliamentary records show that the rationale was a presumed assumption that more serious disfigurements will always elicit worse discrimination. This was questioned during the passage of the Bill through the Lords, as follows:

> The Government protect those with severe disfigurement; but, as the charity Changing Faces makes clear, discrimination is not related to the severity of disfigurement or to the severity of disability. Small wounds can be very disfiguring, whereas a large burn carried by an airman may be worn with pride as a sign of war. Alternatively, mild facial palsy is, for example, very isolating. Therefore, it is not size, it is not seriousness and it is not the conspicuousness of disfigurement which affects the person's ability to cope: it is another person's perception of it. Yet, such a person would not be protected under the provisions of the Bill.[27]

However, the amendment proposed to resolve the issue was one of perceived disability rather than one directed specifically at disfigurement. At the time, perceptive discrimination was not provided for within the DDA (although it has subsequently been incorporated into the Act) and the amendment was not passed. Arguments that 'if the definition of disability is too narrowly drawn, there may well be people who are disabled but who are not protected'[28] were overridden to prevent the net being drawn so widely that 'the issue falls into some form of disrespect; or . . . the provisions cannot be operated and the very people whom we wish to help are not helped'.[29] However, with the benefit of nearly thirty years of hindsight, the binary distinction in the Act between severe and non-severe disfigurements still appears hard to justify for the following reasons:

1. Studies in the field of psychology[30] continue to confirm that this assumption of clinical severity leading to worse consequences is wholly unreliable: reactions to minor or moderate disfigurements, in terms of the psychosocial impact on the individual, can often be as damaging as those experienced by people with severe

[27] HL Deb, 1995, vol 564, col 1642.
[28] Ibid vol 564, col 1650.
[29] Ibid.
[30] See Chapter 4.

disfigurements,[31] and, despite variability, there is evidence that some people with relatively minor disfiguring conditions experience higher levels of both depression and social anxiety than their more severely affected counterparts.[32]

2. The severity threshold for disfigurement is inconsistent with the threshold test for disability in the Act, that of 'substantial adverse effect'. 'Substantial' is defined in the Act as 'more than minor or trivial'[33] which has, in turn, been interpreted as a relatively low standard. An ordinary reading of the word 'severe' denotes a higher threshold than 'substantial' (as evidenced, for example, by national security threat levels where severe is a more serious level than substantial). This suggests that functional impairments are treated by the Act as more disabling than the social barriers of disfigurement, necessitating staggered thresholds for the law to engage. Once again, this sits uncomfortably with a body of evidence which demonstrates that people with a disfigurement are as likely to suffer discrimination in the workplace as people with other types of disability.[34] There appears, therefore, to be little justification for imposing a higher threshold for rights under equality law based on disfigurement than on other types of disability.

Accordingly, there are strong reasons to conclude that the 'severity' threshold for disfigurement is unjustified and inconsistent. In contrast to the CRPD, in which 'the challenge facing a person with a disability is measured in terms of the existing barriers and not on the category or percentage of the impairment',[35] the severity threshold represents a familiar retreat to the ideology of the medical model, pushing the focus back onto the level of impairment. Given the sensitivity of issues of appearance (as recognised by the EAT in *Hutchison*), requiring a person

[31] See, for example, Frances Cooke Macgregor, 'Social and Psychological Implications of Dentofacial Disfigurement' (1970) 40 The Angle Orthodontist 231, 232.

[32] Nichola Rumsey and others, 'Altered Body Image: Appearance-Related Concerns of People with Visible Disfigurement' (2004) 48 Journal of Advanced Nursing 443, 450.

[33] Equality Act 2010 (n 23) s212(1).

[34] Sarah V Stevenage and Yolanda McKay, 'Model Applicants: The Effect of Facial Appearance on Recruitment Decisions' (1999) 90 British Journal of Psychology 221; Anna Stone and Toby Wright, 'When Your Face Doesn't Fit: Employment Discrimination against People with Facial Disfigurements' (2013) 43 Journal of Applied Social Psychology 515, 516. See Section 4.3.

[35] United Nations, *The Convention on the Rights of Persons with Disabilities Training Guide* (n 21) 18.

to prove that he has a 'severe disfigurement' as a precondition to challenging discrimination runs counter to the principles of respect for difference[36] and the inherent dignity of the person[37] and inhibits effective access to justice[38] as required by the CRPD.

7.3 The Legal Dichotomy of Complex Conditions

A further hurdle arises in the interpretation of a disability which 'consists of' severe disfigurement. In *Cosgrove v Northern Ireland Ambulance Service*,[39] the claimant had psoriasis which amounted to a severe disfigurement but which the parties agreed would not, but for the 'deemed disability' provision of severe disfigurement which existed under the DDA 1995 at the time (and which was similar for this purpose to the current provisions under the Act), have satisfied the definition of disability. He was denied a job as an ambulance person due to the risk of irritants aggravating his condition at work, an increased risk of infection for him through broken skin and an increased risk of cross-infection for his patients. Mr Cosgrove argued that this amounted to disability-related discrimination, but his argument hinged on whether the impairment was the psoriasis as a whole (argued by Mr Cosgrove) or merely the disfiguring aspect of the psoriasis. This interpretation was crucial because, while the refusal of the job was causally connected to the symptoms of psoriasis, particularly broken skin, it was not connected to the way it looked.

The Court of Appeal (NI) decided that '[a]n impairment "consisting of" disfigurement means, in common parlance, that the impairment relates solely to the cosmetic aspect of the condition'.[40] Although the claim was decided in relation to disability-related discrimination, it appears likely that it would also apply in relation to other forms, such as discrimination arising from a disability.

It is questionable whether this narrow interpretation of a disability consisting of a severe disfigurement made much practical difference to a claimant in Mr Cosgrove's medical context, as the treatment could perhaps have been objectively justified, subject to a meaningful risk assessment process being carried out. However, the narrow

36 CRPD (n 12) art 3(d).
37 Ibid art 3(a).
38 Ibid art 13.
39 *Cosgrove v Northern Ireland Ambulance Service* [2007] IRLR 397 (NICA).
40 Ibid para 16.

interpretation could make a greater impact in other contexts. Had Mr Cosgrove applied for an office job, for example, the identified risks would presumably have been much reduced and, in consequence, the withdrawal of the offer much less likely to be objectively justifiable. But his claim would still have failed as the withdrawal of the job offer would not arise from the disfiguring aspect of his condition.

The real problem with Cosgrove stems from the statutory wording ('a disability which *consists of* a severe disfigurement'), but the court's literal interpretation missed an opportunity to tackle this; they commented that if someone in Mr Cosgrove's situation was intended to be included with the embrace of the relevant section, 'a phrase such as "includes severe disfigurement" could have been used'.[41] Cosgrove encapsulates the conflict between the social and medical models which is entrenched in the Act itself; its graceless approach implies that someone can be disabled either by attitudes towards people who look different or by functional effects of their impairment – but not by a combination of the two. By implication, the law declares that Mr Cosgrove encountered 'the wrong type of barrier', which is a far cry from the more complex 'interaction with various barriers'[42] envisaged in the CRPD.[43]

Although Mr Cosgrove's claim faltered in establishing that the treatment complained of related to his severe disfigurement, similar conceptual inflexibility in the Act's approach can be found at the earlier stage of proving disability, too. The Act allows multiple minor functional impairments to be considered holistically[44] to meet the definition of disability in section 6 but does not seem to extend the same flexibility to combinations of impairments which include both minor disfigurement and minor functional impairment. These two aspects must be proven separately, meeting the respective thresholds for severe disfigurement or the definition in section 6 independently. This demonstrates once again the Act's inability to embrace the combinations of experiences often encountered by people with complex conditions.

We can conclude from the arguments above that the severity threshold and the drafting of the provision in which it resides represent formidable

[41] Ibid.

[42] CRPD (n 12) art 1.

[43] As a Northern Irish decision, *Cosgrove* (n 39) is persuasive but not binding in England and Wales, which may allow an opportunity for the limitations of the decision to be departed from.

[44] Office for Disability Issues, *Equality Act 2010* (n 2) paras B4–B6.

limitations on the Act's scope and remedial potential. But the concept of perceptive discrimination might mitigate this to some degree.

7.4 Mitigating the Act's Limitations: Perceptive Discrimination

Someone with, say, a moderate disfigurement, who does not satisfy the 'severe' threshold test, may be able to base a claim of direct discrimination or harassment on the respondent's *perception* that he has a severe disfigurement. Perceptive discrimination claims recognise that discrimination can occur on the basis of a protected characteristic which the victim does not have. By way of example, in *English v Thomas Sanderson Ltd*,[45] Mr English brought a successful harassment claim when he was subjected to a campaign of homophobic verbal harassment, despite the fact that he was heterosexual. Perceptive discrimination embodies the social model of disability, in that it recognises that disability can be externally created, not inherent within the individual.

Claims based on perception are permitted under the Act because the wording of both s13 (direct discrimination) and s26 (harassment) is wide enough to allow a claim to be brought where the claimant does not actually have the protected characteristic (in this case, disability). Assume the example of an employee with a small facial haemangioma who is called an offensive nickname at work and told that he cannot be promoted to a client-facing role because of his face. The law's perception of his level of disfigurement may be different from those of his employer and colleagues, in that a Tribunal may find his disfigurement to be only moderate, so not disabling. But a claim that he has been discriminated against and/or harassed because of his employer's perception may enable this gap to be bridged.

However, perceptive disability discrimination claims are not straightforward because disability (unlike, say, race or sex) has a threshold test (set out in s6 of the Act) which a claimant has to meet. To what extent does the decision-maker have to know of, or put his mind to, the elements of that specific legal test before she can be said to perceive disability? In the recent case of *Coffey*,[46] the EAT (subsequently confirmed by the Court of Appeal[47]) confirmed that:

[45] *English v Thomas Sanderson Ltd* (2009) ICR 543 (CA).
[46] *The Chief Constable of Norfolk v Coffey* [2018] IRLR 193 (EAT).
[47] *The Chief Constable of Norfolk v Coffey* [2019] IRLR 805 (CA).

> [T]he answer will not depend on whether the putative discriminator A perceives B to be disabled as a matter of law; in other words, it will not depend on A's knowledge of disability law. It will depend on whether A perceived B to have an impairment with the features which are set out in the legislation.[48]

Although *Coffey*'s confirmation of the application of perceptive discrimination to disability is welcome, the case is in other ways disappointing; it is likely to lead to a series of denials by decision-makers about the scope of their perception. However, this hurdle may be easier for people with disfigurements to overcome than for people with some other types of disability. This is because a moderate disfigurement, which is perceived by the employer to be severe, should be able to bypass the 'substantial adverse effect' test contained in s6; severe disfigurements (presumably including *perceived* severe disfigurements) are *treated as* satisfying that definition. Does this make a difference? Seemingly, yes. It means there is nothing for the respondent to put his mind to save for whether the claimant has an impairment which consists of a severe disfigurement. Comments like those envisaged in our fictional scenario would seem to make it difficult for the respondent to deny this perception. A perceived disability claim may prove a useful alternative where the severity of the disfigurement is contested.

Perceptive discrimination claims can also apply where the perpetrator knew the victim not to have the characteristic which formed the basis of the harassment;[49] in *English*, for example, the people harassing Mr English knew him not to be gay but harassed him with homophobic abuse anyway. One of the judges in that case noted as 'barely perceptible'[50] the distinction between someone harassed because he is believed to be gay and someone harassed *as if he were* believed to be gay. Although the facts of the case are perhaps unusual – claims where people are harassed as if they had a severe disfigurement even when they are known not to have one will be few and far between – the court's approach has important implications for disability law in two respects.

First, the court placed the focal point of its analysis firmly on the discriminatory conduct, not on the characteristic of the victim. This affirms the social model's external focus and contrasts with the Act's

[48] *Coffey* (n 46) para 51.

[49] Equality and Human Rights Commission, *Employment: Statutory Code of Practice* (The Stationery Office Limited 2011) para 7.10.

[50] *English* (n 45) para 38, per Sedley LJ.

approach to severe disfigurement, where the threshold test excludes many claims at the hurdle of proving disability. Second, in *English*, Sedley LJ recognised that sexual orientation is a matter which many people may prefer to keep private,[51] so the law should not require its disclosure in order to challenge discrimination. Given the 'gruelling and personally invasive'[52] process of having one's impairment publicly scrutinised in a disability claim, this recognition of needing to balance privacy with principles of legal process is welcome; requiring someone to undergo a public analysis about whether they are both severely disfigured and disabled is a doubly unreasonable impediment to accessing justice.

Where the claim relates to discrimination on the basis of actual, rather than perceived, disability, it is hard to conceive how to prove disability (as it is currently defined in the Act, at least) without the intrusion of some enquiry. But the CRPD requires procedural accommodations to ensure that justice is accessible.[53] The Employment Tribunals have the power to make anonymity orders and restricted reporting orders,[54] but the requirements for these orders to be made are stringent. This is an area which could be further developed to prevent worthwhile claims being deterred.

A different type of perception connected with appearance is also conceivable; perceptions formed because of the way someone looks can also relate to assumed impairments of other kinds. For example, an employer may assume that a member of staff must be having cancer treatment because she has suddenly lost her hair. Or that a colleague with a red, bulbous nose caused by the skin condition rhinophyma must be an alcoholic. Or indeed that someone who is extremely thin must have an eating disorder.

These examples do expose an inconsistency in the perceptive discrimination concept, though; although the hair loss example might qualify for legal protection (because cancer is a disability under the Act), the rhinophyma/alcoholism example may not because alcoholism is excluded from protection as a disability under the Act.[55] Although the policy

[51] Ibid para 39.

[52] Anna Lawson, 'Disability and Employment in the Equality Act 2010: Opportunities Seized, Lost and Generated' (2011) 40 Industrial Law Journal 359, 361.

[53] See UN Committee on the Rights of Persons with Disabilities, 'Inquiry Concerning the United Kingdom of Great Britain and Northern Ireland Carried Out by the Committee under Article 6 of the Optional Protocol to the Convention Report of the Committee' (2016) CRPD/C/15/R.2/Rev.1, para 33.

[54] The Employment Tribunal Rules of Procedure 2013, rule 50.

[55] Equality Act 2010 (Disability) Regulations 2010 (n 3) reg 3.

reasons for excluding alcoholism would not apply to the person with rhinophyma who was disadvantaged by the perception, it is hard to imagine how the courts would resolve this given the wording of the Act. A similar issue could arise from scars perceived to relate to illegal drug use – also an excluded condition under the Act.

In summary, although perceptive discrimination provides a useful legal tool in some situations, it is not enough on its own to solve the identified shortcomings in the severe disfigurement provision.

7.5 Summary

By protecting only those disfigurements which are 'severe', the Act creates an additional threshold for claimants to meet in challenging discrimination. The application of this threshold is not only uncertain at times, but illogical, and out of line with what we know about the social and psychological experience of looking different. Moreover, it is inconsistent with the Act's treatment of other types of disability, which require a lower threshold of 'substantial' impact. Once again, we see the Act prioritising a model of disability based on functional deficit, by imposing stricter thresholds on claims founded on social, rather than functional, barriers.

Despite case law recognising the sensitive practicalities of proving issues of appearance, the existence of the severity threshold also exacerbates the need for an (often invasive) assessment in order to use the law. This was highlighted as a barrier by some of the participants in Chapter 4 and may contribute to the continued underuse and invisibility of the law.

Case law under the Act has also failed to approach complex conditions (those which are not limited just to aesthetic impact) in a holistic fashion, forcing claimants to compartmentalise their lived experience artificially, and prove each aspect separately. This demonstrates the Act's inability to recognise the interaction of different types of disabling barrier, as required by the CRPD. Although perceptive discrimination might sometimes be useful to backfill some of the shortfalls in the Act's approach, this too is limited in scope, and inadequate to provide an effective remedial mechanism in all cases.

In short, the severity threshold and the case law relating to it serve to restrict an already narrow provision. The resulting law reflects neither the lived experience of looking different nor the standards applied in the rest of the Act.

8

Law and Social Change

Are We Expecting Too Much?

Preceding chapters have highlighted shortcomings in the law. These shortcomings fall mainly into two camps. First, there is conflict caused by different conceptions of disability. This conflict affects understandings and behaviours among both those with visible differences and employers. Second, there is the narrow, uncertain and illogical scope of the severe disfigurement provision in the Act. This excludes many people who are discriminated against for looking different and undermines the implicit logic of the provision. From these shortcomings, there is a temptation to leap to the conclusion that the law should be changed to make it work better. But is it realistic to expect equality law - however drafted - to tackle the deep-rooted bias against visibly different people? And, if so, how can we maximise its chances of success?

Many people tend to assume that law should be able both to deter discrimination and to penalise it when it does occur. Lawyers may be particularly guilty of this, but we are not alone. Roger Cotterrell notes a 'climate of opinion emphasising law's capacity to mould society'.[1] While early social scientists often viewed law as part of the social life of society and reflective (rather than determinative) of its norms,[2] the twentieth century popularised the conception that law can be used as an instrument of state power, acting upon social norms to create change.[3] The reality probably falls somewhere in the middle with a degree of flux depending on the context. After all, many laws are unlikely to reach the statute book unless prompted by some kind of social impetus, even if not universally popular. Accordingly, attention has increasingly turned to identifying the factors which can influence the causal relationship between law and social change.

[1] Roger Cotterrell, *The Sociology of Law: An Introduction* (2nd edn, Butterworths 1992) 50.

[2] See, for example, William Sumner, *Folkways: A Study of the Sociological Importance of Usages, Manners, Customs, Mores, and Morals* (Dover Publications 1906) 55.

[3] Cotterrell, *The Sociology of Law* (n 1) 45.

A preliminary issue here is that 'social change' is a malleable concept;[4] as Albiston and Leachman argue, '[t]he way social change is conceptualized affects conclusions about the law's ability to produce it. Narrow measures of social change may yield pessimistic conclusions, whereas broader definitions of social change may produce more optimistic conclusions'.[5] Clear definitions are crucial. This book focuses on law's potential to achieve the five equality impacts discussed in Chapter 3. In other words, it seeks to identify law's potential to change attitudes, adjust perceived social norms, alter behaviours (whether directly or indirectly) or create an effective remedial mechanism for people with visible differences. (This last aim – an effective remedial mechanism – is harder to conceptualise as an aspect of social change because it is intrinsically linked to continuing negative behaviour. However, an improved remedial mechanism can impact responses to acts of discrimination, which may contribute to social change by altering perceptions of the likely consequences of discrimination.)

This chapter attempts neither to explore the nature and theory of the relationship between law and social change nor to represent the entire body of thought in this area. Others have already noted the difficulty of this in a field as vast, complex and multidisciplinary as the relationship between law and human behaviour.[6] Instead, this chapter groups together five factors which, when implemented in law, have been singled out in wider scholarship for their potential to influence patterns of social change. These relate to (i) the subject matter of the law and how contentious it is; (ii) the type of social change sought; (iii) whether the law has been imposed from the top or grown from civil society activity; (iv) the extent to which the law is publicised; and (v) how effective law's compliance mechanisms are. These factors are used to evaluate the current law's potential to achieve the five potential equality objectives outlined above.

8.1 How Contentious Is the Law?

It is often argued that laws compatible with existing cultural and legal values are more likely to be accepted.[7] The importance of cultural

[4] On this, see Catherine R Albiston and Gwendolyn M Leachman, 'Law as an Instrument of Social Change', in James Wright (ed), *International Encyclopaedia of the Social and Behavioural Sciences* 13 (2nd edn, Elsevier 2015) 543.

[5] Ibid 544.

[6] Thomas S Ulen, 'The Importance of Behavioral Law' in Eyal Zamir and Doron Teichman (eds), *The Oxford Handbook of Behavioral Economics and the Law* (1st edn, Oxford University Press 2014) 94.

[7] Janice Nadler and Kenworthey Bilz, 'Law, Moral Attitudes, and Behavioral Change' in Eyal Zamir and Doron Teichman (eds), *The Oxford Handbook of Behavioral Economics and the*

compatibility may be particularly acute where those laws are value-laden (such as laws regulating family relations, or perhaps individual appearance) rather than emotionally neutral[8] (such as laws regulating commercial transactions). As Roger Cotterrell suggests, 'changes that smack too much of legal or social revolution are likely to be resisted'.[9] Prohibition in the US has been cited[10] as the archetypal example of a law which failed to carry much of the population along with its ideology, leading to flagrant subversion in the form of bootlegging[11] and speakeasies.[12] This idea of resistance to culturally incompatible laws raises the possibility that, if we get it wrong, laws could even make things worse, creating backlash[13] and resistance.

For Cotterrell, equality law meets the requirement of cultural compatibility, as concepts of equality are deeply rooted in British culture.[14] But not all grounds of equality have equal levels of cultural buy-in at a given point in time. A common reaction to the idea of wider appearance equality is that it would be 'an equality too far', something which should fall within the remit of personal resilience, not law. So, while there have been few signs of public resistance to the principle of a law on severe disfigurement equality, the same may not be true of a reformed, wider protected characteristic of appearance. Nor can law's cultural compatibility be judged through a singular lens; multi-cultural societies may mean differing levels of compatibility of a particular law within different parts of the population.[15]

Public resistance may, of course, be a risk worth taking. Catherine Mackinnon points out that '[a]nxiety about backlash, however well founded, keeps one's antennae endlessly attuned to giving power what

Law (Oxford University Press 2014) 246; Cotterrell, *The Sociology of Law* (n 1) 59; Sumner, *Folkways* (n 2) 55; Cristina Bicchieri, *Norms in the Wild: How to Diagnose, Measure, and Change Social Norms* (Oxford University Press 2017) 145; Dan M Kahan, 'Gentle Nudges vs. Hard Shoves: Solving the Sticky Norms Problem' (2000) 67 The University of Chicago Law Review 607, 608.

8 Yehezkel Dror, 'Law and Social Change' (1958) 33 Tulane Law Review 787, 800.

9 Cotterrell, *The Sociology of Law* (n 1) 59 discussing William M Evan, *Law and Sociology: Exploratory Essays/Edited by William M. Evan with a Foreword by Lehan K. Tunks* (Free Press of Glencoe 1962).

10 See, for example, Albiston and Leachman, 'Law as an Instrument of Social Change' (n 4) 542.

11 The illegal manufacturing and sale of alcohol.

12 Nightclubs selling alcohol illegally.

13 Nadler and Bilz, 'Law, Moral Attitudes, and Behavioral Change' (n 7) 242.

14 Cotterrell, *The Sociology of Law* (n 1) 59.

15 Roger Cotterrell, *Law, Culture and Society Legal Ideas in the Mirror of Social Theory* (Ashgate 2006) 84–105.

pleases (and please pacifies) it. This contributes to keeping dominance in place'.[16] If seeking to legislate for social change, a delicate balance must be found between drafting a law for maximum cultural buy-in and creating a weak or narrowly scoped law which lacks both the potential for backlash and positive impact.

8.2 What Aspect of Social Change Is Targeted?

Second, the nature of the intended change may sometimes impact its chances of success. Laws prohibiting behaviours may leave problematic attitudes untouched, pushing unwanted behaviours underground and making them harder to prove.[17] Laws which seek to change attitudes (and ultimately behaviours) *indirectly* are sometimes shown to have greater potential for social change than those which directly prohibit behaviours. The underlying thinking is that we are more likely to change our behaviours when we believe we have reached a particular view ourselves, than when we are conscious of being told what to do.[18] As Bilz and Nadler argue, 'effective propaganda is subtle propaganda'.[19]

Bilz and Nadler give the example of legislation in America taxing the sale of cigarettes and banning smoking inside public venues.[20] This contributed indirectly to changing attitudes to smoking by making it more expensive and less convenient. But more than this, they argue that it brought the issue of smoking into the moral arena by forcing ethical engagement with the problem of passive smoking.[21] A similar example could be the use of plastic carrier bags in the UK; 2015 legislation introducing a small charge for every plastic carrier bag given out by shops has been credited with reducing plastic bag usage by up to 97 per cent in the eight years since its introduction.[22] But it isn't just the

[16] Catharine A MacKinnon, 'Where #MeToo Came from, and Where It's Going' *The Atlantic* <www.theatlantic.com/ideas/archive/2019/03/catharine-mackinnon-what-metoo-has-changed/585313/> accessed 17 October 2023.

[17] Dror, 'Law and Social Change' (n 8) 801.

[18] WK Muir, 'Under What Circumstances Can Law Bring about Attitude Change?' cited in Cotterrell, *The Sociology of Law* (n 1) 61; Nadler and Bilz, 'Law, Moral Attitudes, and Behavioral Change' (n 7) 248.

[19] Nadler and Bilz, 'Law, Moral Attitudes, and Behavioral Change' (n 7) 257.

[20] Ibid 248.

[21] See also Marc Galanter, 'The Radiating Effects of Courts' (*Empirical Theories of Courts 1983*) 125.

[22] DEFRA, *10p Bag Charge Turns the Tide on Plastic Waste* (2022) <www.gov.uk/government/news/10p-bag-charge-turns-the-tide-on-plastic-waste> accessed 18 March 2024.

financial cost of a plastic bag which motivates us to take a reusable bag to the supermarket; more the creeping sense of embarrassment when we forget, given the current environmentally conscious climate. It appears that the social meaning of plastic usage may have changed, as well as the behaviour itself.[23]

This may not, of course, all be due to law.[24] For example, although the 2015 law may have contributed to reducing numbers of plastic bags, this should be seen against a backdrop where 'green' issues have been a hot topic generally. Refill shops have become a common sight on the high street; prime time TV programmes have proclaimed a 'war on plastic';[25] COP 26 attracted enormous public attention to climate change and the environment; and recycling generally has become more mainstream. Isolating law from other factors is difficult, and the reality may often be that a well-timed law forms part of a wider social momentum, not a lone catalyst.

The Act relies mostly on direct prohibitions of certain types of behaviour, rather than indirect 'nudges'.[26] The two main exceptions to this – the positive action provisions and the duty on public bodies under s149 of the Act – are substantively fairly weak[27] and constitute no more than a minor diversion from the Act's main emphasis on classifying certain types of interpersonal actions as discriminatory. Even the duty to make reasonable adjustments, which does promote workplace inclusion to some degree, is rendered largely ineffectual in this context by the Act's primary message that disability means functional deficit.

Behavioural prohibitions can be important, both in creating the ability to challenge individual acts of discrimination and, if communicated, in fostering the perceived social norm that most people consider disfigurement discrimination unacceptable. Richard McAdams refers to this as 'attitudinal signaling',[28] a process by which 'law conveys information about public attitudes concerning the regulated behaviour',[29] often causing them to behave differently to avoid disapproval. But it is clear from

[23] See, for example, Rustam Romaniuc, 'What Makes Law to Change Behavior? An Experimental Study' (2016) 12 Review of Law & Economics 447, 448.

[24] Cotterrell, *The Sociology of Law* (n 1) 62.

[25] BBC, *War on Plastic with Hugh and Anita* (BBC 2020).

[26] Nadler and Bilz, 'Law, Moral Attitudes, and Behavioral Change' (n 7) 248.

[27] See Chapter 3.

[28] Richard H McAdams, *The Expressive Powers of Law: Theories and Limits* (1st edn, Harvard University Press 2015) 137.

[29] Ibid.

the evidence presented already that these behavioural prohibitions are not enough on their own; law and policymakers may need to be more creative and strategic in finding ways to invoke moral judgments about appearance discrimination which nudge attitudes and behaviours in the desired direction.

8.3 Does the Law Have 'Bottom Up' Ownership?

The third factor which has been argued to affect law's ability to contribute to social change is the way the law came about. Anita Bocker argues that laws stemming from the 'bottom-up',[30] perhaps after a long campaign of activism by communities and NGOs, are more likely to be successfully mobilised than those imposed 'top-down'[31] without a prior groundswell of support. She argues:

> civil society groups can play a crucial role in making non-discrimination law a reality on the ground. Non-discrimination laws may be enacted without their involvement, but the chances of 'law in the books' becoming 'law in action' are higher when they are involved in the lawmaking process and perceive the law as 'theirs' once it is in force.[32]

However, conceiving of a particular law as coming from either the top or the bottom is often an oversimplification; even laws which have been won by hard-fought community campaigns may, once on the statute book, be criticised for missing the mark. The Disability Discrimination Act 1995 is a case in point; its introduction followed years of protests and campaigns by disability rights groups.[33] But, once it became law, its flaws were acknowledged by many working within the field.[34] And law can evolve over time through case law too, sometimes taking it further away from the original intent of the community which demanded it.

The provision on severe disfigurement within the 1995 law itself followed a campaign by Sir James Partridge and others to include people

[30] Anita Bocker, 'Can Non-discrimination Law Change Hearts and Minds?' (2020) 13 Erasmus Law Review 21, 25.

[31] Ibid.

[32] Ibid 30.

[33] Philip Lewis, 'Disability Discrimination Act: 1995 and Now' (*House of Lords Library*, 2020) <https://lordslibrary.parliament.uk/disability-discrimination-act-1995-and-now/> accessed 14 February 2024.

[34] For criticisms levelled at the DDA 1995 after its introduction, see Carol Woodhams and Susan Corby, 'Defining Disability in Theory and Practice: A Critique of the British Disability Discrimination Act 1995' (2003) 32 Journal of Social Policy 159, 159.

with visible differences within the scope of equality law.[35] But, despite the significant victory represented by its inclusion, there are reasons to suspect that the community of people with visible differences may not universally claim ownership or the current severe disfigurement provision in the Act. As outlined in Chapter 4, many people with visible differences reject the label of disability. The charity Face Equality International, for example, has campaigned for facial difference to be recognised as an identity and human rights issue separate from disability[36] for this reason. So, despite the severe disfigurement provision being 'bottom-up'[37] in origin, friction between law and community identity may deter some people from using it.

8.4 Has the Law Been Publicised?

Publicity is the fourth factor hailed for its ability to maximise the potential for social change. In its most basic sense, publicity of the law is important to create awareness; people are unlikely to adhere to, or enforce, a law which they have never heard of. Low levels of awareness of the current severe disfigurement provision – both among people with lived experience and employers – were identified earlier as a problem in this regard.[38]

Moreover, publicity of comparable laws – including those in other countries – may carry an important persuasive function, by illustrating the potential for positive outcomes. As later chapters will demonstrate, some countries – including France and the US – do have equivalent laws which are more far-reaching in scope than the severe disfigurement provision. But using these as role models to justify a similar law in Britain is not easy because there are question marks over the efficacy of both.[39]

An alternative route to publicity might be to draw links with high-profile cases brought under other protected characteristics in order to demonstrate the need for greater protection relating to appearance. The

[35] Andrew Jarvis, 'James Partridge Obituary' *The Guardian* (London, 27 August 2020) <www.theguardian.com/society/2020/aug/27/james-partridge-obituary> accessed 6 December 2023.

[36] Face Equality International, 'Face Equality Is a Human Right' (*Face Equality International*, 2022) <https://faceequalityinternational.org/wp-content/uploads/2022/05/Face-Equality-is-a-Human-Right-Report.pdf> accessed 7 November 2023.

[37] Bocker, 'Can Non-discrimination Law Change Hearts and Minds?' (n 30).

[38] See Chapters 1 and 5.

[39] See Section 10.3.

claim brought by BBC presenter Miriam O'Reilly[40] is one example as, although brought using age discrimination legislation, it drew attention to the way that physical appearance is still prioritised in entertainment industries, leading to unjust outcomes.

8.5 What Compliance Mechanisms Does the Law Use?

Finally, the mechanisms through which the Act seeks to ensure compliance can be important. Research highlights the importance of positive motivations for compliance as well as negative sanctions for violation. In other words, the carrot is needed, as well as the stick, because compulsion is often less effective as a way of influencing human behaviour than inducement.[41]

There is little or no direct carrot for employers in the Act itself, but, as Friedman argues, positive motivations for compliance might sometimes be indirect. The desire to do the right thing in moral terms can be an important motivation for some, because 'corporations cannot blush, but executives can'.[42] If other corporations within a particular industry are shouting their EDI credentials from the rooftops, organisations may be motivated to keep up. As one employer that I interviewed said:

> what you don't want to be as an organisation is the one that is taken to task over it, and then, with the benefit of hindsight, other organisations will say 'oh God, look how awful they are. We would never do that'.

There are questions, too, about the stick under the Act – and whether its metaphorical swing is wide enough. The degree to which enacted stigma is actionable depends partly on the type of stigma.[43] For example, the Act provides no remedy for internalised stigma, even when it leads to self-moderated career restrictions. One participant with a visible difference decided not to pursue her dream career on screen or in the theatre, providing a powerful example of this. With a couple of weak

[40] *M O'Reilly v (1) BBC & (2) Bristol Magazines Ltd* [2011] ET2200423/2010 (10 January 2011, unreported, ET).

[41] Laurence Lustgarten, 'Problems of Proof in Employment Discrimination Cases' (1977) 6 Industrial Law Journal 212.

[42] Lawrence Friedman, *Impact: How Law Affects Behavior* (Harvard University Press 2017) 264.

[43] See Valarie K Blake and Mark L Hatzenbuehler, 'Legal Remedies to Address Stigma-Based Health Inequalities in the United States: Challenges and Opportunities' (2019) 97 The Milbank Quarterly 480, 490.

exceptions,[44] the Act does not address structural stigma either. Structural manifestations of stigma are those built into the fabric of society; one example is inadequate regulation of the film industry, which allows disfigurement to be used as shorthand for evil, reinforcing the 'disfigured means bad' stereotype . Instead, the Act's focus is on interpersonal stigma, enacted between individuals. The denial of a job due to visible difference would be a common illustration. Even here, though, the stick of enforcement under the Act can only be used where a particular person is responsible for a specific action which occurs in a set context against an identifiable victim within a certain time frame. As Blake and Hatzenbuehler argue in relation to US equality law, 'one has to have been discriminated against in the "right" time, the "right" place, and by the "right" party (whatever the requirements of any specific antidiscrimination statute) in order for it to count as "unlawful" discrimination and this often has little to do with how unfair, harmful, or blatant the discrimination was'.[45]

Even where a particular act of discrimination is actionable, the law places the burden of enforcement on the victim of discrimination. This means that the person who is least well-positioned to do so must bear the burden of legal proceedings.[46] (This was also highlighted as a barrier during interviews with people with lived experience of visible difference.) Although Employment Tribunals are, theoretically at least, suitable for self-representation by Claimants, those without any legal knowledge may struggle to navigate a complex set of rules about types of discrimination, technical comparators, burdens of proof and procedural wizardry.[47] While some charities offer representation at Tribunal hearings, often this is not accessed in the early stages of claim when arguments often become set in stone. A quick search reveals arguments under the severe disfigurement provision which were dismissed on appeal because they were not pleaded at first instance,[48] often when the claimant was unrepresented.

44 As mentioned earlier, the positive action provisions and the duty on public bodies under s149 are minor exceptions; see Chapter 3 for a more detailed discussion.

45 Blake and Hatzenbuehler, 'Legal Remedies to Address Stigma-Based Health Inequalities in the United States' (n 43) 491.

46 House of Commons Women and Equalities Committee, *Enforcing the Equality Act: The Law and the Role of the Equality and Human Rights Commission* (Tenth Report of Session 2017–2019, HC1470) 7.

47 See, for example, Lizzie Barmes, *Bullying and Behavioural Conflict at Work: The Duality of Individual Rights* (Oxford University Press 2016) 26.

48 See, for example, *Vatcher v Kelly Services (UK) Ltd* [1999] UKEAT 595/99/0510 (5 October 1999, unreported, EAT); *Ellen Mart v Assessment Services Inc* [2019] UKEATS 0032/18/SS (16 May 2019, unreported, EAT).

It is worth noting that the EHRC does have some investigatory and enforcement powers relating to discrimination, as well as the ability to conduct or intervene[49] in strategic litigation and support litigants in particular cases.[50] However, EHRC guidance[51] makes clear that the greater the scale of the action, the more likely the EHRC is to intervene – and indeed the EHRC has been criticised for not being interventionist enough.[52] These powers are not used in the vast majority of cases, and the burden of enforcement remains firmly on the individual.

For the small percentage of people who do bring a claim, the odds are also stacked against them in terms of outcome. Galanter's game-theory analysis of litigation sees the individual claimant as a 'one-shotter' and the employer usually a 'repeat player'.[53] Repeat players have advantages procedurally: greater expertise, resources and the ability to take a risk in what is often, for them, a 'low stakes' environment. One-shotters, by comparison, are often alone in a high-stakes environment, with fears not just about financial consequences but also about reputation and the need for a reference. This often weights the chances against the claimant and may also afford respondents the opportunity to shape case law going forward with employer-friendly precedents. And for the few who succeed, remedies are individual too[54] – compensating the individual claimant rather than improving the landscape going forward for others in that group.[55]

In essence, typically weaker parties in a relationship are disadvantaged at all stages of using legal rights, exposing the flimsiness of the stick under the Act. Some argue that laws like this can discourage other forms of resistance too, by reducing group objections to closely circumscribed opportunities for individual legal action.[56]

[49] Equality Act 2006, s30.

[50] Equality Act 2006, s28.

[51] Equality and Human Rights Commission, 'Our Litigation and Enforcement Policy 2019–2022' (*EHRC*, 2019) <www.equalityhumanrights.com/sites/default/files/our-litigation-and-enforcement-policy-2019-2022_0.pdf> accessed 7 November 2023.

[52] House of Commons Women and Equalities Committee, *Enforcing the Equality Act: The Law and the Role of the Equality and Human Rights Commission* (n 46) 19.

[53] Marc Galanter, 'Why the Haves Come Out Ahead: Speculations on the Limits of Legal Change' (2013) 85 Droit et société 575.

[54] House of Commons Women and Equalities Committee, *Enforcing the Equality Act: The Law and the Role of the Equality and Human Rights Commission* (n 46) 8.

[55] Deregulation Act 2015, s2, requires that any recommendations relate only to the claimant.

[56] Albiston and Leachman, 'Law as an Instrument of Social Change' (n 4) 545.

These five factors offer an additional perspective on the severe disfigurement provision's apparent lack of impact. The first factor – whether the subject matter of the law reflects existing cultural principles – has been satisfied to some degree, in that the equality objective of the severe disfigurement provision has produced no discernible public criticism since its introduction. But the remaining four factors highlight missed opportunities to maximise the severe disfigurement provision's potential for real-world impact. The Act does little to nudge attitudes in the right direction, relying primarily on categorising certain behaviours as unlawful. Moreover, by bolting the severe disfigurement provision onto wider disability provisions based on a model of functional deficit, the law creates an identity conflict which may prevent people with visible differences from mobilising the law and creating a collective sense of identity around it.

There is also a lack of publicity about the existence or meaning of the law which has been exacerbated by nearly thirty years of underuse. While most people know of laws against sex or age discrimination, relatively few people have heard of the severe disfigurement provision. And those that have heard of it may find its message eroded by wider cultural messaging about the importance of beauty that does little to recognise respect for difference. This has ensured that the Act's potential to send a symbolic message has been all but silenced. Finally, the Act's failure to motivate people to buy into its aims through positive incentives is mirrored by its failure to provide effective, forward-looking negative sanctions for violations. Winning a claim under the severe disfigurement provision often means navigating a series of practical, legal, financial, reputational and emotional hurdles in a game where the odds are often stacked against the victim and the outcome is set up to avoid the need for wider change.

The application of these five factors is context-dependent and probably an oversimplification of the full social picture. Nevertheless, this analysis raises the possibility that even the very limited framework of potential equality objectives in Chapter 3 may be asking more of the current law than it was ever likely, on its own, to be able to offer. This reinforces the case for a new approach.

8.6 Summary

The literature on law and social change stresses the complexity of that relationship. A 'one size fits all' approach to legislating for social change is not possible; much depends on the context of the law and the change sought. As Lawrence Friedman concludes in his recent review of the literature, 'Much more research is needed. More replications. More attempts at pulling the strands together. Otherwise, everything depends. On time. On place. On situation'.[57]

It is often unrealistic to assume that law – however drafted – can induce targeted social change. But, while context is key, certain factors may sometimes affect a particular law's chances of doing so. First, the extent to which the law aligns with social values can help to determine how people react to it, with resistance more likely to laws which do not accord with current values. Second, laws which nudge towards change indirectly can sometimes be more effective than those which seek to alter behaviours and attitudes through overt instruction. Third, grassroots organisations and their supporters are important, creating a sense of ownership which can influence how the law is used once in place. Fourth, law is not immune to the power of PR; awareness and positive messaging about the potential of a law can increase likely impact. And finally, the quality of the law's enforcement mechanism is important, ensuring that it is not seen as toothless and that carrot and stick both play a part in motivating compliance.

Applying these principles to the severe disfigurement provision provides disappointing results. While the current provision is not controversial, it relies on overt prohibitions of discrimination and avoids subtler nudges towards appearance-inclusivity. Grassroots support in this space does exist and has grown over recent years. There are charities doing important work supporting people with visible differences, and at least one[58] dedicated to promoting the human rights of people with visible differences across the globe. This activism provides an important impetus for a growing collective identity. However, that impetus is hindered by the law's categorisation of severe disfigurement as a disability, because that label is rejected by many people with visible differences who see disability in purely functional terms. Publicity and awareness of the law is also low, both among employers and employees. This further inhibits its impact. Finally, the Act's enforcement mechanism is hamstrung by limitations of context, unequal burdens and differential power relations, as well as by a failure to include enough positive motivation to change behaviours.

In sum, the severe disfigurement provision's potential for impact has been hampered by its form, history and social environment. A different approach is needed.

[57] Friedman, *Impact: How Law Affects Behavior* (n 42) 249.

[58] Face Equality International, see www.faceequalityinternational.org.

9

Alternative Approaches in Law and Policy

Little evidence has been uncovered so far to suggest that law has succeeded in improving attitudes or behaviours towards people who look different, nor that it has altered the perceptions held about relevant social norms. The evidence has also revealed serious flaws in the remedial mechanism for challenging instances of discrimination towards people with disfigurements. A consideration of alternative regulatory and policy-level solutions to the problem of visible difference inequality at work is sorely needed.

The approaches mooted below draw on stigma-reduction interventions trialled in other areas – such as those relating to mental health and HIV – which provide useful comparisons in the absence of sufficient issue-specific data. The discussion considers wider interventions as well as those focused on the workplace, given the potential for change in one area of society to impact another.

9.1 Changing Attitudes, Perceived Social Norms and Behaviours

The approaches discussed in this section fall broadly into six categories. The first category relates to interpersonal contact and increasing the visibility of people with visible differences. The second relates to education – not just in schools but other areas of life too. The third category addresses advertising industry practices, with their focus on narrow beauty ideals. The fourth considers measures designed to motivate employers to achieve greater levels of visible difference equality. The penultimate category concerns technology, and the need to ensure that the rapidly changing world of AI does not exacerbate existing appearance equalities. And the last consists of influential changes *outside* the work context, which may shape practices *inside* the workplace. These categories will be considered in turn.

9.1.1 *Regulatory Interventions Focused on Contact and Visibility*

Law can be used to create situations where different groups of people mingle in contexts conducive to positive attitudinal change. This means bringing together people with and without visible differences to reduce prejudice as they get to know each other. As Monroe Berger argued: 'by altering the situations in which attitudes and opinions are formed, law can indirectly reach the more private areas of life it cannot touch directly in a democratic society'.[1] Promising results have been shown using contact to reduce prejudice against people with mental health conditions,[2] among other stigmatised groups.

To channel this approach, law could be utilised to increase opportunities for equal workplace participation. In theory, the Act already addresses workplace inclusion – by prohibiting actions which exclude people with severe disfigurements. But more extensive options could be introduced. This might mean job applicants with disabilities and visible differences being given the right to a paid work trial, to allow personal contact to dislodge stereotypes. One HR participant that I interviewed already had experience of this, having supported a visibly different employee in transitioning successfully from a work experience placement organised by a charity partner to a full-time paid role.

There are some complications in applying this contact hypothesis to visible difference in the workplace, however. The first is that a right to a paid work trial relies on relevant job applicants wanting to use it. Given the evidence in Chapter 4 – that many people with visible differences choose not to single themselves out by requesting adjustments or using guaranteed interview schemes – minimal use of such a right would be a significant possibility. The second complication is ensuring that the conditions of the contact are conducive to positive outcomes. It has been suggested that contact is most effective when groups work side by side with equal status and common goals.[3] This is difficult in hierarchical

1 Monroe Berger, *Equality by Statute: The Revolution in Civil Rights* (1968) cited in Anita Bocker, 'Can Non-discrimination Law Change Hearts and Minds?' (2020) 13 Erasmus Law Review 31.

2 Sarah Parry and others, 'Interventions to Reduce Mental Illness Stigma and Discrimination at the Person-Level for Individuals and Small Groups' in David L Vogel and Nathaniel G Wade (eds), *The Cambridge Handbook of Stigma and Mental Health* (Cambridge University Press 2022) 370.

3 Gordon W Allport, *The Nature of Prejudice* (Addison-Wesley 1955) 274–278.

workplaces;[4] if individuals with visible differences are in lower paid roles, assumptions and perceived status differentials may instead be reinforced.

The third complication is that research on the contact hypothesis may not yet be sufficiently nuanced to adjust for what Jasmine Harris terms the 'aesthetics of disability'.[5] Harris argues that contact is less likely to result in positive attitudinal change towards people with disabilities which trigger emotional affective responses in other people – such as visible disfigurements. These can elicit an avoidance response even within an integrated setting, defeating the power of integration. Harris argues that further research is needed on ways to overcome these affective responses – perhaps by varying the speed or conditions of integration.[6] Further analysis would be needed to understand this – including the extent to which different types of visible difference are impacted – and to establish the optimum conditions.

The potential benefits of increased contact could perhaps be facilitated indirectly by law in other ways, too. Visibility in social media is one example. Currently, abuse from other users may deter some people from engaging in online social platforms.[7] There are also anecdotal reports of platform algorithms blocking visibly different users from posting content of themselves or posting warning labels on their videos.[8] This may further reduce positive visibility, as well as leading to social exclusion.

The TV and film industry is another example. On-screen representation of people with visible differences generally is sparse. A 2009 study conducted at Cardiff University found that, in 7,650 hours of primetime television, there were only 293 representations of people with disfigurements, and many of these were at off-peak times.[9] The same year, Sir

[4] Bocker, 'Can Non-discrimination Law Change Hearts and Minds?' (n 1) 32.

[5] Jasmine E Harris, 'The Aesthetics of Disability' (2019) 119 Columbia Law Review 895, 895. See also Gwen Jones and Dianna Stone, 'Perceived Discomfort Associated with Working with Persons with Varying Disabilities' (1995) 81 Perceptual and Motor Skills 918.

[6] Harris, 'The Aesthetics of Disability' (n 5) 970.

[7] A survey by Changing Faces found that one in ten respondents with a visible difference had been the target of appearance-related abuse on social media, such as a meme or other content, and 29 per cent said that they chose not to use a photo of themselves as their profile. Changing Faces, 'Disfigurement in the UK' (*Changing Faces*, 2017) 25.

[8] See, for example, Natalie Keegan, 'Instagram Removed Photo of Boy with Facial Deformity for Violating "Guidelines"' *The Sun* <https://nypost.com/2017/09/13/instagram-removed-photo-of-boy-with-facial-deformity-for-violating-guidelines/> accessed 17 October 2023.

[9] Claire Wardle and Tammy Boyce, *Media Coverage and Audience Reception of Disfigurement on Television* (Cardiff University/The Healing Foundation 2009) 5.

James Partridge, who founded the charity Changing Faces and had a burns injury, read the lunchtime news on Channel five for a week – but despite a broadly positive reaction,[10] this did not trigger a significant increase in representation of visibly different faces on our screens.

When people with disfigurements do appear on our screens, they are often portrayed either as villains,[11] victims or curiosities. For example, research shows that 11 per cent of characters in James Bond films have a visible difference; of these, 80 per cent are villains (often with more severe and highly visible differences), 17 per cent are allied with Bond, and 3 per cent are double agents. So far, none are Bond girls.[12] Some progress has been made in this space; the British Film Institute has promised not to fund films which feature someone with a disfigurement in the role of the villain,[13] and some commentators suggest a trend towards more balanced portrayals of people with skin conditions in US movies over time.[14] Despite this, there remains a steady flow of fictional disfigured villains ready to (dis)grace our screens.[15]

On-screen visibility (whether on TV, in films or in social media) can either be educational – in the form of programmes or content about the

[10] Catherine Bennett, 'At Long Last, a Newsreader Who Made Us Face Reality' *The Guardian* <www.theguardian.com/commentisfree/2009/nov/22/james-partridge-tv-news readers> accessed 8 November 2023.

[11] The list includes numerous James Bond films, Freddie Krueger in *Nightmare on Elm Street*, Darth Vader in *Star Wars*, the Joker in *Batman*, Scar in *The Lion King* and Dr Poison in *Wonder Woman*. See also Wardle and Boyce, *Media Coverage and Audience Reception of Disfigurement on Television* (n 9) 39; Julie Amthor Croley, Vail Reese and Richard F Wagner, 'Dermatologic Features of Classic Movie Villains: The Face of Evil' (2017) 153 JAMA Dermatology 559; Laura Elliott, 'What's So Scary about Disability?' (*The Establishment*, 2018) <https://theestablishment.co/whats-so-scary-about-disability/index.html> accessed 7 February 2024; Cornelia Klecker and Gudrun M Grabher, *The Disfigured Face in American Literature, Film, and Television* (1st edn, Routledge 2021) 3.

[12] MKY Chen and others, 'The Spectre of Visible Difference: Semiotics of Disfigurement and Moral Character in James Bond Films' (2022) 47 Clinical and Experimental Dermatology 767, 767.

[13] Andrew Pulver, 'BFI to Refuse Funding for Films with Facially-Scarred Villains' *The Guardian* <www.theguardian.com/film/2018/nov/29/bfi-to-refuse-funding-for-films-with-facially-scarred-villains> accessed 8 November 2023.

[14] Y Ishida and others, 'Skin Findings of Twenty-first Century Movie Characters' (2017) 32 Journal of the European Academy of Dermatology and Venereology 98.

[15] See, for example, Jenny Kattlove, 'Open Letter – The Impact of Portraying Villainous Character, Frank Nakai, with Scars in TV Series *Dark Winds*' (*Face Equality International*, 2022) <https://faceequalityinternational.org/2022/09/openletter-dark winds/> accessed 8 November 2023; Philip Kirby, 'Battle Scars: Wonder Woman, Aesthetic Geopolitics and Disfigurement in Hollywood Film' (2020) 25 Geopolitics 916.

lived experience of looking different – or simply more appearance-diverse in its cast. There is evidence that both types of content might *sometimes* be capable of changing attitudes.[16] But there are still many challenges and unknowns. Research studies conducted using volunteer participants may not mirror results in the real world,[17] when viewers have a choice over what to watch.[18] The conditions in which content is watched may be different in daily life too; people may view multiple programmes or content-streams in quick succession,[19] either with friends or alone, and while in public places or privately. This might affect the way they respond to them. The nature of the representation is also crucial, with portrayals of minority groups on-screen capable of reinforcing stereotypes and biases.[20] One US study found that participants who watched an episode of 'The Biggest Loser', a reality TV programme about weight loss, demonstrated increased dislike for overweight people after the intervention.[21] In short, there are both opportunities and risks in

[16] In relation to visible difference specifically, see, for example, Jacob M Burmeister and others, 'Reducing Obesity Stigma via a Brief Documentary Film: A Randomized Trial' (2017) 2 Stigma and Health 43; Anna Stone and Veronica Fisher, 'Changing Negative Perceptions of Individuals with Facial Disfigurement: The Effectiveness of a Brief Intervention' (2020) 42 Basic and Applied Social Psychology 341; Abbi Matthews, Bruna Costa and Diana Harcourt, '"Scars: How Our Wounds Make Us Who We Are": Improving Appearance-Based Stigma, Conceptualisation of Beauty and Body Esteem through a Documentary' (2023) 9 Scars, Burns and Healing. In other contexts, see, for example, Bradley J Bond, 'The Development and Influence of Parasocial Relationships with Television Characters: A Longitudinal Experimental Test of Prejudice Reduction through Parasocial Contact' (2021) 48 Communication Research 573; Sohad Murrar and Markus Brauer, 'Entertainment-Education Effectively Reduces Prejudice' (2018) 21 Group Processes & Intergroup Relations 1053; Bartosz G Zerebecki and others, 'Can TV Shows Promote Acceptance of Sexual and Ethnic Minorities? A Literature Review of Television Effects on Diversity Attitudes' (2021) 15 Sociology Compass; cf Traci K Gillig and Sheila T Murphy, 'Fostering Support for LGBTQ Youth? The Effects of a Gay Adolescent Media Portrayal on Young Viewers' (2016) International Journal of Communication (Online) 3828.

[17] Zerebecki and others, 'Can TV Shows Promote Acceptance of Sexual and Ethnic Minorities?' (n 16) 12.

[18] Ibid 11.

[19] Ibid 12.

[20] Max Weisbuch, Kristin Pauker and Nalini Ambady, 'Subtle Transmission of Race Bias via Televised Nonverbal Behavior' (2009) 326 Science 1711, 1714; Zerebecki and others, 'Can TV Shows Promote Acceptance of Sexual and Ethnic Minorities?' (n 16) 11.

[21] This effect was more pronounced in those viewers with lower BMIs. See Sarah E Domoff and others, 'The Effects of Reality Television on Weight Bias: An Examination of *The Biggest Loser*' (2012) 20 Obesity 993, 996.

seeking to change attitudes through television and social media, and the risks are significant given the wide reach of these mediums.

Despite this, regulation could still be useful in some respects. Legislation banning the screening of content featuring a disfigured villain would be a simple step forward and one which already has considerable grassroots support.[22] While not likely to induce positive changes in attitudes, it would at least prevent the constant reinforcement of negative stereotypes.[23] One approach might be to apply such a law to prospectively generated content only, at least for now; any law that effectively banned popular pre-existing films would likely promote significant public opposition which could endanger the underlying message.

Legislating to prevent harassment of people with visible differences online is another potentially important step in upholding the right to equal participation and respect, even if positive attitudinal changes cannot be guaranteed to flow from the increased online visibility which may follow.[24] At the time of writing, the Online Safety Act 2023 has just become law and includes a provision under which social media users may block contact from non-verified users (such as anonymous accounts),[25] as well as options to filter out certain types of harmful content.[26] It is unclear how effective this will be in practice.

Regulation to force broadcasters to increase the degree of appearance diversity is a bigger challenge. A law which required broadcasters to increase the representation of people with visible differences could simply end up supercharging existing stereotypes of villainy, victimhood and curiosity. The qualitative nature of the representation is, of course, important as well as the number of representations on-screen.[27] A law

[22] See Changing Faces, 'I Am Not Your Villain: Equal Representation of Visible Difference in Film' (*Changing Faces*, undated) <www.changingfaces.org.uk/get-involved/campaign-with-us/i-am-not-your-villian/> accessed 7 December 2023. The sale of Halloween masks of people with visible differences could also be banned.

[23] In a similar vein, checks may be needed to ensure that AI image generators do not reinforce negative representations of visibly different faces.

[24] One (as yet unpublished) study conducted at the Centre for Appearance Research found that seeing people with visible differences on social media did not necessarily reduce prejudice without some form of educational/informative content too. However, the study was small scale so these findings require further testing. See Amy Slater, Ella Guest and G Treneman-Evans, *Utilising Social Media to Increase Acceptance of Appearance-Altering Conditions: A Two-Part Experimental Study* (2023).

[25] Online Safety Act 2023, s15.

[26] Online Safety Act 2015, s15 and s16.

[27] This point is implicitly acknowledged by the BBC's 50:50 project. This project aims to increase the representation of women on screen, and factors in both the nature and

which managed to engage broadcasters with the aim of improving visible difference equality[28] might encourage a more nuanced, considered and evaluated response than, say, a blunt requirement to include more people with disfigurements on-screen.

9.1.2 Reform Focused on Education

Reform could touch on education by putting appearance-linked content on the curriculum in schools. One or more books about the lived experience of disfigurement[29] could join the literature curriculum; models of disability could be taught alongside biology classes; history and art classes could study Henry's Tonks' portraits of soldiers with facial injuries returning from war,[30] and so on. If successful, this could promote awareness, familiarity and empathy in the next generation of colleagues and managers. But the big caveat here – and indeed throughout the suggestions in this chapter – is that these interventions would need to be thoughtfully designed and their cumulative impact carefully evaluated.[31] Well-meaning but poorly executed interventions designed to manipulate perceptions and acceptance of physical appearances can

perspective of the representation as well as the number of appearances of women on screen. See www.bbc.co.uk/5050.

28 Broadcast content is excluded from the duty on public sector bodies under s149 of the Equality Act 2010 by schedule 19. But see Ofcom, *Equity, diversity and inclusion Guidance for broadcasters* (Ofcom, 2 November 2022) <https://www.ofcom.org.uk/siteassets/resources/documents/tv-radio-and-on-demand/diversity-and-equality/guidance-diversity-in-broadcasting?v=323925> accessed 23.4.2025.

29 Examples include RJ Palacio, *Wonder* (Penguin Books 2020); Benjamin Zephaniah, *Face* (Bloomsbury 1999). For an analysis of the former, see Sandra Tausel, 'Writing against the Stigma: Facial Disfigurement in RJ Palacio's Wonder' in Cornelia Klecker (ed), *The Disfigured Face in American Literature, Film and Television* (Routledge 2021) 92.

30 Henry Tonks was a surgeon-turned-artist in the first world war, and he painted portraits of soldiers returning from battle with significant facial injuries.

31 PhD research conducted at the Centre for Appearance Research at UWE produced a guide to help primary school educators have conversations with children about appearance diversity. See Jade Parnell, 'Promoting Acceptance of Diverse Appearances in Primary School-Aged Children', UWE 2021. See also Lindsay Dell and Jess Prior, 'Evaluating a Schools' Service for Children with a Facial Disfigurement: The Views of Teaching and Support Staff' (2005) 20 Support for Learning 35; Melissa Jayne Atkinson, Phillippa C Diedrichs and Kirsty M Garbett, 'Evaluating a School-Based Intervention for Body Image (Dove Confident Me: 5-Part Body Confidence Workshops for Schools) Among Adolescent Girls and Boys: Results from a Cluster Randomized Controlled Effectiveness Trial' (2017) 60 Journal of Adolescent Health s5.

not only be ineffective but also counterproductive and can even cause psychological harm to vulnerable students.[32]

While young people represent an obvious target for educational intervention, other groups[33] in positions of power could also be targeted by mandated training. One-off organisational training sessions designed specifically to reduce unconscious bias are widely criticised for being ineffective.[34] But training on relevant profession-specific processes could hold more immediate potential. For example, research by Changing Faces suggests that many police officers lack awareness of the problem of disfigurement hate crime or don't know the correct reporting procedures.[35] Addressing this professional knowledge gap in training may lead to better support and justice for victims, and greater representation in statistics. A similar point could be made in relation to healthcare workers; surveys suggest that healthcare workers often fail to accommodate the psychosocial impact of visible difference.[36] Specific training with frontline staff to embed an appropriate psychosocial support pathway for patients with visible differences could be valuable.[37]

9.1.3 *Reform of Advertising*

Much has been written elsewhere about the increasingly narrow beauty ideals promoted by advertisers and influencers seeking to take advantage

[32] Lucy Foulkes and Argyris Stringaris, 'Do No Harm: Can School Mental Health Interventions Cause Iatrogenic Harm?' (2023) BJPsych Bulletin 1, 268.

[33] See Stephen P Hinshaw, *The Mark of Shame: Stigma of Mental Illness and an Agenda for Change* (Oxford University Press 2006) 404; Parry and others, 'Interventions to Reduce Mental Illness Stigma and Discrimination at the Person-Level for Individuals and Small Groups' (n 2) 373, for discussions of targeting interventions towards specific groups. For an international example, see Yin-Yi Lien and others, 'Challenging Mental Illness Stigma in Healthcare Professionals and Students: A Systematic Review and Network Meta-analysis' (2021) 36 Psychology & Health 669.

[34] See, for example, Julia Lopez, 'Unconscious Bias Training' (UK Parliament, HCWS652, 15 December 2020) <https://questions-statements.parliament.uk/written-statements/detail/2020-12-15/hcws652> accessed 7 December 2023.

[35] Changing Faces, *Evidence (*EQD0131*)* (of Lords Select Committee on the Equality Act 2010 and Disability 2015) para 31.

[36] See, for example, Changing Faces, 'Disfigurement in the UK' (n 7) 32, in which two-fifths of respondents said their healthcare professionals had very little understanding of the psychosocial impact of their condition.

[37] For an example, see Wyona M Freysteinson and others, 'Educating Nurses on Supported Mirror Viewing for Patients after Amputation and Other Visible Disfigurements' (2021) 46 Rehabilitation Nursing 43.

of the halo effect of beauty to sell products. The main criticism of this practice often relates to the potential for body image harms, as we become ever more conscious and critical of our own bodies' inability to meet these exacting and unrealistic standards.[38] But the corresponding potential for dominant beauty ideals to increase appearance-shaming directed towards other people is rarely explored. Heather Widdows argues that, as appearance matters more and society expects ever more demanding minimum standards of beauty, this increases the likelihood of discrimination against people with physical features that fall outside the (increasingly narrow) normal range.[39] So would a relaxation in the strictness of beauty ideals lead to greater acceptance of people with visible differences, and how could this be achieved?

Appearances in advertising are already regulated in Britain to some degree.[40] For example, guidance by the Committee of Advertising Practice (CAP) provides that advertisers should not 'portray particular body types in an irresponsible manner or present an unhealthy body image as aspirational, exploit people's insecurities about their body image, or suggest that happiness or wellbeing depends on conforming to a particular physical appearance, or gender stereotypical body type or physical features'.[41] But, while this is useful in some contexts – such as where adverts glamourise bodies which appear unhealthily thin,[42] or make promises of greater happiness dependent on having cosmetic surgery[43] – it currently stops far short of requiring advertisers to portray

[38] See, for example, Jennifer C Selensky and Robert A Carels, 'Weight Stigma and Media: An Examination of the Effect of Advertising Campaigns on Weight Bias, Internalized Weight Bias, Self-Esteem, Body Image, and Affect' (2021) 36 Body Image 95, 101.

[39] Heather Widdows, *Perfect Me: Beauty as an Ethical Ideal* (Princeton University Press 2018) 149.

[40] See in particular BCAP, *The UK Code of Broadcast Advertising (BCAP Code) v12.2.52* (*Advertising Standards Agency*, undated); CAP, *UK Code of Non-broadcast Advertising and Direct & Promotional Marketing (CAP Code) Edition 12 v12.2.88* (*Advertising Standards Agency*, 2014).

[41] Committee on Advertising Practice, 'Social Responsibility: Body Image' (*CAP*, 2022) <www.asa.org.uk/advice-online/social-responsibility-body-image.html> accessed 8 March 2024. For more detail, see the principles on social responsibility and avoiding harm in both the CAP code (n 40 rule 1.3 and 4) and BCAP code (n 40 rule 1.2 and 4).

[42] Committee of Advertising Practice, 'ASA Adjudication on Yves Saint Laurent SAS t/a Saint Laurent Paris A15-292161' (*ASA*, 2015) <www.asa.org.uk/rulings/yves-saint-laurent-sas-a15-292161.html> accessed 11 March 2024.

[43] ASA, 'ASA Ruling on MYA Cosmetic Surgery Ltd' (*ASA*, 2018) <www.asa.org.uk/rulings/mya-cosmetic-surgery-ltd-a18-459775.html> accessed 11 March 2024. Specific rules have also been introduced regarding advertisements for cosmetic interventions

positively a more representative range of appearances and visible differences. Nor are advertisers always prevented from using digitally altered images, provided that 'the resulting effect is not one which misleadingly exaggerates the effect the products are capable of achieving'.[44] The emphasis here is not on the realism or diversity of the image, but whether it unjustly exaggerates what consumers can expect from the product. CAP (and their broadcast counterpart, BCAP) are presently reviewing the evidence about body image and advertising[45] so a change in approach may soon be forthcoming.

Some countries have already gone further. Israel,[46] France[47] and Norway,[48] for example, have all legislated to require some advertising images in which body size or shape[49] has been retouched to carry a disclosure label. However, studies suggest that the power of the image subsists despite the knowledge that it isn't real, so disclosure labels are often ineffective at preventing the internalisation of the idealised (and mostly unachievable) beauty standard.[50] An alternative might be to ban all commercial photoshopped images completely, as was suggested by the House of Commons Women and Equalities Committee in their recent report into body image.[51] But this might encourage advertisers to use only the very few models without any visible physical 'flaws', reducing the diversity of images even further. And you don't have to be a model to be airbrushed to perfection today; photo filter apps give all

aimed at children; see ASA, 'Guidance on the Marketing of Surgical and Non-surgical Cosmetic Procedures' (*ASA*, 2023) <www.asa.org.uk/resource/cosmetic-interventions.html> accessed 11 March 2024.

44 Advertising Standards Agency, 'Beauty and Cosmetics: The Use of Production Techniques' (*ASA*, 2021) <https://bit.ly/3TaHDck> accessed 7 December 2023.

45 Committee of Advertising Practice and Broadcast Committee of Advertising Practice, 'Digitally Altered Images – Update Statement' (*CAP/BCAP*, 2023) <www.asa.org.uk/resource/digitally-altered-images-update-statement.html> accessed 11 March 2024.

46 See Marilyn Krawitz, 'Beauty Is Only Photoshop Deep: Legislating Models' BMIs and Photoshopping Images' (2014) 21 *Journal of Law and Medicine* 859.

47 See Yann Basire and Caroline Le Goffic, 'To Be or Not to Be . . . Photoshopped?' (2018) 13 Journal of Intellectual Property Law & Practice 177. France has also passed a law regulating altered photos posted by social media influencers; see Law No.223-451 (9 June 2023) art 5.

48 Marketing Control Act 2009, s2 (as amended by Inst. 146L, 2020–2021).

49 The Norwegian law also includes changes to skin.

50 Sarah E McComb and Jennifer S Mills, 'A Systematic Review on the Effects of Media Disclaimers on Young Women's Body Image and Mood' (2020) 32 Body Image 34, 48.

51 House of Commons Women and Equalities Committee, *Changing the Perfect Picture: An Inquiry into Body Image* (Sixth Report of Session 2019–2021, HC274) 32.

of us the ability to morph our image into something unrealistic and to post it for others to see.

In 2022, a parliamentary bill which promised to add disclosure labels to photoshopped online images in Britain failed to pass through the legislative process.[52] But a voluntary scheme exists under which organisations pledge not to use retouched imagery to promote their brands,[53] and past campaigns have embraced other realities of appearance too.[54] Some household names have signed up to the body image pledge demonstrating that, in some quarters at least, there is a will to be seen to be making changes. The limitations of voluntary schemes are obvious and discussed further below, but they could perhaps offer a useful base for law to build on. For example, regulation could require social media platforms to provide filters for content from organisations who have not signed the pledge,[55] perhaps with a mandatory opt-out for children. The success of such a scheme would depend on whether organisations felt enough pressure from public sentiment to conform.

9.1.4 *Reforms Designed to Motivate Employers*

We saw earlier that HR functions are under increasing pressure to pursue initiatives which support wider commercial goals, often related to profits. It was also noted that laws combining motivations and sanctions can have more impact than sanctions alone when seeking to change behaviours. So motivating employers is another key consideration of reform and one which is under increasing pressure from changing global priorities, notably the Trump administration's war on diversity initiatives in corporate America.

It is often argued that, as a motivating factor, diversity carries its own commercial rewards; diverse workforces tend to be more innovative and profitable.[56] Breaking down the barriers faced by people with visible

52 Digitally Altered Body Images Bill, HC Bill (2021–2022) [227].

53 Luke Evans, 'Body Image Pledge' (undated) <www.drlukeevans.org.uk/body-image> accessed 7 December 2023. See also Nadia Craddock and others, 'Can Big Business Foster Positive Body Image? Qualitative Insights from Industry Leaders Walking the Talk' (2019) 30 Body Image 93.

54 For example, 'Be Real' campaign run by Dove.

55 Some social media platforms allow some content opt-outs already. But I found none relating to appearance diversity.

56 See, for example, Cedric Herring, 'Does Diversity Pay? Race, Gender, and the Business Case for Diversity' (2009) 74 American Sociological Review 208; Mark Kaplan, *The*

differences at work could enable a talented group of staff to thrive in their jobs and bring significant commercial benefits. As one HR participant explained:

> I think there is a business case and an ethical case and a moral case for employers being proactive about, you know, visible difference.... You know, the fact that in 30 years of HR I have so little experience says to me there are people – talented people – hiding away because they don't feel like they're wanted in the world of employment, they don't feel like there's a place for them. So when we're looking at skills shortages, talent shortages, this is just such a huge opportunity and it's a win win for everybody, isn't it?

Disability Confident,[57] the employer charter mark scheme, is one example of a voluntary scheme which seeks to attract employers with promises of saving recruitment costs, retaining talent and reducing sickness costs.[58] Some employer participants in my study felt that obtaining this kind of external recognition was important – even if only to be *seen* to be doing the right thing. While signing up to numerous different charter marks was judged by some to be impractical, there was support for umbrella charter marks which find commonalities between groups and recommend changes that work across the board – provided that they are not so generic as to be unclear in practice. Ensuring that visible difference is sufficiently accounted for in a wider scheme, such as Disability Confident, could help to embed appearance-inclusive practices within employer members.

However, the challenge with voluntary schemes is not just in getting organisations to sign up, but in ensuring that compliance is ongoing and substantive. By way of example, one employer admitted that their main driver for participating in equality charter marks was just to get the badge and move on because 'it's very helpful for tenders'. Charter marks may therefore fail without a continuing programme of monitoring, consultation and sanctions. As Kate Malleson argues, where the case for diversity is inked to profitability, it is liable to be overridden if changing

Inclusion Dividend: Why Investing in Diversity & Inclusion Pays Off (Bibliomotion 2013) chapter 2.

57 Department for Work and Pensions, 'Disability Confident Employer Scheme' (*UK Government*, 2021) <www.gov.uk/government/collections/disability-confident-campaign> accessed 7 December 2023.

58 Department for Work and Pensions, 'How to Sign Up to the Disability Confident Employer Scheme' (*UK Government*, 2019) <www.gov.uk/guidance/disability-confident-how-to-sign-up-to-the-employer-scheme#why-you-should-become-disability-confident> accessed 16 February 2024.

market conditions offer better financial incentives.[59] And the balance of past experience suggests that a purely voluntary approach to engaging employers with equality objectives is unlikely to succeed.[60]

Voluntary approaches could be externally incentivised, perhaps with corporate tax breaks for hitting equality objectives. But, even in the unlikely event that the political will and budget for this purpose could be found, financial incentives can backfire. Christina Bicchieri argues that linking morally desirable conduct with monetary motivation can remove the moral impetus (and corresponding feel-good factor) which would be felt if the behaviour remained voluntary.[61] And the idea of rewarding corporations with public money for meeting diversity targets may feel uncomfortable, given the evidence that a diverse workplace is a commercial advantage[62] in its own right.

An alternative approach might be to require corporations to disclose their performance against additional equality standards – such as the numbers and pay rates of people with visible differences throughout the workforce. Required disclosure may nudge organisations to do better – peer pressure can be an important motivator for compliance,[63] and public perceptions of the organisation may affect profits. This link between social responsibility and profit was highlighted by *Nadia Craddock et al.* in their study on corporate motivations to foster positive body image, which identified profit as 'central to business success and thus the sustainability of social purpose agendas'.[64] Regrettably, though, there is mixed evidence about the extent to which the most comparable disclosure duty in the law – that relating to gender pay gap reporting – is proving effective. A few

[59] Kate Malleson, 'Diversity in the Judiciary: The Case for Positive Action' (2009) 36 Journal of Law and Society 376, 384. See also Alysia Blackham, 'Reflexive Change? A Quantitative Review of the Impact of the Equality Act 2010 on Age Equality Measures in Organizations' (2016) 16 International Journal of Discrimination and the Law 122, 135.

[60] Simon Deakin, Colm Mclaughlin and Dominic Chai, 'Gender Inequality and Reflexive Law: The Potential of Difference Regulatory Mechanisms' in Linda Dickens (ed), *Making Employment Rights Effective* (Hart 2012) 116–118; Sara Benedi Lahuerta, Peter Rejchrt and Alex Patrick, 'The UK Pay Transparency Regulations: Apparent Transparency without Accountability?' (2023) Legal Studies (Society of Legal Scholars) 1, 3.

[61] Cristina Bicchieri, *Norms in the Wild: How to Diagnose, Measure, and Change Social Norms* (Oxford University Press 2017) 153.

[62] For a similar reaction to profitable companies accepting furlough payments during the pandemic, see Ben King, 'Ladbrokes Claimed £102m Furlough Despite Online Boost' *BBC* <www.bbc.co.uk/news/business-59900249> accessed 16 February 2024.

[63] Lawrence Friedman, *Impact: How Law Affects Behavior* (Harvard University Press 2017) 153.

[64] Craddock and others, 'Can Big Business Foster Positive Body Image?' (n 53) 104.

studies suggest that the gender pay transparency rules are helping to narrow the wage gap to some extent, at least in the short term.[65] But others have doubted the ability of the transparency rules to lead to the kind of systemic change which is needed. Not only do the rules apply only to larger organisations, but also their 'narrow scope and simplistic reporting requirements'[66] have been argued by some to hinder the effectiveness of gender pay gap reporting. *Sara Benuedi Lahuerta et al.* highlight in particular the low integrity of the data produced by the duty, which makes evidence-based actions harder to accomplish and produces 'apparent transparency without accountability'.[67] So, in terms of equality objectives, there are reasons to question the likely effectiveness of both purely voluntary schemes and legal transparency requirements.

Between these two approaches, the concept of reflexive regulation occupies a middle ground. Reflexive regulation is based on systems theory and the idea that the messages transmitted by law do not necessarily translate easily into sub-system organisations.[68] Accordingly, rather than law commanding organisations to take particular actions and controlling how they do it, reflexive regulation seeks to stimulate organisations to self-regulate. Academic debate highlights the potential for reflexive regulation to engage employers in meeting equality objectives.[69] But the risk of short-lived compliance is significant here too; reflexive regulation relies on embedded dialogue and enforcement mechanisms to ensure that self-regulation doesn't collapse into inaction. This might, for example, require different levels of engagement with employees, service users, trade unions and civil society, backed by an enforcement body such as the EHRC. Others have argued that the need for these layers of cooperation and enforcement does not fit easily within the UK's institutional and legal structures.[70] For example, although trade unions

[65] Emma Duchini and others, 'Pay Transparency and Gender Equality' (2020) arXivorg 29. The narrowing was largely attributed to reductions in men's wages rather than increases in women's wages.

[66] Benedi Lahuerta and others, 'The UK Pay Transparency Regulations' (n 60) 19.

[67] Ibid 1.

[68] For more on this, see Blackham, 'Reflexive Change? (n 61) 124; Bob Hepple, 'Enforcing Equality Law: Two Steps Forward and Two Steps Backwards for Reflexive Regulation' (2011) 40 Industrial Law Journal 320, 320; Colm McLaughlin, 'Equal Pay, Litigation and Reflexive Regulation: The Case of the UK Local Authority Sector' (2014) 43 Industrial Law Journal 1, 4.

[69] See, for example, Hepple, 'Enforcing Equality Law' (n 28) 321.

[70] Catherine Barnard, *Reflexive Law, Corporate Social Responsibility and the Evolution of Labour Standards: The Case of Working Time* (ERSC Centre for Business Research,

represent perhaps the most obvious partner for this structured engagement, recent decades have witnessed the declining influence of trade unions in private sector workplaces.[71] Trade union equality representatives do not receive the same protections (such as the right to paid time off for training) as some other representatives, which may limit their ability to hold organisations to account. Moreover, many disabled people's organisations are struggling financially since the pandemic after a drop in income,[72] reducing their ability to act as watchdogs for industry practice. And EHRC funding has seen swathing cuts since its creation in 2007, hindering the exercise of its powers. Accordingly, a lack of effective dialogue and enforcement could represent a major hurdle for the principle of reflexive regulation.

In summary, although motivating employers to achieve equality objectives is a key goal for many equality campaigns, the mechanics of how to do this – and any role for law in achieving it – remain unclear.

9.1.5 Law Reform of AI in HR Processes

Regulation may also need to address automated behaviours resulting from increased reliance on technology. AI is used by some employers for purposes including conducting automated recruitment interviews and screening CVs.[73] Video interview software also has the technological capability to analyse the candidate's facial expressions and voice inflection – although concerns about the potentially discriminatory impact of this have led some AI providers to remove this capability.[74]

We don't yet fully understand the impact of this technology on people with visible differences, but there is cause for concern. One concern relates to deterrence. One employer, whose organisation uses the technology to

University of Cambridge 2004) 23–25; McLaughlin, 'Equal Pay, Litigation and Reflexive Regulation' (n 68) 23.

71 McLaughlin, 'Equal Pay, Litigation and Reflexive Regulation' (n 68) 6; Barnard, *Reflexive Law, Corporate Social Responsibility and the Evolution of Labour Standards* (n 70) 23.

72 Amie McWilliam Reynolds, 'What New Research about the Impact of COVID-19 on Charities' (*Charities Commission*, 2021) <https://charitycommission.blog.gov.uk/2021/10/28/what-new-research-tells-us-about-the-impact-of-covid-19-on-charities/> accessed 16 February 2024.

73 Trades Union Congress, 'Technology Managing People: The Worker Experience' (*TUC*, 2020) 18.

74 Madhumita Murgia, 'Emotion Recognition: Can AI Detect Human Feelings from a Face?' *Financial Times* (London, 12 May 2021) <www.ft.com/content/c0b03d1d-f72f-48a8-b342-b4a926109452> accessed 7 December 2023.

shortlist candidates, admitted to me that 'a lot of people drop out at that stage . . . because they don't feel comfortable answering questions into a computer, I guess'. Many people with visible facial differences are reluctant to appear in videos or photographs, so the potential for deterrence is troubling. Another concern relates to the creation of a transparency problem; the organisation operating the AI may not be sure why a particular decision has been made, and, in some cases, may be powerless to change it. One HR professional that I interviewed recalled the difficulty of being unable to override – or even fully understand – recruitment decisions taken by a computer. A third concern is that, if this capability is still being used, analysing facial expressions or tones of voice could discriminate against people with certain conditions, such as facial palsy (which can prevent facial movement) and cleft palate (which can affect intonation).[75]

Further regulation in this area is growing – at the time of writing, the EU has just passed its AI Act,[76] which lists some uses of AI in the employment context as 'high risk', prompting a need for the products to be regularly assessed. In the meantime, the Special Rapporteur to the United Nations under the Convention on the Rights of Persons with Disabilities has recommended a moratorium on the use of AI applications which carry the greatest risk of discrimination against people with disabilities – including the use of facial recognition technology.[77] Regulation is needed to create this pause while further investigations into risks and necessary safeguards take place.

9.1.6 Reform at Wider Institutional Level

Making changes to influential systems and institutions *outside* the work context may also shape attitudes and practices *inside* the workplace. By way of example, evidence from America suggests that appearance bias can impact the outcomes of criminal trials, with defendants perceived as better-looking less likely to be convicted[78] and, if convicted, likely to be

[75] For a discussion about other factors with the potential to influence AI decisions, see Eleanor Drage and Kerry Mackereth, 'Does AI Debias Recruitment? Race, Gender, and AI's Eradication of Difference' (2022) 35 Philosophy & Technology 89.

[76] Artificial Intelligence Act (2024).

[77] Gerard Quinn, *Report of the Special Rapporteur on the Rights of Persons with Disabilities on Artificial Intelligence and the Rights of Persons with Disabilities* (United Nations, 2021).

[78] NA Schvey and others, 'The Influence of a Defendant's Body Weight on Perceptions of Guilt' (2013) 37 International Journal of Obesity 1275, 1279; Kevin M Beaver and others,

sentenced for shorter periods[79] or given significantly lower fines for minor offences.[80] Formal recognition of the impact of appearance within the law could prompt a rethink on court procedures – perhaps even an evaluation of non-visual courtrooms which prevent someone's appearance from being taken into account. The use of neutral digital avatars might allow facial expressions to be seen, without bodily appearance being apparent.[81] (It is worth noting, however, that virtual courtrooms have already been criticised for losing the benefit of non-verbal clues; a non-visual courtroom would exacerbate this.)

Although changes within the justice system do not impact the work context directly, they would bring significant publicity to the issue. There clearly are normative links between the justice system and employment practice. Principles of natural justice (including the right to be heard by an unbiased adjudicator) run through organisational practices, such as the conduct of disciplinary and grievance hearings. Accordingly, changes applied within the justice system may inform re-evaluations in workplace practice too.

Also influential is the education system. Research suggests that teachers' biases can sometimes affect the expectations they have of their students and the grades they award.[82] Although the evidence is mixed, this includes

'Physical Attractiveness and Criminal Justice Processing: Results from a Longitudinal Sample of Youth and Young Adults' (2019) 26 Psychiatry, Psychology and Law 669; Bonnie Berry, *Appearance Bias and Crime* (Cambridge University Press 2019) 7. See also Leslie A Zebrowitz and Susan M McDonald, 'The Impact of Litigants' Baby-Facedness and Attractiveness on Adjudications in Small Claims Courts' (1991) 15 Law and Human Behavior 603 on the impact of physical attractiveness in small claims court cases in the US.

79 See, for example, Michael G Efran, 'The Effect of Physical Appearance on the Judgment of Guilt, Interpersonal Attraction, and Severity of Recommended Punishment in a Simulated Jury Task' (1974) 8 Journal of Research in Personality 45; John E Stewart, 'Appearance and Punishment: The Attraction-Leniency Effect in the Courtroom' (1985) 125 The Journal of Social Psychology 373.

80 A Chris Downs and Phillip M Lyons, 'Natural Observations of the Links between Attractiveness and Initial Legal Judgments' (1991) 17 Personality & Social Psychology Bulletin 541, 544.

81 See Vincent Denault, 'Guilty or Innocent? In Virtual Courtrooms, the Absence of Non-verbal Cues May Threaten Justice' *The Conversation* <https://theconversation.com/guilty-or-innocent-in-virtual-courtrooms-the-absence-of-non-verbal-cues-may-threaten-justice-145371> accessed 21 November 2023.

82 See, for example, Lewis Doyle, Matthew J Easterbrook and Peter R Harris, 'Roles of Socioeconomic Status, Ethnicity and Teacher Beliefs in Academic Grading' (2023) 93 British Journal of Educational Psychology 91, 104; Giulietta Zanga and Elena de Gioannis, 'Discrimination in Grading: A Scoping Review of Studies on Teachers' Discrimination in School' (2023) 78 Studies in Educational Evaluation 101284, 7.

appearance,[83] with some studies finding that physically attractive students tend to be evaluated more positively by teachers.[84] One recent study in Sweden found the correlation between physically attractive students and good grades to be particularly pronounced in subjects which involve greater teacher–student interaction and, for girls, in those classes which are taught face-to-face rather than online.[85]

But addressing this is complex. Unlike the criminal justice system, teachers usually have long-term interaction with particular students and pastoral responsibilities too. Hiding students' appearances from teachers to remove the opportunity for appearance bias to operate would be both grotesquely impersonal and impractical. Summative assessment methods may be more apt to intervention, though. Traditionally visual assessments – such as university admissions interviews, PhD vivas and spoken language exams – are one-off events usually conducted by someone who does not know the student. A non-visual format would be more feasible here and may create publicity and debate with the potential to shape practices outside of education too. But this non-visual assessment format could also bring significant risks. Would students struggle to do their best without the reassurance of two-way visual cues? Might appearance anonymity measures lead to an increase in exam fraud? Or, deprived of face-to-face contact, might examiners subconsciously be more influenced by differences in the candidates' voices, rather than the content of their answers? Evaluation would be critical, and redoubling efforts to create effective educational interventions for teachers and examiners may ultimately prove more practical.

9.2 Creating an Effective Remedial Mechanism

The approaches discussed above focus on social structures, practices and technologies to change the way people think and act towards people who

[83] There is some evidence about the impact of disfigurement on teacher expectations and actions, but this is currently underdeveloped.

[84] See, for example, Pamela Kenealy, Neil Frude and William Shaw, 'Influence of Children's Physical Attractiveness on Teacher Expectations' (1988) 128 The Journal of Social Psychology 373. Some suggest that these positive evaluations are due to the favourable treatment of attractive people creating a self-fulfilling prophecy of positive traits. On this, see Judith H Langlois, 'Maxims or Myths of Beauty?: A Meta-analytic and Theoretical Review' (2000) 126(3) Psychological Bulletin 400–402.

[85] For boys, the correlation between teacher ratings and physical attractiveness was found to have held in the remote classroom too. See Adrian Mehic, 'Student Beauty and Grades under In-person and Remote Teaching' (2022) 219 Economics Letters 110782.

look different. This section focuses instead on potential reforms to equality law. The main objective here is to consider how law reform could create a more effective remedial mechanism for instances of disfigurement discrimination.

The reforms in this section divide broadly into two groups. The first group are those designed to ensure that meritorious claims relating to visible difference succeed, by resolving some of the limitations of the current law. The second group are those aiming to foster greater enforcement, so that more instances of discrimination are challenged. These are explored in turn below.

9.2.1 Reforms to Improve Claim Success Rates

In order to ensure that claims, once brought, can succeed if meritorious, the inconsistencies and technicalities identified earlier in the book must be addressed. Three main options will be discussed. These are discrete changes to the severe disfigurement provision, a hybrid definition of disability and a new protected characteristic of either disfigurement or appearance.

9.2.1.1 Discrete Changes to the Severe Disfigurement Provision

The most discrete level of equality law reform would mean tweaking the drafting of the severe disfigurement provision. This could include the following:

- Reducing the threshold for disfigurement from severity to substantiality. This would bring the standard into line with the main test for disability contained in section 6 of the Act and make it easier to satisfy. Progressively disfiguring conditions, such as neurofibromatosis type 1, could be expressly included too.
- Enabling the functional and aesthetic effects of a condition to be considered holistically. This would make it easier for people with complex conditions to demonstrate disability,[86] and sometimes easier to prove discrimination too.[87]
- Including better definitions of 'disfigurement' and 'impairment' in the statutory guidance to bring clarity. The definition could take into

[86] See Section 7.3.

[87] This was the problem in *Cosgrove v Northern Ireland Ambulance Service* [2007] IRLR 397 (NICA) – see Section 7.3.

account the individual's personal context (age, sex, etc.), helping to delineate the right approach to conditions such as hair loss and short stature.[88] More examples could be included to provide greater clarity.

These discrete changes together might make it slightly easier for lawyers to understand whether potential claimants fall within the scope of the Act. They should also remove some of the very technical hurdles to winning a claim. And these small changes are unlikely to provoke resistance among the public, as the case for disfigurement equality has not proved contentious. But the biggest disadvantage of this path to reform is its ability to go unnoticed, barely making a ripple in the surface of societal awareness and leaving the disability identity conflict untouched. These hurdles are significant, and accordingly there are few reasons to suppose that these small tweaks would lead to greater awareness, enforcement or positive social change.

9.2.1.2 A Social/Hybrid Approach to Disability

A second method of law reform to improve the remedial function of the law is to bring the Act's definition of disability into line with the social model approach taken in the CRPD. A definition which focused at least partly on external barriers could include people who are visibly different without the friction caused by trying to bolt on a separate disfigurement provision. People with other types of impairments could benefit from this approach too. A social model focus creates a natural progression towards wider, preventative changes because it shifts the attention to society – perhaps via more robust positive action and related measures – and away from individual medical limitations.

The adoption of the same description of disability[89] as contained in the CRPD might seem logical. But this open-textured description might be less suited to an enforceable statutory provision than to a convention

[88] An instructive comparison on this can be found in the Interpretive Guidance to the Americans with Disabilities Act, which assists the interpretation of the relevant equality legislation in the US. Title 29 CFR Appendix to Part 1630, 1630.2(h) of this guidance refers to an impairment of cosmetic disfigurement as excluding 'physical characteristics such as eye colour, hair colour, left-handedness, or height, weight or muscle tone that are within "normal" range and are not the result of a physiological disorder'. See EEOC, 'Interpretive Guidance of Title 1 of the Americans with Disabilities Act' <www.law.cornell.edu/cfr/text/29/appendix-to_part_1630> accessed 18 March 2024.

[89] UN Convention on the Rights of Persons with Disabilities (12 December 2006) A/RES/61/106, art 1.

designed to provide principles for lawmakers. Whereas a definition of disability based on the medical model provides set criteria against which functionality can be measured, a fully social model description involves measuring external barriers, such as attitudes, which are harder to prove. Under a social model definition, the expert evidence of medical professionals may need to yield to evidence about stereotypes, structural disadvantage and accessibility. If external barriers were judged at the individual level, the requirement to prove disability could ultimately be subsumed into a finding of discrimination, because discrimination itself is a form of disabling social barrier; treatment and disability status become merged. On the other hand, if judged at group level by reference to statistics of barriers encountered by people who share a particular characteristic, complications arise in defining relevant groups with common experiences. This is particularly troublesome when employers are seeking to make reasonable adjustments since they might claim to need the clarity that comes with an occupational health report rather than vague assumptions about what external barriers might be encountered. In this respect, the social model in legislative form might become a reactive concept which is hard to balance with legal duties to accommodate and be proactive, creating an impractical remedial mechanism.

But a social model perspective could be incorporated into the Act in other ways. One option is to make claims based on perceived disability (which are already permitted under the Act) easier to win. Perceptive discrimination honours the spirit, if not the letter, of the social model, because it places the focus on the assumptions made by other people. In 2008, the US chose to relax its equivalent provision concerning people 'regarded as' disabled,[90] making it – in theory at least – easier to prove. However, despite being hailed by many as a step forward in rights protection, the amended US provision does not appear to have had a significant impact on chances of success. EEOC data between 1997 and 2018 does not show a consistent increase in the number of merit factor resolutions after 2008 relating to disfigurement.[91] Perceptive discrimination is also subject to another limitation – the duty to make reasonable adjustments is unlikely to apply to someone who is perceived to be

[90] Americans with Disabilities Act 1990 (as amended) Title 42 s12102 (1) (c) and (3).

[91] See US Equal Employment Opportunity Commission, 'ADA Charge Data by Impairments/Bases – Merit Factor Resolutions (Charges Filed with EEOC) FY 1997–FY 2022' (undated) <https://bit.ly/43kwmeb> accessed 8 November 2023.

disabled without meeting the Act's definition of disability. Accordingly, the net result of any legal reform which focused more extensively on perception could actually be a narrowing of rights.

A different approach is to introduce a hybrid definition of disability. This would mean retaining the existing functional definition of s6 in the Act but incorporating an additional prong to cover impairments causing appearance-related disadvantage. A basic statutory provision might be as follows:

> (1) A person (P) has a disability if P has a physical or mental impairment, and the impairment has a substantial and long-term adverse effect on:
> (a) P's ability to carry out normal day-to-day activities; or
> (b) P's appearance.
>
> (2) The effects under sub-paragraph (1) (a) and sub-paragraph (1) (b) may be considered either separately or cumulatively in determining whether section 1 is satisfied.
>
> (3) For the purposes of sub-paragraph (1) (b), an impairment excludes appearance characteristics which are within the normal range for someone of P's age, sex [and other relevant personal characteristics].

Although not fully social model compliant given the continued inclusion of a functional test, a hybrid definition of this kind has some advantages. The proposed wording might be more readily acceptable to some people with lived experience of looking different because it avoids the problematic word 'disfigurement'. It also avoids the discomfort of having one's appearance compared to a notional external standard; instead, the effects on the claimant's own appearance are examined. And allowing functional and appearance effects to be combined under proposed sub-section (2) allows people with complex conditions to have their conditions considered holistically, rather than having to prove both aspects separately. Someone whose impairment has a minor impact in terms of function and a borderline impact on their appearance may be able to show a substantial adverse effect overall.

Perhaps most importantly, this approach might begin a wider conversation about how to conceptualise disability. In both research interviews and the undergraduate classroom, asking the question 'what is disability?' tends to prompt answers using the wording contained in the Act's definition; this suggests that law is shaping social meanings. Changing the legal definition may therefore help to change how people understand disability, paving the way for wider acceptance of the social model.

If this hybrid definition were to be adopted, some existing case outcomes may well be unaffected. The decision in *Campbell*[92] relating to male pattern baldness, for example, may not be affected, because hair loss within the normal range for a man in his sixties may not class as an impairment under proposed sub-section (3). Other cases, however, could lead to a different outcome. The height of 4′8″ in *Hussain*[93] seems more likely to fall outside the normal height range for an adult male, so a finding of impairment could well follow. The proposed definition might also impact on a minority of cases relating to body size; given the prevalence of mild to moderate obesity, a finding of impairment (i.e. weight outside of the normal range) may be limited to cases of much larger body size. But once impairment was established, it may be possible to argue that this level of body size has a substantial adverse effect on someone's appearance, to bring them within the remit of the Act.

9.2.1.3 A New Protected Characteristic?

As an alternative, creating a new protected characteristic – either of disfigurement or appearance – would be a much more visible change engaging the public consciousness. There is some international precedent for a protected characteristic of general appearance – with France and the US being the best-known examples.

9.2.1.3.1 Appearance Discrimination in France Let us turn to France first. The French Labour Code was amended in 2001 to add physical appearance to existing protected categories.[94] Both civil and criminal penalties (including imprisonment and a substantial fine) are available. The concept of physical appearance in the legislation is broad, including not just immutable characteristics such as skin colour, facial features, scars or body size – but also characteristics chosen by a person: piercings, clothes, hairstyle and so on. The related characteristics of 'disability' and 'health condition' are also protected.

The right to appearance equality is not unqualified in France – justifications are available to employers.[95] Case law sometimes reveals a difficult balance between the employer's desire to create a particular brand

[92] *Campbell v Falkirk Council* [2008] S/136261/07 (9 April 2008, unreported, ETS).

[93] *Hussain v Sky In-Home Services Ltd* [2017] ET/2300908/16 (10 January 2017, unreported, ET).

[94] Code du travail, art 1132-1. See also n 47.

[95] See, for example, Code du travail, art 1133-1 and art 1121-1.

image to increase profitability and the employee's right not to be discriminated against on the basis of physical appearance. France's equality body, the Défenseur des Droits (DfD), gives the example of an image requirement for fashion models which could be justified – whereas Abercrombie and Fitch's aesthetic recruitment criteria for sales staff in its French stores were not, despite labelling staff as store 'models'.[96]

9.2.1.3.2 Appearance Discrimination in the US In the US, the legal position on appearance equality is more fragmented. On one level, the Americans with Disabilities Act prohibits discrimination against disabled people nationally, including people who have – or are perceived as having – an impairment (including a cosmetic disfigurement).[97] However, there is no federal law prohibiting wider appearance discrimination. Appearance is sometimes relevant in claims brought under other protected characteristics though. One example related to maximum weight restrictions for female flight attendants to maintain a corporate image. The requirements did not apply equally to male stewards, resulting in a finding of sex discrimination.[98]

Some justifications are available under US anti-discrimination law too, including an exception for bona fide occupational qualifications (broadly equivalent to the occupational requirement exception under the Act[99]) but case law has interpreted this exception narrowly. Accordingly, being a woman (and wearing hotpants) was not an occupational qualification for being a flight attendant because the primary business purpose was air transportation, not sexual attractiveness.[100]

Where general appearance – rather than disfigurement – discrimination is concerned, some states and cities have enacted their own appearance discrimination laws. By way of example:

[96] Le défenseur des droits, Decision MLD-2014-147 of 3 November 2014 on discriminatory recruitment procedures in relation to the physical appearance of candidates <https://juridique.defenseurdesdroits.fr/index.php?lvl=notice_display&id=12325> accessed 7 December 2023.

[97] Regulations to Implement the Equal Employment Provisions of the Americans with Disabilities Act, as amended, 29 CFR 1630.2(h).

[98] *Gerdom v Continental Airlines, Inc.*, 692 F.2d 602 (9th Cir. 1982).

[99] Equality Act 2010, sched 9 s1.

[100] *Wilson v Southwest Airlines Co.*, 517 F. Supp. 292 (N.D. Tex. 1981). See Frank J Cavico, Stephen C Muffler and Bahaudin G Mujtaba, 'Appearance Discrimination in Employment' (2012) 32 Equality, Diversity and Inclusion: An International Journal 83, 96.

- The Local Ordinance of Santa Cruz prohibits discrimination on the basis of height, weight and physical characteristic[101] (defined as 'a bodily condition or bodily characteristics of any person which is from birth, accident or disease, or from any natural physical development, or any other event outside the control of that person including individual physical mannerisms'). This scope was reportedly a compromise from the original intention to protect all appearance traits – both mutable and immutable – due to public outcry;[102]
- Both San Francisco[103] and most recently New York[104] prohibit height and weight discrimination;
- The District of Columbia Human Rights Act prohibits discrimination on grounds of personal appearance;[105] and
- Regulations also exist in Urbana,[106] several counties within Maryland,[107] Madison[108] and Michigan.[109] Some other places – including New Jersey and Massachusetts – are reported to be considering some form of regulation.

Creating a protected characteristic of appearance in Britain would almost certainly provoke significant media attention and debate, helping to raise awareness of the law and the underlying problem of appearance bias. It would also remove the need for a threshold test by encompassing everyone, without the hurdle of proving that one's appearance met a specific level of difference. However, if the severe disfigurement provision were replaced by a protected characteristic of general appearance, the goal of fighting visible difference discrimination could become a hostage to a much larger fortune; the case for a wider protected characteristic of appearance would be based not just on the disadvantage experienced by people with visible differences but on the disadvantage experienced by all

[101] Santa Cruz Municipal Code, chap 9.83 §9.83.010-030.
[102] Heather James, 'If You Are Attractive and You Know It, Please Apply: Appearance Based Discrimination and Employers' Discretion' (2008) 42 Valparaiso University Law Review 629, 653.
[103] San Francisco, Cal., Administrative Code chap 12A §12A.1.
[104] New York City Administrative Code, Title 8 chap 1 §8-107 (1).
[105] District of Columbia Code, §2-1401.01.
[106] Urbana, Ill., Municipal Code chap 12 art 3 div 1 §12-37–§12-39.
[107] Prince George's County, MD, Code, subtitle 1 div 12 subdiv 1 §2-186(21) and §2-185; Howard County, MD, Code title 12 subtitle 2 §12.200 (ii) and §12.201 (xv); and Harford County, MD, Code chap 95 §95-3 and §95-5.
[108] Madison, Wisconsin, Code of Ordinances chap 39 §39.03(1) and §39.03 (2)
[109] Elliott-Larsen Civil Rights Act, Michigan, No. 453 of 1976 art 1 §372202(1).

of us – from those judged most to least beautiful – because of our looks. So the limitations of a protected characteristic of appearance – whether imposed by statute, developed through precedent or shaped by public reactions – may have a very significant impact on the ability of people with visible differences to challenge discrimination. With this in mind, Chapter 10 will evaluate whether appearance is a viable protected characteristic in its own right.

The creation of a new protected characteristic of disfigurement, on the other hand, continues the difficulty and intrusion of defining and proving disfigurement. As Jerome Bickenbach argues, 'what could be more demeaning than having to earn one's right to equality and eligibility to "special treatment" by proving that one is a member of a socially discredited group?'[110] The terminology of disfigurement may, for some, be a deterrent to enforcement.[111]

Creating a new protected characteristic of either disfigurement or appearance enables visible difference discrimination to be challenged without acquiring the label of disabled,[112] which is difficult for many people with lived experience of visible difference. But separating visible difference from disability may have unintended consequences. Ensuring sufficient permeability for complex disfiguring conditions (involving both visible difference and functional impairment) might be harder under a separate legislative structure; people might have to claim under the characteristic of disability as well as under the new characteristic of disfigurement or appearance. In addition, under a separate protected characteristic, the duty to make reasonable adjustment might no longer apply to people with disfigurements. Although there is little evidence that the duty is frequently being applied to support people with disfigurements, it does have the potential to do so in some cases.[113]

9.2.2 *Reforms to Increase Enforcement*

The suggestions above focus on removing some of the uncertainties, flaws and illogicalities of scope which characterise the current law on

[110] Jerome Bickenbach, 'Disability Human Rights, Law and Policy' in Gary Albrecht, Katherine Seelman and Michael Bury (eds), *Handbook of Disability Studies* (Sage 2001) 577.

[111] Changing Faces, 'What Is Visible Difference?' (*Changing Faces*, undated) <www.changingfaces.org.uk/about-visible-difference/what-is-visible-difference/> accessed 8 November 2023.

[112] See Section 4.3.3.

[113] See Sections 4.3.3 and 5.2 and Appendix 1.

severe disfigurement equality. However, ensuring that meritorious claims (when brought) can succeed is only half the battle. Wider impact relies on greater breadth of enforcement too, in order to disrupt unchallenged patterns of negative behaviour against people who look different.

On this, the interests of people with visible differences elide with the interests of other minority groups across the field of equality law. Serious concerns have long been raised about numerous aspects of the procedures and systems for challenging discrimination under the Act, including the following:

- The burden of enforcement being placed on the victim of discrimination. The House of Commons Women and Equalities Committee in their 2019 inquiry into the Equality Act 2010 recommended that this burden should be removed,[114] but this has not been acted on. Instead, the gradual restriction of trade union rights[115] over recent years may have exacerbated it by removing a source of advice and support in many workplaces.
- The evidential burden on claimants within the Tribunal system (which many participants in my study perceived to be a significant hurdle)[116] and the erosion of procedures to assist claimants finding evidence before claiming.[117]
- The formality and procedural technicality of the Tribunal process, which may deter potential claimants[118] and increase the potential cost[119] of challenging discrimination with legal representation. One commentator, for example, notes the investigative and consultative approach of the French equality body compared with the 'adversarial procedure with cross-examination at its heart' found in the British employment tribunal system.[120]

[114] House of Commons Women and Equalities Committee, *Enforcing the Equality Act: The Law and the Role of the Equality and Human Rights Commission* (Tenth Report of Session 2017–2019, HC1470) 9. Others have noted its limitations, too. See, for example, Fredman, 'The Public Sector Equality Duty' (n 28) 407; Michael Ford, 'Employment Tribunal Fees and the Rule of Law: R (Unison) v Lord Chancellor in the Supreme Court' (2018) 47 Industrial Law Journal 1, 6; Alysia Blackham, 'Abandoning Individual Enforcement? Interrogating the Enforcement of Age Discrimination Law' (2023) 43 Legal Studies (Society of Legal Scholars) 3, 4.

[115] See Alan Bogg, 'Beyond Neo-Liberalism: The Trade Union Act 2016 and the Authoritarian State' (2016) 45 Industrial Law Journal 299, 303.

[116] See Section 4.3.3.

[117] See Section 3.1 and Enterprise and Regulatory Reform Act 2013, s66.

[118] See Sections 4.3.3 and 8.5.

[119] See Section 4.3.3.

[120] Susan Corby, Laura William and Sarah Richard, 'Combatting Disability Discrimination: A Comparison of France and Great Britain' (2019) 25 European Journal of Industrial

- The individualisation of the problem of discrimination. Remedies are focused on the individual claimant rather than improving conditions for other people in similar situations.[121] This misses an opportunity where policies – perhaps relating to uniform or website photos – are introduced to the detriment of multiple people with visible differences in the organisation.
- The reality of abuse from customers and third parties at work is ignored.[122] The new statutory duty on employers to take reasonable steps to prevent harassment of staff by third parties only extends to sexual harassment,[123] not harassment because of visible differences or other personal characteristics. This is so despite frequent reports from this community of harassment by customers.
- The insufficient collation of disaggregated data. In the US, Blake and Hatzenbuehler argue for the creation of a population-wide data collection effort[124] to monitor the experiences of stigmatised characteristics and map them against enforcement measures and laws over the long term. This is a problem in the UK too; as Chapter 4 identified, the little public data about employment rates of people with disfigurements is aggregated with other health conditions and lacks sufficient detail. Better data would be an invaluable resource both in understanding the scale and nuances of the problem and tracking the impact of regulation.

Relations 41, 48. Mediation is available in the Employment Tribunals but is infrequently used and has been criticised – see, for example, Peter Urwin and Paul L Latreille, 'Experiences of Judicial Mediation in Employment Tribunals' in William K Roche, Paul Teague and Alexander JS Colvin (eds), *The Oxford Handbook of Conflict Management in Organizations* (1st edn, Oxford University Press 2014) 343.

121 Deregulation Act 2015 s2 requires that any recommendations relate only to the claimant. See also Section 8.5. For a discussion of some exceptions to this general principle of individualisation, see Ford, 'Employment Tribunal Fees and the Rule of Law' (n 114) 5.

122 The Worker Protection (Amendment of Equality Act 2010) Bill 2022–2023 originally contained proposals to make employers liable in some circumstances for third-party harassment on various grounds, including disability. However, this aspect was removed during parliamentary debates. Note that a claimant might sometimes be able to show that their employer has failed to protect them from harassment by third parties and this inaction was on grounds of disability; see *Unite the Union v Nailard* [2018] EWCA Civ 1203.

123 Worker Protection (Amendment of Equality Act 2010) Act 2023, s1.

124 Valarie K Blake and Mark L Hatzenbuehler, 'Legal Remedies to Address Stigma-Based Health Inequalities in the United States: Challenges and Opportunities' (2019) 97 The Milbank Quarterly 494.

Removing these barriers would require far-reaching changes to the Employment Tribunal and equality law system as a whole, not just its application to disfigurement discrimination claims. There appears to be little cause for optimism on this front; others have highlighted a trajectory in the opposite direction, towards a narrowing of rights and increased barriers to enforcement.[125] So, while reform of the severe disfigurement provision is sorely needed to achieve fair outcomes in the relatively small number of claims brought, the potential for broader impact from even an improved law on disfigurement equality is doubtful given the challenges inherent in the equality law system as a whole. Campaigners may conclude that, for now, limited resources are better spent researching other forms of intervention, such as those discussed in the first half of this chapter.

9.3 Summary

While it is tempting to assume, or hope, that equality law reform alone could provide an effective answer to the social problem of disfigurement inequality, that is unlikely to be the case. Bias against people who look different is deeply ingrained and regularly reinforced by cultural messaging. The severe disfigurement provision does at least serve one function; it provides a financial remedy to the tiny minority of people who are able and willing to bring claims based on fact patterns that can be squeezed into law's narrow set of requirements and assumptions. Although it is easy to criticise the lack of impact of these rights, their value may be more keenly appreciated if they were taken away, allowing discrimination against people who look different to be openly practised.[126]

Improvements could be made to the severe disfigurement provision to make it easier to use in the Tribunal. These range from small legislative tweaks to the application of social model or hybrid definitions of disability, through to the creation of a new protected characteristic of either disfigurement or appearance. But, to increase the breadth of enforcement, far-reaching changes would also be needed to equality law systems as a whole.

For wider social change – tackling problematic attitudes, perceived social norms and behaviours towards people with visible differences – a combination of other measures would likely be needed as well. These

[125] See, for example, Ford, 'Employment Tribunal Fees and the Rule of Law' (n 114) 9–11.

[126] Carol Smart, *Feminism and the Power of Law* (Routledge 1989) 142.

range from measures to increase contact between people with disfigurements and others in the workplace and beyond, to educational interventions, to altering influential systems outside the workplace (including the criminal justice system and governance of the advertising industry). There is a pressing need for further interdisciplinary research in this area to evaluate the likely impact of options for reform in greater detail.

10

Beyond Disfigurement

This chapter considers whether equality law should extend its scope beyond disfigurement to other aspects of the way we look. Do the justifications for the inclusion of people with severe disfigurements within equality law apply to other aspects of appearance too? Would a wider protected characteristic of appearance offer viable legal rights to the many millions of us who do not have a disfigurement but are less-than-beautiful in some way? And, if so, would we even be willing to use it?

10.1 Is a Protected Characteristic of Appearance Justified in Principle?

I argued earlier in the book that there are several rationales underpinning the need for a disfigurement equality law. To recap briefly, disfigurements are almost always immutable (in that they are involuntary not chosen) and many result from a significant life event outside the individual's control – such as an illness, an accident, a war or being the victim of a crime. Discriminating against someone because of visible difference violates their dignity, as identity and self-esteem are closely connected with the way we look.[1] And people with disfigurements are widely stigmatised in society, with common reactions ranging from staring and awkwardness to abuse and hate crime. The widespread use of disfigurement in the media and film industry to symbolise evil helps to maintain this stigma.[2] For these reasons, the Act's inclusion of people with severe disfigurements is uncontroversial. But justifying law's chosen

[1] G Patzer, 'Improving Self-Esteem by Improving Physical Attractiveness' (1997) 9 Journal of Esthetic Dentistry 44, 44.

[2] Changing Faces, 'I Am Not Your Villain: Equal Representation of Visible Difference in Film' (*Changing Faces*, undated) <www.changingfaces.org.uk/get-involved/campaign-with-us/i-am-not-your-villian/> accessed 8 September 2023.

scope gets more problematic when we ask ourselves why disfigurement is treated differently in equality law from the wider concept of appearance. I will argue that general appearance also seems to satisfy these rationales yet remains outside of the scope of equality law.

In terms of immutability, setting aside (sometimes) malleable characteristics like hairstyle and clothing, there are some aspects of our appearance which we can't change except through surgery. Admittedly, the line between mutable and immutable appearance traits is blurring thanks to the increased availability of medico-cosmetic treatments. Clinics offering services such as permanent make-up, fillers and fat-freezing treatments can be found across the UK, often offering lunch hour 'tweakments'.[3] But law should not expect us to change our natural appearance traits, even if we could hand over a credit card in our lunch hour in order to do so. In her book *Intact*, the philosopher Clare Chambers offers a defence of the unmodified body and demands: 'we must insist: our bodies are good enough just as they are'.[4] The Act implicitly endorses this message in its disability provisions by ignoring the ameliorative effects of medical aids in deciding whether the threshold for disability is met. To provide otherwise would import an expectation that physical differences which can be treated *should* be treated, and legal rights denied accordingly. Rejecting societal pressures to modify our bodies in line with societal expectations means accepting that our bodies, and the way they look, are immutable.

Similarly, we can make a case that appearance discrimination violates our right to dignity. The close connection between appearance and identity applies not just to visible difference but to *all* appearances. Being harassed or judged negatively because of our appearance degrades and humiliates us,[5] and potentially harms us emotionally – especially when so many of us already struggle to view our bodies in a positive light.[6] As well as this emotional impact, appearance discrimination can

[3] Incidentally, it was allegedly a fat freezing treatment which caused the supermodel, Linda Evangelista, to proclaim herself 'deformed'; a legal action is understood to have been settled. See 2022, 'Linda Evangelista Settles Lawsuit over Cosmetic Procedure That Left Her "Permanently Deformed"' (*The Independent*, 20 July 2022) <www.independent.co.uk/life-style/fashion/linda-evangelista-coolsculpting-lawsuit-settle-b2127213.html> accessed 5 September 2023.

[4] Clare Chambers, *Intact: A Defence of the Unmodified Body* (Penguin Books 2022) 4.

[5] See Adam Etinson, 'What's So Special about Human Dignity?' (2020) 48 Philosophy and Public Affairs 353, 364.

[6] House of Commons Committee on Health and Social Care, *The Impact of Body Image on Mental and Physical Health* (Second Report of 2022–23, HC114) 3.

also harm us materially. Being treated differently because of how we look compromises our autonomy and the control we have over our lives to pursue employment on an equal basis with others.[7] Appearance bias makes opportunities for jobs, promotions and fair pay harder to obtain for some of us, impacting our ability to achieve the basic human capabilities[8] which should be available to all of us.

Physical appearance can also provide a window into other aspects of someone's social context. Race and religion, for example, are often evident (or at least perceived) from someone's appearance, as are familial and cultural roots. Social and economic factors such as poverty and class can be evident too, not just through available clothing and styling choices but through features such as dental health, height and weight which can be impacted by access to nutritious food during childhood and beyond.[9] Appearance can even sometimes provide clues to occupation as when callouses on hands might be assumed to be associated with manual labour. Far from being a neutral wrapper, physical appearance often holds clues as to individual history, context, values and choice, providing a porthole into other inviolable aspects of humanity. In sum, appearance discrimination offends our moral worth.

In terms of stigma, appearance-related disadvantage is not confined just to people with a disfigurement; there is some level of relative disadvantage attached to just looking 'plain' rather than beautiful. Our inbuilt belief that beauty equates to goodness[10] results in a raft of positive personality traits being subconsciously attributed to aesthetically beautiful people, with the converse true for the rest of us. Heather Widdows argues that beauty functions increasingly as an ethical ideal[11] – importing a moral expectation that we should present an attractive front, and moral condemnation for any failure to do so. Everyday language reinforces this ethical ideal – with phrases like 'letting yourself go' and 'you owe it to yourself'

[7] Martha C Nussbaum, *Creating Capabilities: The Human Development Approach* (Harvard University Press 2011) 34.

[8] Martha C Nussbaum, *Women and Human Development: The Capabilities Approach*, vol 3 (1st edn, Cambridge University Press 2000) 80.

[9] Andrea Rodriguez-Martinez and others, 'Height and Body-Mass Index Trajectories of School-Aged Children and Adolescents from 1985 to 2019 in 200 Countries and Territories: A Pooled Analysis of 2181 Population-Based Studies with 65 Million Participants' (2020) 396 The Lancet 1511, 1511.

[10] Karen Dion, Ellen Berscheid and Elaine Walster, 'What Is Beautiful Is Good' (1972) 24 Journal of Personality and Social Psychology 285.

[11] Heather Widdows, *Perfect Me: Beauty as an Ethical Ideal* (Princeton University Press 2018) 2.

importing a demeaning moral judgment for those who don't comply,[12] not just an aesthetic one. Accordingly, when our appearance fails to meet beauty ideals, we face moral blame, as well as aesthetic judgment.

So the logic underpinning disfigurement equality law also applies to wider appearance. The distinction, perhaps, is one of degree. Should equality law address the whole breadth of appearance-related stigma by granting anti-discrimination rights to everyone, from the most beautiful[13] to those with the more severe disfigurements? Or should we expect a degree of stoicism from the many of us whose disadvantage stems from just being less-than-beautiful, and instead focus the efforts of law on a central core of deeper disadvantage outside the 'norm' (as experienced by many people with a disfigurement)?

Similar questions have arisen in relation to other characteristics. David Wasserman has argued that 'many physical and mental differences not classified as impairments elicit equally contemptuous, dismissive, patronizing and over solicitous responses, that can be equally handicapping'.[14] This suggests that the scope of relative 'ability' disadvantage extends beyond the law's narrow definition of disability. A similar argument can be made of general appearance disadvantage, which extends to the many of us who are unprepossessing but not disfigured. Interestingly, though, Wasserman does acknowledge that within this widened group some people with significant impairments would be 'the most salient and aggrieved victims',[15] suggesting a more nuanced reality.

In general terms, the law's approach on related issues has tended to focus on breadth rather than depth. In that sense, a protected characteristic of appearance would be in good company. This breadth of equal treatment is also found in the specification of 'symmetrical' characteristics such as sex and race, rather than the deeper disadvantage of women and black people. And in the 'spectrum' characteristic of age, rather than in, say, the more commonly stigmatised 55+ age group only. Kate Malleson argues that this breadth comes at the expense of greater

[12] Ibid 30.

[13] There is some evidence that physically beautiful women sometimes struggle to get taken seriously in work contexts: see Nancy L Etcoff, *Survival of the Prettiest: The Science of Beauty* (Little, Brown 1999) 83.

[14] David Wasserman, 'Stigma without Impairment' in Leslie Pickering Francis and Anita Silvers (eds), *Americans with Disabilities* (Routledge 2000) 151.

[15] Ibid 148.

intervention to prevent deeper group inequality.[16] By protecting everyone equally, breadth encourages blindness to difference rather than targeted actions to reach fair outcomes for the most disadvantaged. But others see value in the default of legal abstraction (rights that apply to everyone in the same way), arguing that asymmetric laws can easily become a mechanism of abuse if not properly targeted.[17]

When it comes to appearance, differing degrees of stigma attaching to disfigurement and appearance respectively can be evidenced historically. In the West, people with disfigurements have, even in relatively recent years, been oppressed by societal practices and legal institutions. Until the mid-1970s, numerous cities in America had in place laws which criminalised unsightly or disfigured beggars who were seen in public.[18] And in Britain, if they wanted to avoid the workhouse in the early twentieth century, people with disfigurements often had little economic choice but to appear in travelling 'freak shows' to be stared at – the life story of Joseph Merrick,[19] known as the 'Elephant Man', provides one such example. People with some other protected characteristics, such as women and racial minorities, have endured social and legal oppression too. But the public history in relation to appearance more generally is less structural in nature. People have not been criminalised, enslaved or denied the right to vote because they have a bigger-than-average nose, unfashionably shaped eyebrows or sticking-out ears. With the exception of specific social contexts in which appearance has been treated as a proxy for another oppressed trait,[20] general appearance stigma, though

[16] Kate Malleson, 'Equality Law and the Protected Characteristics' (2018) 81 Modern Law Review 598, 598.

[17] William Lucy, 'Abstraction and the Rule of Law' (2009) 29 Oxford Journal of Legal Studies 481, 501.

[18] For a detailed exposition, see Susan M Schweik, *The Ugly Laws: Disability in Public* (New York University Press 2009).

[19] Greig Watson, 'Elephant Man City Statue Plan Faces "Freak Show" Criticism' *BBC News Online* <www.bbc.co.uk/news/uk-england-leicestershire-51012975> accessed 8 September 2023.

[20] For example, Edwin Black argues that physical appearance was one of many factors relevant in the eugenics practices in America and Germany in the late 1800s and early 1900s. In particular, he argues that people of Nordic heritage were so prized that even brunette hair 'constituted an ancestral stigma that proved a non-Nordic bloodline'. Accordingly, physical appearance as an indicator of a racial group seems to have played a part in the atrocity of eugenics. See Edwin Black, *War against the Weak: Eugenics and America's Campaign to Create a Master Race* (Four Walls Eight Windows 2003) 30. See also Bonnie Berry, *The Power of Looks: Social Stratification of Physical Appearance* (Ashgate 2008) 18.

undoubtedly real, has historically been seen as a low-profile social problem, not an explicit social or legal outrage.

But, in our increasingly visual and virtual world, the way that stigma operates seems to be changing, creating a more compelling case for the legal regulation of appearance discrimination. Our faces and bodies are now visible to large numbers of people in online contexts as wide-ranging as employer website profiles, remote learning classrooms, email headers, social media posts and dating apps, to name just a few. This increases the speed and breadth of stigma, and the ways it can be directed. Easy online accessibility of images means that cross-context judgments can be made, too. (Around 70 per cent of employers view a job applicant's social media profile when recruiting,[21] which leaves the door open to appearance-related judgments even before a decision has been made on who to interview.) And appearance-related bullying is now sometimes cited as the most prevalent form of bullying,[22] often with serious mental and physical health consequences for those affected.

Two examples illustrate this point. The first is the image of 'four lads in jeans' – a photo taken in 2019 of a group of male friends all wearing tight jeans, ready for an evening out. The photo went viral because of their clothes, resulting in such a media storm that the photo was even immortalised into a public statue. The publicity resulted in the lads receiving a wave of online abuse, including offensive telephone calls both at work and at home, and having some of their family members targeted by trolls.[23] The second example is the singer Jesy Nelson, who has openly admitted to the mental health impact and attempted suicide, resulting from being trolled about her appearance while working in the music industry. It is hard to reconcile these examples – and the many like them involving both celebrities and normal people – with the suggestion that

[21] CareerBuilder, 'Number of Employers Using Social Media to Screen Candidates at All-Time High, Finds Latest CareerBuilder Study' *PR Newswire* <https://prn.to/3IGytQ1> accessed 5 September 2023.

[22] Heather Widdows, 'Be Ashamed of Body Shaming' (*Sussex Publishers LLC*, 2020) <https://bit.ly/3Pm9y84> accessed 10 January 2020. The anti-bullying alliance defines bullying as 'The repetitive, intentional hurting of one person or group by another person or group, where the relationship involves an imbalance of power. Bullying can be physical, verbal or psychological. It can happen face-to-face or online'. See <https://anti-bullyingalliance.org.uk/tools-information/all-about-bullying/understanding-bullying/definition> accessed 25 September 2023.

[23] Jennifer Savin, 'The Men from the "Four Lads in Jeans" Meme Discuss the Down Sides of Going Viral' (*Cosmopolitan*, 19 January 2021) <www.cosmopolitan.com/uk/entertainment/a35249416/four-lads-jeans-meme/> accessed 13 March 2024.

appearance stigma is not deep enough to merit legal intervention. This changing social context allows many more of us than before to judge a book by its (rather mundane) cover and to express those judgments much more forcefully. This context behoves us to look again at the case for wider legal protection.

Counterarguments against a protected characteristic of appearance can of course be made. Perhaps the most common is economic; given customer preferences for good-looking staff in certain public-facing sectors, appearance-based hiring maximises profits, thereby encouraging economic growth and job creation.[24] On that analysis, appearance is a useful qualification for the job which business can – and perhaps even should – exploit for the greater economic good. Where this argument fails, however, is that similar reasoning can be – and sometimes has been – directed at other protected characteristics. Economic arguments based on customer preference could be made in relation to other traits too – such as religious belief – but the law has refused to indulge this indirect prejudice[25] – at least where the customer preferences are not intrinsic to the role.[26] To allow customer bias free rein as a justification would undermine the impact of the equality legislation significantly, enabling businesses to act lawfully on the least acceptable prejudices of their customers.

The second counterargument is that a protected characteristic of appearance is not necessary, because the most egregious forms of appearance-based discrimination are already protected under existing protected characteristics. The severe disfigurement provision is one example, of course, but there are others: hair policies prohibiting corn-rows, for example, may be indirect race discrimination;[27] an instruction to remove a religious symbol at work may sometimes constitute religious discrimination;[28] and, as we saw in Chapter 6, calling a man a 'bald cunt'

[24] Robert J Barro, 'So You Want to Hire the Beautiful. Well Why Not?' (*Business Week*, 16 March 1998). <https://scholar.harvard.edu/files/barro/files/98_0316_hire_bw.pdf> accessed 1 March 2018.

[25] See, for example, C-188/15 *Bougnaoui v Micropole SA* [2016] 7 WLUK 275.

[26] Equality and Human Rights Commission, *Employment: Statutory Code of Practice* (The Stationery Office Limited 2011) para 13.8.

[27] For a case example in an educational context, see *G v Head Teacher and Governors of St Gregory's Catholic Science College* [2011] EWHC 1452 (Admin).

[28] The case law on the wearing of visible religious symbols at work is complex; see Equality and Human Rights Commission, *Religion or Belief: Dress Codes and Religious Symbols* (2018) <www.equalityhumanrights.com/guidance/religion-or-belief-workplace/religion-or-belief-dress-codes-and-religious-symbols> accessed 19 March 2024.

at work may be harassment related to sex. However, these examples are the tip of the iceberg when it comes to appearance discrimination. They leave large gaps and create illogical distinctions – protecting men with male pattern baldness but perhaps not people with alopecia,[29] or an obese person who finds it hard to walk upstairs but not an obese person with no functional limitation,[30] or someone who is short due to restricted bodily development but not someone of the same height without a proven medical cause.[31] As Andrew Mason and Francesca Minerva argue: 'the idea that appearance discrimination is a serious problem in practice when, and only when, it constitutes indirect discrimination on some other basis, fails to recognise that direct appearance discrimination in the context of employment is both systematic and consequential'.[32]

A third, more persuasive, argument against the principle of a protected characteristic of general appearance relates to likely public reactions. This is a concern because if laws are met with derision and scepticism, victims may be less willing to take on the mantle of enforcement and employers less likely to abide by them. While few people would suggest that a disfigurement equality law is not justified, reactions to the idea of a protected characteristic of appearance are often much more mixed. Without reliable survey data, we can't know what public attitudes might be to this proposal, but anecdotal evidence and existing literature suggest two key reservations about a protected characteristic of appearance.

The first tends to be expressed in terms equating to personal resilience – an idea that differential treatment on the basis of appearance is something we should all have to cope with, not need a law to protect us from. This may stem from the fact that appearance shaming is so ubiquitous that it is something most people will experience in their lives. After all, even the most physically beautiful eventually find themselves eclipsed as they age. Ubiquity can be easily confused with inevitability. Appearance shaming may be felt as something which we all have to deal with; not a disadvantage visited on a minority but an unpleasant and unavoidable fact of life. That sense of inevitability may be sharpened if we acknowledge that most of us judge others on their appearance

29 *Finn v British Bung Manufacturing Company Ltd* [2022] ET/1803764/2021 (11 May 2022, unreported, ET).

30 Case C-354/13 *FOA v Kommuneres Landsforening (Kaltoft)* [2015] 2 CMLR 19.

31 *Hussain v Sky In-Home Services Ltd* [2017] ET/2300908/16 (10 January 2017, unreported, ET).

32 Andrew Mason and Francesca Minerva, 'Should the Equality Act 2010 Be Extended to Prohibit Appearance Discrimination?' (2022) 70 Political Studies 425, 434.

sometimes – how many of us can honestly say that physical appearance played no part in our thought processes when dating or choosing friends? As Barth and Wagner argue, 'Each in turn is tormentor and victim of this criterion, and so accepts the game of appearance-related appraisal'.[33]

But ubiquity is not a good reason to shun an approach to inequality based on rights. Over the years, equality law has embraced many other expressions of disadvantage which were, at the time, widespread – and perhaps even seen as the norm. Sexual harassment is a good example. In her seminal 1979 book on sexual harassment at work, Catherine Mackinnon cites an array of evidence showing the ubiquity of sexual harassment against women at the time, including a magazine poll in which nine out of ten respondents had experienced sexual harassment at work.[34] Mackinnon argues that the prevalence of the problem (in that case sexual harassment) reinforces it as a group-based, structural issue, rather than as isolated incidents between individuals. The same could be said of appearance-shaming and discrimination; its ubiquity underlines its macro-level presence and the cultural beauty norms and mechanisms which underscore it.

The second commonly expressed reservation about a protected characteristic of appearance is a lack of collective identity. As every person's appearance is unique (save for identical twins), appearance shaming feels individual and personal[35] – not an affront to people who look a certain way, but just to *me* and how *I* look. That might impact how we respond to it. We may feel angry on behalf of women generally when we experience sexism, but our reaction to appearance discrimination is often one of individual embarrassment. When Heather Widdows launched a campaign (#everydaylookism) asking members of the public to post their anonymous experiences of appearance discrimination,[36] it was feelings of shame which came through as the defining reaction in a majority of stories posted.[37]

[33] Isabelle Barth and Anne-Lorraine Wagner, 'Physical Appearance as Invisible Discrimination' (2017) 4 International Perspectives on Equality, Diversity and inclusion 127, 145.

[34] Catharine A MacKinnon, *Sexual Harassment of Working Women: A Case of Sex Discrimination* (Yale University Press 1979) 27.

[35] This is particularly the case when the appearance shaming focuses on overall appearance, rather than one aspect, such as weight.

[36] Heather Widdows, 'Everyday Lookism' (undated) <www.everydaylookism.com/> accessed 8 June 2023.

[37] Heather Widdows, 'Lookism: The Last Acceptable Discrimination' (Appearance, Identity and the Law Conference, Queen Mary University of London, 7 September 2022).

Of course, feeling shamed is not unique to appearance. For example, research has documented the feelings of shame experienced by many LGBTQIA+ people when interacting within a homophobic society.[38] But alongside this, gay pride has enabled many within this community to reject the negative reactions of others, creating resilience and positive collective identity, at least in some contexts. Former slurs such as the term 'queer' have in some cases been reclaimed and worn as a collective badge of pride. But this process of identifying as a group may feel more of a challenge where appearance is concerned, because we all look different from each other.

When the campaign for reforms against sexual harassment was in its infancy, similar feelings of individual shame were powerfully expressed. As Mackinnon summarised:

> Sexual subjects are generally sensitive and considered private; women feel embarrassed, demeaned and intimidated by these incidents. They feel afraid, despairing, utterly alone and complicit. This is not the sort of experience one discusses readily.[39]

One reason that Mackinnon identified for the reluctance to talk about these experiences was a lack of acceptable terminology. Naming this sort of conduct as sexual harassment helped to unite women in recognising their experiences as group based. The same is arguably also true of appearance, which lacks an acceptable vocabulary; we can talk of the practice of 'appearance-shaming' with relative confidence but struggle to find suitable words to describe the group of people united by their experiences of it (the ugly? the unsightly? the plain?). Commonly accepted terminology may help to establish appearance-shaming as a collective affront, rather than an individual insult.

To summarise: it is hard to argue that disfigurement justifies the intervention of equality law, but general appearance does not. Many of the rationales underpinning the former also extend to the latter. And the arguments against a protected characteristic of appearance are less persuasive when viewed in the context of social and historical changes and the passage of other equality laws which are now readily accepted as necessary. In the next section, I will argue that the difficulty with a protected characteristic of appearance is instead better conceptualised as one of practicality, not principle.

[38] Simona Giordano, 'Understanding the Emotion of Shame in Transgender Individuals: Some Insight from Kafka' (2018) 14 Life Sciences, Society and Policy 23, 1.

[39] MacKinnon, *Sexual Harassment of Working Women* (n 34) 27.

10.2 Is a Protected Characteristic of Appearance Viable in Practice?

Let us assume for a moment that Parliament chose to introduce a protected characteristic of appearance into the Act tomorrow, with the rest of the law remaining the same. Several questions would likely be raised about the practicability of the new provision.

The first of these is how to define 'appearance'. Whether to protect both mutable and immutable traits would be a primary issue, to determine whether features such as hairstyles, tattoos, clothing choices and so on are within the scope of the law. The approach taken on this point may also determine whether cosmetically altered appearances (such as enlarged lips from botox or a newly reacquired head of hair due to hair transplantation) are protected too.

Determining where appearance starts and stops can be challenging. Take facial expressions: some faces tend to rest in a frown, while others fall more naturally into an apparently friendly expression. These default expressions do not necessarily represent our personalities or our moods – but could make us seem more or less approachable to other people. Employers may consider this important, especially in a customer service role. Similarly, we could argue that the degree of facial animation during social interactions can affect the way that we perceive appearance. Some people may be thought better looking thanks to cute dimples when they smile, twinkling expressive eyes or a broad grin, while a tendency to sweat or blush visibly may produce the opposite effect. All of these features may alter the way we judge appearance, so drawing a clear line in the law to distinguish appearance traits from other physical traits could be difficult. This is perhaps why some of the local laws in the US (discussed below) have tended to focus on specific appearance traits (height, weight, etc.) rather than just 'appearance'.

The second likely question is how a protected characteristic of appearance would impact the more image-conscious industries, such as advertising and fashion. In the fashion industry, good looks and tall, slim body shapes are the norm. Advertising executives regularly rely on good-looking actors to market products, because the halo effect of beauty can tempt consumers to buy the product.[40] A protected characteristic of appearance may threaten these long-established practices, unless an exemption within the law could be relied on. The current exception is

[40] Widdows, *Perfect Me* (n 11) 41.

found in Schedule 9[41] and provides, in summary, that direct discrimination is not proven where, having regard to the nature or context of the work, possessing a particular protected characteristic is an occupational requirement which is a proportionate means of meeting a legitimate aim. However, this exception is both narrowly drafted and narrowly applied.[42] It might well justify a requirement for a fashion model to look a certain way, because the central purpose of modelling is to make the clothes look good. But the position may be different when advertising other products and services. Would physical attractiveness really be a requirement to be pictured eating a piece of toast, even if more loaves might be sold as a result? Looks are not intrinsic to bread adverts in the way they are to fashion modelling. A broader construal of the occupational requirement exception would risk opening the floodgates in other protected characteristics, allowing customer preferences to justify almost any discriminatory practice. A protected characteristic of appearance may therefore force us either to confront these long-standing practices head-on or to undermine the new legislation with additional exceptions.

Ironically, an equivalent problem could arise in reverse, too. Some brands have begun to take steps to display greater appearance diversity in their promotions – particularly when it comes to showing different body sizes and shapes. This representation may be important in the fight against negative body image and related disorders. But a protected characteristic of appearance – if drafted symmetrically to grant rights to everyone – could make it unlawful to choose someone because of their larger body size, visible cellulite or other realistic appearance traits.[43] To do so could discriminate against their appearance 'advantaged' counterparts, at least where the context falls within the scope of the Act. So the unintended consequence of making appearance discrimination unlawful may be to encourage organisations to row back on appearance diversity measures in favour of a policy of appearance blindness.

41 Equality Act 2010, sched 9(1).

42 See, for example, *A Kinlay v Bronte Film and Television Limite*d [2021] ET/2200251/2020 (18 July 2021, unreported, ET), in which a requirement to not be visibly pregnant as an actor to play a particular character was not upheld as an occupational requirement.

43 For the same point in another context, see Lizzie Barmes and Kate Malleson, 'The Case for Caution in Making Social Class a Protected Characteristic under the UK's Equality Act 2010' (3 August 2023) <https://ohrh.law.ox.ac.uk/the-case-for-caution-in-making-social-class-a-protected-characteristic-under-the-uks-equality-act-2010/> accessed 3 August 2023.

The third likely question relates to proof: how would Claimants be able to show that their appearance was the reason for the negative treatment complained of?[44] This may be somewhat of a red herring. Proving discrimination is rarely easy, but the mechanisms already in place in relation to other protected characteristics should be no less applicable in relation to appearance. Section 136 of the Equality Act 2010 provides that:

> . . .
>
> (2) If there are facts from which the court could decide, in the absence of any other explanation, that a person (A) contravened the provision concerned, the court must hold that the contravention occurred.
>
> (3)But subsection (2) does not apply if A shows that A did not contravene the provision.

In other words, if the claimant can show facts from which an inference of discrimination can be drawn, the burden of proof shifts to the respondent to prove that appearance was not the reason for the decision. While explicit evidence pointing to appearance bias – such as an overheard comment by the decision-maker criticising the claimant's appearance[45] – would make the claimant's job easier, other forms of evidence might sometimes be enough to shift the burden of proof to the respondent. For example, the organisational context may be such that a certain 'look' appears to be a prerequisite, whether written in a formal policy or inferred from the fact that all existing staff fit a narrow appearance formula (e.g. blonde, tall, slim and clear skin) which the Claimant does not meet.[46] Or the decision at issue may sometimes be inferred from relevant circumstantial evidence – imagine a less qualified (but better-looking) candidate being promoted over a better qualified candidate, and an employer without an equal opportunities policy who refuses to explain their decision. But the difficulty of proof may be more acute where the potential claimant has multiple grounds on which to base their claim.

[44] Heather James, 'If You Are Attractive and You Know It, Please Apply: Appearance Based Discrimination and Employers' Discretion' (2008) 42 Valparaiso University Law Review 661; Francesca Minerva, 'The Invisible Discrimination before Our Eyes: A Bioethical Analysis' (2017) 31 Bioethics 180, 186.

[45] See, for example, *Cromwell Garage Ltd v Doran* [2011] UKEAT/2011/036 (8 April 2011, unreported, EAT) for an example relating to pregnancy.

[46] See *West Midlands Passenger Transport Executive v Singh* [1988] IRLR 186 for a discussion on similar facts relating to race discrimination.

In the latter example, if the stronger but unpromoted candidate is not only less physically attractive than her successful colleague but also older and of a different religion – adding the extra ground of appearance into the mix of possibilities may muddy the waters.

The final likely question relates to objectivity: can concepts such as physical attractiveness, as one aspect of appearance, be objective and fixed enough to provide a sufficient degree of legal certainty?[47] With the exception of disability, the existence of the cited protected characteristic in a discrimination claim (such as age, race or religion) is usually uncontentious, and the claimant's self-categorisation is simply accepted. But assertions relating to appearance are more likely to be contested. This is a particular problem where the allegation relates not to a characteristic such as height or weight which can be measured, but to general attractiveness or beauty.

10.2.1 The Problem of Pretty

Attractiveness and beauty are difficult to pin down in concrete terms – although plenty have tried. But there is increasing agreement about the physical features possessed by the most good-looking people in contemporary Western culture. Nancy Etcoff highlights beauty ideals of appearing young,[48] tall[49] and with good skin,[50] as well as possessing certain (often symmetrical and mathematical) bodily proportions.[51] Etcoff's analysis of beauty rests on biological determinism; hence we are attracted to features which might often be associated with good health and fertility.[52] Societally 'average' appearances, which are close to the population mean, are often beautiful for this reason.[53] She argues that facial features which appear youthful and feminine are a particular draw in female faces[54] – large eyes, high cheekbones and plump lips. And

47 Lynn T Vo, 'A More Attractive Look at Physical Appearance-Based Discrimination: Filling the Gap in Appearance-Based Anti-Discrimination Law' (2002) 26 Southern Illinois University Law Journal 339, 356.

48 Etcoff, *Survival of the Prettiest* (n 13) 63.

49 Ibid 172.

50 Ibid 113.

51 Ibid 140.

52 Note that Bonnie Berry argues that the case for biological determinism has diminished in contemporary society. See Berry, *The Power of Looks* (n 20) 18.

53 Etcoff, *Survival of the Prettiest* (n 13) 145.

54 Ibid 152.

masculine features such as prominent bone structures, visible muscles and height are attractive in men, provided not taken to extremes.[55]

Although beauty ideals have historically varied significantly from culture to culture, Heather Widdows argues that these cross-cultural differences are converging[56] due to our increasingly visual, virtual culture. Features such as 'large round eyes, cheek bones, smallish-straightish noses, and plump lips'[57] are fast becoming a global mean. And the evidence suggests that these ideals are commonly shared. Studies show that, within a given culture, ratings of attractiveness given to others have a high degree of consistency, even among raters of different ages, genders and social backgrounds.[58] Beauty may be in the eye of the beholder, but the eyes of most beholders are surprisingly consistent.

This consistency might suggest that sufficient objectivity could be identified to bring physical attractiveness (as a subset of appearance) within the realm of the Act. But there are surely practical difficulties replicating that apparent quasi-objectivity in a legal environment. For one, making findings about the relative attractiveness of the claimant and their comparator in a direct discrimination would be a lot to ask personally of employment judges. It would also be hard to stop the deliberate manipulation of appearance comparisons. Would it not be in the interests of both a claimant and her comparator in a direct discrimination claim to 'glow down'[59] on the day of the hearing, turning up with greasy hair, wearing a stained, unflattering tracksuit and a scowl? And would it be fair for employers to ask a 'comparator' employee – who often has no responsibility for the decisions complained of – to have their appearance publicly judged in order to aid the employer's defence of a discrimination claim?

The challenge of evaluating appearance becomes even more problematic when we consider indirect discrimination claims based on physical attractiveness. Indirect discrimination claims under s19 of the Act require the claimant to show not just that they have been disadvantaged individually, but collectively too; in other words, that other people who

55 Ibid 157.

56 Widdows, *Perfect Me* (n 11) 74. See also Berry, *The Power of Looks* (n 20) 72.

57 Widdows, *Perfect Me* (n 11) 84.

58 See, for example, Daniel S Hamermesh, *Beauty Pays* (Princeton University Press 2011) 24; Etcoff, *Survival of the Prettiest* (n 13) 137.

59 A 'glow down' is the opposite of a 'glow up'; it refers to a period in which an individual loses attractiveness, style and confidence.

share the appearance characteristic would also be disadvantaged.[60] To illustrate this point, imagine a company policy which links staff pay and bonuses to customer feedback scores from shoppers. We know that customers are likely to rate physically attractive sales staff higher because they may assume them to be more sociable, successful, trustworthy and have a range of positive personality traits.[61] So the less attractive sales staff might be disadvantaged in their potential for feedback scores, and therefore in their pay. A shop assistant wanting to challenge this policy as indirectly discriminatory would have to show not just that *she* has been disadvantaged by it but that other 'less attractive' colleagues were too.

The prospect of categorising the attractiveness of large proportions of the workforce feels instinctively wrong, but it may not be insurmountable. On occasions, tribunals make findings based on 'social facts', showing a willingness to accept a proposition based on commonly understood social evidence rather than individual circumstances. This approach has sometimes been used in sex discrimination cases, for example, to establish the proposition that women are more likely to have childcare responsibilities.[62] Acceptance of the tendency to associate beauty with positive traits as a social fact could help to establish group disadvantage in an indirect discrimination claim.

Another potential workaround – in theory at least – is to use AI to determine relative attractiveness for the purpose of an appearance discrimination claim. Apps already exist which claim to apply prevailing beauty standards to images of individuals and award them a beauty score. However, there are serious questions to be asked about the use of this technology. To begin with, there is increasing evidence highlighting the possibility of racially biased outcomes. In 2016, this technology was used to judge an international beauty contest – and almost all of the forty-four competition winners it selected were white.[63] The makers of the app involved in the beauty contest – who were themselves surprised by its outcome – suggested that the data set may have been to blame;[64] insufficient data, or biased data, can effectively 'train' the algorithm to produce

[60] Note also s19A which provides for indirect discrimination by association. This is not addressed further here.

[61] Dion and others, 'What Is Beautiful Is Good' (n 10) 288.

[62] See, for example, *London Underground v Edwards (No2)* [1988] IRLR 364 (CA).

[63] Sam Levin, 'A Beauty Contest Was Judged by AI and the Robots Didn't Like Dark Skin' (*The Guardian*, 8 September 2016) <https://bit.ly/3TBBQxH> accessed 5 September 2023.

[64] Ibid.

biased results, replicating the prejudice inherent in the data set used to programme it. This potential for hidden malleability of outcomes is troubling. The second obvious problem with the use of computer-generated assessments of physical attractiveness relates to individual dignity, and the possible mental health impact of putting parties in a tribunal claim through a potentially demeaning process.

There are also practical limitations associated with applying current understandings of good employment practice to a protected characteristic of appearance. While we generally accept that the individual is the expert on her own beliefs, race, age and so forth, the societal standard is that the 'expertise' of appearance is placed in the hands of observers. Many employers monitor their own diversity compliance – particularly for race and gender – and some undertake positive action to fill identified gaps in their diversity. But asking managers to rate the attractiveness of their staff would run counter to every tenet of good employment practice and may fill up the employment tribunals with constructive dismissal claims! Asking staff to self-rate their own attractiveness would also be of limited use; the way we see our own appearance tends to be different from the way that others see us,[65] so even our honest self-ratings are unlikely to be representative of wider social reactions. Of course, the inability to monitor appearance diversity does not cancel out the potential benefits of a protected characteristic of appearance – but it does remove one of the more reflexive aspects of compliance.

In essence, categorising attractiveness is difficult, and that creates friction with a system of equality law which relies heavily on groups and categories. Appearance may not be alone in this regard, however. As identities evolve, other protected categories are fragmenting too. For example, societal recognition of multiple (and sometimes fluid) identities and sexualities is challenging the Act's simplistic approach. Wider identity fragmentation may ultimately require the Act to rethink its approach to group definition. As Kenji Yoshino argues:

> we must shift away from claims that demand equality for particular groups toward claims that demand liberty for us all. This is not an exhortation that we strip protections from currently recognized groups. Rather, it is a prediction that future courts will be unable to sustain a

[65] John B Pittenger and Linda Musun Baskett, 'Facial Self-Perception: Its Relation to Objective Appearance and Self-Concept' (1984) 22 Bulletin of the Psychonomic Society 167, 170.

> groupbased vision of civil rights when faced with the broad and irreversible trend toward demographic pluralism.[66]

In the meantime, the problem of evaluating attractiveness remains, but the frequency with which it would arise should not be overstated. Most appearance discrimination claims would not hang on such an evaluation. For example, appearance claims relating to a specific characteristic – such as height, weight or hair loss – would be easier to measure than attractiveness. Claims about *perceived* (un)attractiveness would often provide an alternative to an evaluation of *actual* attractiveness.[67] And claims relating to narrow brand image requirements (as might be found in a teen clothing store, for example, where all the sale staff have a certain 'look') would not need to venture into findings of physical attractiveness. In short, difficulties determining claims based on nuances of generalised physical attractiveness may be few and far between, and employment tribunals would doubtless find ways of dealing with them. This is not necessarily a reason to ignore the wider potential of a protected characteristic of appearance.

10.3 Would a Protected Characteristic of Appearance Be Enforced?

If appearance were to be added to the list of protected characteristics in the Act, its potential effectiveness would hinge on whether victims of discrimination were willing and able to bring a legal claim. As set out earlier in the book, this is already a problem under the severe disfigurement provision, with a common reluctance and powerlessness to use the law reflected in the tiny number of claims brought. Would a protected characteristic of appearance in Britain be similarly underused? International comparisons are instructive here. Chapter 9 gave an overview of appearance equality laws in France and the US. But the evidence from those countries suggests that appearance equality laws have had little impact.

A quick internet search reveals a steady stream of debate in France on this topic of appearance discrimination, in which law at least plays a part.

[66] Kenji Yoshino, 'The pressure to cover' *New York Times Magazine Online* (New York, 15 January 2006) <www.nytimes.com/2006/01/15/magazine/the-pressure-to-cover.html> accessed 25 October 2023.

[67] Mason and Minerva, 'Should the Equality Act 2010 Be Extended to Prohibit Appearance Discrimination?' (n 32) 435.

The most recent example is the unsuccessful claim brought by three rejected Miss France contestants,[68] backed by a feminist organisation, who alleged that the contest's rules (including that contestants must be over 1.7 m tall) were discriminatory.[69] But, despite this, a significant body of research in France suggests that appearance discrimination is still very much a problem. Of French workers in a survey who claimed to have been discriminated against or harassed in their jobs, 40 per cent believe this was linked to appearance,[70] with women often worse affected.[71] In its 2019 guidance,[72] the French equality body notes that appearance has become one of the most common grounds of discrimination. Yet the number of complaints based on physical appearance discrimination in France remains low – making up only 2.6 per cent of complaints.[73] Some commentators in France have suggested that these low levels of enforcement may, ironically, flow from the fact that appearance discrimination is so prevalent that it is implicitly legitimised:

> its omnipresence makes it something that is rarely called into question and leads to very few complaints. In effect, we may presume that everyone has assimilated and legitimised it because it just seems so natural.[74]

So the ongoing tension between legal provision and legal enforcement remains a problem in France as well as in Britain, despite its much wider-ranging provisions.

In the US, local laws exist protecting a variety of characteristics including height and weight, and physical characteristics. What these local laws have in common is low levels of enforcement.[75] Deborah Rhodes posits a variety of possible reasons for low enforcement rates

[68] See, for example, Le Monde, 'French Court Backs Miss France Beauty Contest against Feminists' (*Le Monde*, Paris) <https://bit.ly/3VsxR84> accessed 22 March 2023.

[69] For the organisation's comment on the decision, see Osez Le Feminisme, 'Décision justice MISS France' (2023) <https://osezlefeminisme.fr/decision-justice-miss-france/> accessed 8 December 2023.

[70] Le Defenseur des droits et L'Organisation internationale du travail, *13e barometre: La perception des discriminations dans l'emploi* (Defenseur des droits 2020) 4.

[71] Jacques Toubon, *Décision-cadre n°2019-205 relative aux discriminations dans l'emploi fondées sur l'apparence physique* (Defenseur des Droits 2019) 4.

[72] Ibid.

[73] Ibid 3. This figure relates to complaints to the Défenseur des droits in 2018.

[74] Barth and Wagner, 'Physical Appearance as Invisible Discrimination' (n 33) 137.

[75] Deborah Rhodes, *The Beauty Bias* (Oxford University Press 2010) 125. Some have argued that the law may be being enforced by mediation rather than litigation; see Linda Hamilton Krieger, 'Afterword: Socio-Legal Backlash' (2000) 21 Berkeley Journal of Employment and Labor Law 476, 502.

under these laws. Evidential difficulties may be deterring claims, particularly as employers become more aware of the need to disguise any appearance-motivated decisions.[76] Broadly interpreted exceptions could be impacting as well, allowing employers considerable leeway to direct their employees' appearance standards.[77] Low success rates could be putting people off claiming too.[78] And she suggests that the very limited remedies available under some local ordinances might be dissuading complaints[79] (although it is notable that low enforcement is still a problem in jurisdictions with heavier penalties available, such as France). Just like France, the US experience suggests that concerns about an appearance equality law opening the floodgates to an unmanageable number of claims are without foundation. The much bigger concern is adequate enforcement.

So, despite good potential for awareness-raising, a protected characteristic of appearance under the Act faces significant questions about its likely enforcement and effectiveness. It would probably provide remedies for a proportionately small number of victims of appearance discrimination at work. And it may also provoke debate and media coverage, as it has to some extent in France, helping to raise the profile of the issue.[80] But, akin to the severe disfigurement provision, an under-used appearance equality law seems unlikely, on its own, to bring about wider attitudinal or behavioural change. Its potential for social transformation of appearance bias and discrimination therefore appears limited unless accompanied by another impetus for change.

10.4 Summary

There are persuasive reasons to take seriously the problem of general appearance discrimination. Those reasons are becoming ever more compelling in our digital world where images of us are not only expected but also more widely distributed than ever before. Despite this, the idea of a law against appearance discrimination is often accused of being an 'equality too far' – responding to a type of discrimination which needs

[76] Rhodes, *The Beauty Bias* (n 75) 133.
[77] Ibid.
[78] Ibid.
[79] Ibid 140.
[80] Mason and Minerva, 'Should the Equality Act 2010 Be Extended to Prohibit Appearance Discrimination?' (n 32) 436.

to be tolerated in a liberal society, rather than something for which a legal remedy should be available. As one managing partner of a US labour law firm opined: 'The noble purpose of the laws requiring equal employment opportunity is already undermined by too many frivolous lawsuits. These laws would only be further trivialized by allowing employees who do not succeed at work to blame it on their looks'.[81] I argue instead that the reasons which often underpin this objection – namely the ubiquity of appearance bias and the sensation of individual shame rather than collective identity – actually reinforce the theoretical case for a legal response.

Instead, the real challenges lie not in the principle of making appearance discrimination unlawful, but in the practicalities. These challenges include the lack of acceptable terminology about appearance; the difficulties making categorisations of attractiveness, and the difficulties which employers would face implementing positive action programmes on the basis of particular appearance traits or creating records of staff attractiveness for the purpose of diversity monitoring. And, for the provisions to be effective, employees must be willing to declare themselves unattractive and to accept the financial, reputational and emotional risks inherent in bringing a discrimination claim. Given both our domestic experience with low enforcement of the severe disfigurement provision and international comparisons with France and the US, this seems unlikely. Although social change rejecting wider appearance inequality is long overdue, equality regulation alone is unlikely to effect this transformation.

[81] James J McDonald, 'Lookism: The Next Form of Illegal Discrimination' (Bloomberg Law Reports, 11 October 2010) <www.fisherphillips.com/en/news-insights/lookism-the-next-form-of-illegal-discrimination.html> accessed 8 December 2023.

11

Conclusion

This book began by describing a mismatch between high numbers of reported experiences of disfigurement discrimination and very low numbers of claims under the severe disfigurement provision in the Equality Act 2010. Research which began as an attempt to understand this mismatch developed into a much broader critique of the relationship between disfigurement, the workplace and the law. The problems identified relate not just to low levels of individual enforcement but also to flaws, inconsistencies and limitations of scope in the law itself, to conceptual confusion about the social meaning of disability and to uncertainty and wariness among HR professionals and people with lived experience of visible difference, respectively. In short, the analysis has revealed concerns on every level.

The opening chapters highlighted inconsistency in the approach to disability taken in the Act and the international legal framework surrounding it. The severe disfigurement provision is something of an anomaly in the Act; it bypasses the need for functional impairment (which is prioritised by the Act's usual definition of disability in section 6) and implicitly recognises the disabling potential of social barriers. However, this refreshing difference in approach is short-lived; the detail of the Act and the case law under it instead return to the primacy of the functional, medical model approach. By way of example, the Act applies a more demanding threshold (severity) to disfigurements than it does to disabilities based on functional impairment (substantiality), even though there is good evidence that the social barriers of disfigurement are not limited to those which are severe. In addition, the Act's narrow concepts of disfigurement and impairment may exclude many appearance-altering conditions (such as obesity and hair loss) in favour of others despite shared experiences of common social barriers. Moreover, both the Act and some of the case law under it[1] create rigid distinctions between

[1] *Cosgrove v Northern Ireland Ambulance Service* [2007] IRLR 397 (NICA).

aesthetic and functional impairments which fail to recognise the holistic experience of people with complex conditions that encounter more than one type of barrier. In essence, the severe disfigurement provision is undermined by technicalities which emphasise the law's lack of commitment to the social model logic which, at first glance only, seems to underlie it.

The analysis has also traced this conceptual tension between the social and medical models of disability into real life. Employers are accustomed to thinking of disability in functional terms too. This impacts not just their understanding of what disability is, but how they should respond to it. The duty to make reasonable adjustments is often seen as a response to functional deficit, such as impairments affecting hearing, mobility or eating. Accordingly, many HR managers are puzzled about how to apply the duty to counter the social barriers of disfigurement. This uncertainty is compounded by awkwardness engaging with appearance-related issues, and by the common worry that talking about visible difference will cause offence. This may lead to the possibility of support simply being ignored.

The tension between differing concepts of disability is also evident in the accounts of people with lived experience of visible difference. Some people with visible differences express a feeling of 'falling between the gaps', not fitting into the category of disabled, but still disadvantaged by the attitudes of others. Many do not consider themselves disabled because, again, disability is seen as something which affects what you can do, not what you look like. This conflicts with a legal system which requires claimants to wear a metaphorical badge of 'disabled' as well as 'disfigured' in order to challenge discrimination.

Accordingly, medical model understandings are bound up in the legal consciousness and lived experiences of both employers and employees with visible differences. It is probable that definitions in the law have influenced these real-world understandings to some extent, although this was not tested specifically in the research.

Awareness of the severe disfigurement provision appears to be low among both HR staff[2] and people with visible differences. Levels of awareness within the general public have not, to my knowledge, been measured, but low (or even lower) awareness is plausible, given the

[2] Around 80 per cent of HR participants knew or assumed that severe disfigurement might fall under the disability provisions in the Act, but only around 25 per cent appreciated that the Act's usual test of function would not apply.

reduced relevance of the provision outside these interested groups. And the tiny number of cases brought under the severe disfigurement provision has ensured that publicity of it – even within the professional press – has been negligible, allowing it to remain largely invisible.

Limited awareness of what the law requires is likely to reduce compliance. Low numbers of claims may compound this, encouraging disregard for the potential sanctions of the law even where awareness is present. The prevalence of real-world understandings of disability based on the medical model further limits any expressive, value-shaping power of the severe disfigurement provision. Law's dissemination of a symbolic message about the disabling impact of looking different is likely to be eroded by the persistent perception that disability is about what you can't do, not what you look like.

Any remaining positive symbolism is further eroded by the steady stream of negative portrayals of people with visible differences which drown out law's message of equality and respect. People with the visible difference of proteus syndrome are parodied in 'elephant man' masks sold in mainstream British shops;[3] west end musicals portray characters with scars as bitter, twisted and dangerous;[4] and 'ugly photo' apps encourage users to enjoy uglifying their photos by adding spots and boils, bulbous noses and squints. In sum, the law's whispered expression of disfigurement equality is persistently drowned out by low awareness, conceptual conflict and wider cultural messaging. The law whispers much too quietly to be heard above all this societal noise.

Consistent with this, while acknowledging a frustrating lack of longitudinal data, the analysis has revealed very little evidence of the severe disfigurement provision producing any kind of positive impact on attitudes, behaviours or perceived social norms in the real world. Surveys and research studies – including the empirical work summarised in this book – regularly report accounts of continuing prejudice and discrimination against people who look different. The few partial (and not disaggregated) statistics available about employment rates present a mixed picture but do still suggest that people with disfigurements are less likely to be employed than people without disabilities. In interview, some of the

[3] This was for sale in Amazon UK at the time of writing.

[4] In *The Phantom of the Opera*, the title character has a facial deformity and has hidden himself away for years before taking a young woman hostage. In *The Lion King*, Scar is the main antagonist who has murdered another character.

HR participants candidly recognised the possibility of bias against visibly different people within their own organisations.

Even the least ambitious potential equality outcome – the creation of a remedial mechanism by which disfigurement discrimination can be challenged effectively if the victim so chooses – appears flawed in its implementation. As well as placing a significant burden (financial, emotional, temporal, reputational) on the victim of discrimination, the structure of the law creates conflict with the non-disabled self-identity of many people with visible differences, deterring claims. The technicalities of the law make it uncertain, narrow in scope and often hard to win. And the process is commonly perceived as intrusive and difficult. In the real world, wariness about using rights under equality law is often cited as a reason to walk away, with an underlying sense that challenging discrimination in the courts is just not an option for many people.

In short, I found little evidence of effectiveness even when the law judged against the very limited ambitions of the framework of potential equality impacts outlined earlier in the book. Having begun the book pondering a lack of clarity in what law was trying to achieve, I end it with a lack of clarity over what, if anything, law has achieved. A small number of claims have been brought – some successfully – but I uncovered little evidence of impact beyond this. The limited evidence available suggests that the severe disfigurement provision is largely ineffective.

While disappointing, this conclusion is perhaps not wholly surprising; research in the social sciences emphasises the complexity of the relationship between law and social change. There are no 'givens' and no 'absolutes'; much depends on context. But some key characteristics which have been suggested as likely indicators of impactful laws in other contexts are noticeably absent in the context of the severe disfigurement provision. It offers no indirect nudges to guide attitudes, no publicity to demonstrate its worth, few positive motivations for compliance and little grassroots support due to the identity conflict which it creates for many people with visible differences who do not self-identify as disabled.

This rather sobering conclusion needs to be put into context, though. This book is a product of a particular time and place. The world (and the virtual world in particular) has changed significantly in the last couple of decades, altering the social meanings and experiences of physical appearance. Further change is likely. While visible difference inequality has to date remained largely invisible, wider concerns relating to physical appearance are increasingly pressing and well recognised. With dramatic increases in reports of body image concerns,[5] eating disorders[6] and associated mental health conditions,[7] our changing relationship with our bodies and the way they look has come into sharper focus. This is already starting to shine a light on factors such as idealised beauty standards, the growing importance placed on looks (with corresponding increases in rates of plastic surgery) and high rates of appearance-related bullying and shaming.[8] This very worrying social context creates an impetus for change which may bring increased recognition to the campaign for visible difference equality too.

This impetus could spark research and data gathering to fill the identified gaps in knowledge. That means disaggregated, detailed employment statistics covering everything from the numbers of people with visible differences, pay rates, job types and degree of job security to quantify the problem and understand nuances in patterns of disadvantage. It means longitudinal research measuring attitudes and social norms about how people with disfigurements should be treated and responses to interventions. And it means funding for regular large-scale consultations with people in this community to ensure that the full range of experiences and views continue to be heard.

Greater knowledge in this area may bring renewed attention to the need for law reform too. Laws could be designed to increase contact with people who look different in the workplace and beyond, and both educational initiatives and advertising regulation could seek to foster acceptance of appearance diversity. As AI evolves, additional legal safeguards may be needed to stop human negative judgments of difference being replicated through technology, and policies could be implemented to motivate employers to develop communities of good practice. Of course, equality laws could be reformed too, both to mitigate the heavy burden of challenging discrimination and to remove some of the limitations in the law's current structure and scope. A key priority would

[5] House of Commons Women and Equalities Committee, *Changing the Perfect Picture: An Inquiry into Body Image* (Sixth Report of Session 2019–2021, HC274) 9.

[6] Children's Commission, 'Young People with Eating Disorders on the Rise in England' (*Children's Commission*, 2023) <https://www.childrenscommissioner.gov.uk/media-centre/young-people-with-eating-disorders-on-the-rise-in-england/> accessed 8 December 2023.

[7] House of Commons Women and Equalities Committee, *Changing the Perfect Picture* (n 5) 15.

[8] See, for example, Anti-Bullying Alliance, 'Appearance-Targeted Bullying' (undated) <https://anti-bullyingalliance.org.uk/tools-information/all-about-bullying/at-risk-groups/appearance-targeted-bullying> accessed 6 December 2023.

be to resolve the underlying tension about the meaning of the word 'disability' which has hindered the effectiveness of the law on disfigurement equality to date. In short, there is no shortage of possible interventions, but a pressing need for further research to ensure that any interventions are effectively targeted.

Perhaps the most immediate and tangible potential for change exists in motivating and assisting employers to become more appearance-inclusive. The model of good practice at Appendix 1 suggests a series of small, practical steps which organisations can adapt and develop within their own contexts – such as adjusting recruitment processes to reduce the impact of appearance prejudice and training managers how to have productive, comfortable conversations about support needs with staff with a visible difference. A community which builds on this could be capable of succeeding where law has failed: creating awareness, shared understandings of good practice and positive steps towards the inclusion and equality of people with visible differences at work.

Appendix 1

Model of Good Practice

Creating Appearance-Inclusive Workplaces for People with a Visible Difference

What Is Visible Difference?

A 'visible difference' is any condition, injury or side-effect of medical treatment which alters or affects someone's appearance. It is used as an alternative to the word 'disfigurement' which some people with a visible difference prefer not to use. It can include both acquired appearance differences and those present from birth. Although visible difference affects appearance, sometimes it can affect the person in other ways too. For example, some facial visible differences (such as a cleft) can affect the person's speech, hearing or facial expressions, and living with a visible difference can be psychologically challenging. For some, visible difference may fluctuate or change over time; for others, it may remain constant and unchanged. The social experience of visible difference – in terms of the reactions, attitudes and bias of other people towards someone who looks different – can be disabling.

Purpose and Scope

This model of good practice for employers has been written to help make inclusive workplace environments in Britain for people with a visible difference as at June 2023. It is designed to give practical guidance only which can be adapted within different contexts, but it is not intended to be comprehensive. Although this model is written with people with a visible difference in mind, some of the guidance suggested may also be useful for reducing the impact of bias based on general physical appearance too.

Some people with more severe visible differences may have rights as disabled people under the Equality Act 2010. In particular, Schedule 1 to the Act provides that an impairment which 'consists of a severe disfigurement' shall be treated as a disability provided it is long term. In that case, as an employer you may have a duty not to discriminate, including a legal duty to make reasonable adjustments at work. Although there may be some points of overlap, this model of good practice is **not** designed to mirror the scope of these legal duties. If the duty to make reasonable adjustments applies in a particular case, additional or different steps from those discussed here may be needed.

Also be careful to **ensure that any steps taken comply with data protection laws and obligations**. For example, video or images of a person with a visible difference could amount to special category data for data protection purposes which will place certain additional obligations on the control, disclosure and processing of such videos or photos. Data protection is beyond the scope of this note.

Always Take HR and Legal Advice on Individual Circumstances

Guiding Principles The good practice suggestions set out below are informed by four guiding principles:

- Be proactive. Rather than waiting for individual difficulties to occur, employers can take proactive steps to create an appearance-inclusive culture.
- Reduce the opportunity for bias – both human and automated – to operate, whether unknowingly or knowingly.
- Don't make assumptions. Research shows that the experience of living with a visible difference can vary significantly from person to person, and also over time. Championing the needs and preferences of the individual, and taking into account the context, is key.
- Be respectful with language. Some terminology (e.g. the words 'disabled' or 'disfigured') can be difficult for some people. Take your cue from the individual on their preferred terminology.

Suggestion 1: Audit Your Policies, Procedures and Branding

- Decide whether to make a commitment to appearance equality as part of wider equality policies. You may wish to define the extent of this commitment (e.g. do you wish to include tattoos and clothing choices too?) and think about how it will be put into practice. Consider, too, including a brief diversity commitment in job advertisements.
- Ensure that up-to-date policies are in place and communicated to deal with any instance of bullying or harassment between colleagues.
- Check that your policies are accessible and enable all staff to understand what entitlements to sick leave and sick pay they have (such as when considering having surgery). Encourage a culture where staff feel able to use entitlements in appropriate cases without fear of negative judgment or unfair treatment.
- People with a visible difference can receive intrusive questions and abuse – and potentially even hate crime – from customers and third parties at work.

Ensure that you have processes in place to prevent this and to deal with any occurrences, so that the employee and their colleagues know how to handle such a situation calmly and without putting themselves at risk, either physically or emotionally. You may wish to set out measures to prevent repeat occurrences too (for example, prohibiting customers – if possible – who are repeatedly abusive to staff). Consider how such incidents can be reported (whether internally or externally to relevant authorities if appropriate) and what support or counselling can be offered to staff involved.[1]

- Audit the images you use to promote your brand for inclusivity, as this may affect how your employees and job applicants perceive the company. Note that the charity Changing Faces runs a campaign for employers called Pledge to be Seen which employers can apply to join.

Suggestion 2: Introduce Staff Training on Appearance and/or Visible Difference Equality

- When running staff equality training, consider including a section on appearance and disfigurement equality.[2] Getting buy-in from senior management may help to ensure training is taken seriously.

Suggestion 3: Review Job Adverts and Forms

- Check the proposed wording of your job adverts to ensure they do not disadvantage or deter applications from people with a visible difference. For example, asking for applications from 'smiley' candidates or for people to be 'the welcoming face on reception' may deter applications from candidates with a visible facial difference. If some kind of description really is needed, focus on attitudes instead, for example, 'committed to helping customers'.
- Health-related questions can only be asked pre-employment in very narrow circumstances.[3] Where needed and permitted, be very careful how any such

[1] For a guide to preventing workplace harassment, see Equality and Human Rights Commission, 'Sexual Harassment and Harassment at Work' (*EHRC*, 2020) <www.equalityhumanrights.com/sites/default/files/sexual_harassment_and_harassment_at_work.pdf> accessed 22 March 2024.

[2] The charity Changing Faces offers some resources and training materials – including an online Implicit Attitudes Test – about appearance bias specifically; see Changing Faces, 'Visible Difference and Unconscious Bias Training' (*Changing Faces*, undated) <www.changingfaces.org.uk/for-professionals/employers/training-guidance/unconscious-bias-training/> accessed 25 March 2024.

[3] There is a government quick start guide about this area of the law: see Government Equalities Office, 'Equality Act 2010: What Do I Need to Know? A Quick Start Guide to the Ban on Questions about Health and Disability during Recruitment' (UK Government, 2011) <https://assets.publishing.service.gov.uk/government/uploads/system/uploads/attachment_data/file/85013/employment-health-questions.pdf> accessed 25 March 2024.

questions are phrased, bearing in mind the purpose for which the question is being asked. Many people with a visible difference are uncertain whether their difference is a disability in law or unwilling to label it so. Disability tick boxes ('Do you have a disability? Tick yes or no') can cause significant anxiety and uncertainty for some people. For example, if asking for the purpose of diversity monitoring, you could ask whether the individual *considers themself* to be disabled and could provide options for 'prefer not to say' and/or 'don't know' as well. Where appropriate, consider explaining the reason for the question and how the information will be used.

Suggestion 4: Plan Inclusive Recruitment Processes

- Train recruiters and interviewers. Acknowledge that some interviewers may feel awkward meeting a candidate who looks different for the first time but provide strategies to move quickly beyond this[4] and to make the applicant feel comfortable. Training should also discuss the existence and impact of appearance bias[5] (the judgments which people make based on how someone looks). Plan interview questioning techniques in advance to reduce the opportunity for judgments about appearance and other biases to operate.[6] Consider having multiple decision-makers interviewing together to help reduce the impact of individual bias.
- If using interviews, consider carefully which interview medium to use. Non-visual interviews (e.g. by telephone or an online 'camera off' interview) can mitigate the appearance bias of interviewers and may make some candidates feel more relaxed. But non-visual interviews do not suit all candidates with visible differences, including those whose differences have an impact on speech or hearing, and those who feel more confident face to face. Some people with lived experience would like to be offered a choice of interview medium. But some of the HR experts we spoke to warned that it might be easier to form a rapport with the candidates who were interviewed face to face, so offering a choice of interview medium to candidates might disadvantage those who chose a non-visual interview. If providing a choice of medium, training for interviewers about how to assess equally across different mediums, and not to be suspicious of a candidate's reason for preferring a non-visual interview, would be an important safeguard. The nature of the

4 The charity Changing Faces has some resources: Changing Faces, 'Recruiting Someone Who Has a Visible Difference' (*Changing Faces*, undated) <www.changingfaces.org.uk/for-professionals/employers/training-guidance/fair-recruitment/> accessed 25 March 2024.

5 See Changing Faces, 'Visible Difference and Unconscious Bias Training' (n 2).

6 You can find some suggestions about planning interview questions to limit the operation of bias at CIPD, 'Selection Methods' (*CIPD*, 24 November 2023) <www.cipd.org/uk/knowledge/factsheets/selection-factsheet/#7263> accessed 25 March 2024.

job may impact too, and of course it is important to find a recruitment process which is suitable for people with lots of different types of impairment and circumstance, not just visible difference.

- In summary, we did not find one clear 'one size fits all' best approach to interview medium because there are lots of competing considerations at play, and taking into account the context is important.
- Outside of careers such as acting, it is rarely warranted to request photographs with job applications.[7] But if a candidate with a visible difference **chooses** to send an unsolicited explanation, photo or brief video of their visible difference in advance of a visual interview, asking for their consent to share this with the interviewing panel beforehand may reduce the potential for awkward reactions and increase the comfort of all involved.
- One caveat to this is that, if the unsolicited information goes beyond discussing the visible difference, it may not be appropriate to share this with interviewers. If, for example, the familiarisation video proceeds to discuss the individual's experience or suitability for the role, forwarding this to interviewers could unfairly impact the recruitment decision. Where additional information is disclosed, it may be preferable simply to relay the disclosure of a visibly different appearance, rather than all of the content. Note that it is usually not permitted to follow up by asking health-related questions to the applicant during recruitment.[8]
- Be wary of using AI to sift applications during recruitment. Depending on the technology and how it is used, there are some concerns and piecemeal evidence (yet to be fully investigated) about whether candidates could be inadvertently sifted out because a CV reveals different life experiences, or because someone's face does not conform to an expected pattern. For example, the Special Rapporteur on the Rights of Persons with Disabilities concluded in his recent UN report that 'Artificial intelligence tools are often unable to, or improperly, read the facial expressions of persons with disabilities. That can lead to their exclusion as candidates'.[9] A further indication of unintended consequences of using AI in recruitment comes from a 2021 study conducted by journalists in Germany.[10] This found that AI can itself favour candidates based on factors as diverse and whether they are

[7] Equality and Human Rights Commission, *Employment: Statutory Code of Practice* (The Stationery Office Limited 2011) para 16.42.

[8] For summary guidance on when pre-employment health questions can be asked, see Government Equalities Office, 'Equality Act 2010' (n 3).

[9] Report of the Special Rapporteur on the Rights of Persons with Disabilities for the 49th Session of the UN Human Rights Council (2022) A/HRC/49/52, 10.

[10] J Fergus (2021), 'A Bookshelf in Your Job Screening Video Makes You More Hireable to AI' (*Input*, 18 February 2021) <www.inputmag.com/culture/a-bookshelf-in-your-job-screening-video-makes-you-more-hirable-to-ai> accessed 21 March 2022. See also

wearing glasses or sitting in front of bookshelves during the interview. Until more is known about this, if using AI in recruitment, ensure that you fully understand both its deliberate parameters and its possible effects. Consider having human safety checks as well. Also be wary of blanket sifting CVs looking for unexplained gaps in employment, in case any gaps relate to visible difference or disability in some way.

- Be alive to the challenge posed by requiring candidates to undergo Automated Video Interviews or to give videoed presentations during recruitment. For some people with a visible difference, this may act as a deterrent to applying, and for others the pressure of being videoed may make it harder to perform well. Also be wary of requiring a job applicant to have their photo taken on interview day. If a photo really is necessary, could candidates be offered the chance to bring a headshot from home instead?

Suggestion 5: Consider Support Measures

- Many employers in our study chose to highlight to all staff, irrespective of health condition or disability, the opportunity to request support measures at work. This wider approach can benefit people for a number of reasons (e.g. caring responsibilities) and may be useful to people with a visible difference, many of whom do not self-identify as disabled.
- Beyond this open approach to receiving support requests, it can be very difficult for employers to know whether to offer support to an employee individually relating to a visible difference. Many employers are justifiably wary about starting this conversation for fear of offending the individual, intruding on their privacy or making unfounded assumptions. These are valid concerns. At the same time, however, many people with a visible difference may be reluctant to start the conversation, even though some of them would benefit from support measures. And it isn't always easy to tell how someone feels, because some people use outgoing social skills as a coping mechanism to hide their discomfort. We suggest that, if the employee chooses neither to request support nor to mention their visible difference to you, it may be appropriate not to raise it *unless* you become aware of a workplace 'trigger' which suggests the individual may be likely to be disadvantaged, such as:
    - Noticing that the employee is uncomfortable about performing a particular aspect of the role where appearance is highlighted, such as having their camera on during Teams calls, or speaking up during a group meeting;

Eleanor Drage and Kerry Mackereth, 'Does AI Debias Recruitment? Race, Gender and AI's "Eradication of Difference"' (2022) 35 Philosophy & Technology 89.

  - Sensing awkwardness or that they are being treated differently by other colleagues in their team;
  - Awareness that the individual has had to explain their condition to colleagues on multiple occasions;
  - Hearing third parties make insensitive remarks to or about the employee's appearance.
- Suggestions about ways for managers to start this conversation can be found below. Some employers may have access to an occupational health service which may be useful to find out about the individual's position and recommend possible adjustments.
- The type of support (if any) which might be relevant depends on the individual's preferences, the employer's context, the job requirements and the nature of any trigger event. Not everyone with a visible difference will need, or want, support or adjustments. Examples which might be relevant for some situations include the following:

  - Adjustments to hours, for example, reduction in working hours or flexible hours.
  - The ability to work from home when needed.
  - An adjustment to any Teams/Zoom policies, allowing the individual to use 'audio' only if desired.
  - Uniform adjustments (e.g. looser clothing, different fabric and long sleeves) or adjustments to 'looks' policies (e.g. relaxing a requirement to wear make-up or vice versa).
  - The ability to bring a photo from home if needed for security pass, or not to have a photo on the website if preferred.
  - Somewhere quiet to apply topical medication/change dressings if needed.
  - A locker to keep any medicines needed at work.
  - Adjustments to duties (including moving to a non-customer-facing role for a period of time if desired by the individual).
  - A mentor/buddy for difficult days.
  - Time off for medical appointments, psychological therapy, physio and related appointments.
  - Allowing a job applicant to submit a piece of written work instead of a video self-tape.
  - Allowing the individual to make contributions in writing in advance of a meeting, rather than verbally in front of others.
  - Some flexibility on seating arrangements, to ensure the individual feels as comfortable as possible.
  - The option (at the employee's request) to explain one's condition to colleagues during an information session, so that others can understand the impact it has on them. Some of the charities working in this area are willing to support these information sessions if required.

- In addition to general staff equality training, it may sometimes be appropriate to provide mentoring in private to a member of staff about how to develop an effective working relationship with a colleague who looks different. Should the person's behaviour persist and/or go beyond awkwardness, consider whether formal HR processes are appropriate.

Suggestion 6: Help with Return-to-Work Plans

- If the employee is due to return to work after acquiring a visible difference (perhaps due to an accident or sudden illness), talk to the employee about what, if anything, they would like you to say to colleagues about their return; it is important that the employee approves any messaging. A message could cover things like:
  - How they are feeling now
  - Plans for their return (e.g. whether they will undertake a reduced workload for a while, or get straight back to normal)
  - Whether they want people to ask about what happened or would prefer not to talk about it.
  - Thanks for well wishes and how they are looking forward to catching up with colleagues.
  - A photo, only if they wish.
- The employee may also value the chance to meet up socially with a trusted small circle of colleagues before returning to the office.

How to Have a Conversation about Support

Choose somewhere quiet and private, and a time where there are no deadlines looming so the employee is likely to feel relaxed. Some employees can be nervous about being summoned to see a manager or HR, so you may want to give some reassurance about the purpose of the meeting in advance.

Ask simple, open questions and let that person explain in their own words how their visible difference affects them at work and what support (if any) they feel they need. To help the person feel comfortable, it is often a good idea to mirror the language that the individual uses about their condition.[11] For example:

◦ you mentioned [your health condition/your visible difference / your birthmark]. How does that affect you at work? Is there anything we can do to support you?.

[11] Regarding appropriate language, see also Changing Faces, 'Training: Providing Good Customer Service to People with a Visible Difference' (*Changing Faces*, undated) <www.changingfaces.org.uk/for-professionals/employers/training-guidance/good-customer-service/> accessed 25 March 2024.

If the individual hasn't mentioned their condition to you at all, you could introduce the conversation another way. For example, if you have noticed that the person has encountered a difficulty of some kind at work, you could start by asking about that experience, such as follows:

- 'I wanted to have a chat about how you are finding the team meetings' or
- 'I understand that a customer was rude yesterday. Do you mind sharing with me what happened'?

Listen. What is helpful or difficult for one person may not be for another.

Beware of placing too much of a burden on the individual. It can be tempting just to ask the individual what adjustments they would like – but they may not know what would be available and may struggle to answer. It may be appropriate to raise some suggestions for the individual to consider as well, particularly those which are relevant to particular difficulties which the individual has expressed. You may want to give the individual some time to think about possible support measures and to chat it through with a friend before responding.

Consider confidentiality. Who will the conversation be shared with? How will changes be communicated if they affect others, to ensure the individual doesn't feel awkward?

Keep the conversation going. Perhaps set a review date to meet again and see how any adjustments are working out. Arrangements may also need reviewing after any transition, for example, a move to another part of the business.

Bear in mind that it may sometimes be appropriate to seek advice from Occupational Health or to refer the employee for medical or specialist support externally. Also bear in mind that some visible differences may be combined with other types of symptoms, so remember to consider adjustments there too if appropriate.

Employers may wish to provide interactive training to managers about having conversations about support to embed these principles.

****

This production of this model was funded by the VTCT Foundation.

Appendix 2

Empirical Study Information

This appendix summarises the methodology of the empirical studies referenced primarily in Chapter 4 (on the lived experience of visible difference) and Chapter 5 (on employer perspectives).

Lived Experience Study

The lived experience study took place in 2018–2019, with approval from Durham University Ethics Committee. The target group of participants was adults with a visible difference who had experience of the workplace or job market in the UK. Participants responded to adverts placed by relevant charities and on message boards for people with conditions associated with visible difference.

All interviewees self-identified as having a visible difference (defined as 'any condition or injury which alters appearance'); for both ethical and logistical reasons, no attempt was made to assess externally the extent to which any participants met this definition. Accordingly, it is possible that some of the participants would not have had a severe disfigurement (or disability) under the Act.

A full consent process – including written information and consent and an opportunity to ask questions – was carried out, and participants were offered a support sheet containing details of relevant support organisations and, where appropriate, places where legal advice on disfigurement discrimination at work could be sought.

The demographic breakdown of participants was as follows:

Interview method	Work situation	Age band	Gender identity	Race/ethnic origin
Face to face: 5 Telephone: 12	Employed: 10 Self-employed: 2 Retired: 2 Unemployed/not working: 3	0–30: 1 30–40: 3 40–50: 3 50–60: 6 60–70: 3 70+: 1	Female: 15 Male: 2 Non-binary: 0	White British: 17

Table showing the numbers of participants with figures broken into categories of interview method, work situation, age band, gender identity and race/ethnic origin.

A lack of racial and gender diversity here is acknowledged, as is minimal representation of younger people. This flowed from the self-selecting sample and the decision not to turn any willing participant away. Institutional and ethical constraints prevented the use of direct or snowball approaches, so the study relied entirely on volunteers responding to adverts. This made it very difficult to influence the diversity of the sample.

As some participants were in their 50s, 60s and 70s when interviewed, some of their recollections related to periods prior to the coming into force of the Equality Act 2010 (and its predecessor, the Disability Discrimination Act 1995). Some also referred to experiences as self-employed people, as well as during an employment relationship.

In addition, the range of conditions identified by the participants did not cover the full range of potentially appearance-altering conditions. For example, while seven participants had facial palsy, none had a burns injury, and this limited the ability to understand different experiences according to aetiology. The fact that all participants were recruited through charitable mediums may also have biased the sample towards those people in contact with relevant charities.

Employer Study

The employer study took place in 2022 with approval from Queen Mary University Ethics Committee. Participants were those who were working – or had previously worked – in an HR, people management, or equality diversity and inclusion role in a UK organisation. Advertisements were placed on relevant message boards, through relevant charities, and on various professional networking sites. Direct approaches were made to a wide range of organisations in the private, public and third sectors. Snowball sampling was also used; participants were asked to forward details of the study to any contacts who might be interested, and this yielded a small number of extra participants. Again, a full consent process was undertaken and participants were offered a support sheet containing details of relevant support organisations.

The participants came from a wide range of organisations. In total, thirteen interviews were conducted, of which ten were HR professionals (either in-house or working as a consultant) and three were in an EDI role. Demographic data of these participants was not collected as it was not directly relevant to the professional nature of the interview topic.

Both studies began with a series of questions to explore. This enabled participants' accounts to be heard with few restrictions. Given the small sample sizes, this research does not claim to represent the views of a wider community, but to create a deep understanding of the realities, experiences, meanings and perceptions described by these participants within an interpretivist framework. Once transcribed, thematic analysis (as expounded by Braun and Clarke)[1] was used to analyse the interview data.

Focus Groups

After both sets of interviews were complete, the resulting themes were used to inform the drafting of a model of good practice on appearance-inclusive workplaces. The initial draft was written by me, with feedback from colleagues in the fields of both psychology and law and from one practising employment lawyer.

Focus groups were then convened in 2023 to consult on the draft model of good practice. This was included within the ethics consent from Queen Mary University Ethics Committee. Focus group members were recruited in the same ways as the participants in the respective interview studies outlined above. A full consent process was carried out.

Two focus groups took place involving people with lived experience of visible difference, and a charity representative. Separately, an additional focus group took place with employer representatives and a different charity representative. The participants in each group were asked for their thoughts on the draft model of good practice.

After the first round of focus groups, the draft model was amended, and a further round of lived experience focus groups were conducted to review the changes made and to agree on additional amendments to the satisfaction of the groups.

[1] Virginia Braun and Victoria Clarke, 'Using Thematic Analysis in Psychology' (2006) 3 Qualitative Research in Psychology 77.

REFERENCES

Advertising Standards Agency, 'ASA Ruling on MYA Cosmetic Surgery Ltd' (ASA, 2018) <www.asa.org.uk/rulings/mya-cosmetic-surgery-ltd-a18-459775.html> accessed 11 March 2024

'Beauty and Cosmetics: The Use of Production Techniques' (ASA, 2021) <https://bit.ly/3TaHDck> accessed 7 December 2023

'Guidance on the Marketing of Surgical and Non-surgical Cosmetic Procedures' (ASA, 2023) <www.asa.org.uk/resource/cosmetic-interventions.html> accessed 11 March 2024

Albiston CR and Leachman GM, 'Law as an Instrument of Social Change' in Wright J (ed), *International Encyclopaedia of the Social and Behavioural Sciences*, vol 13 (2nd edn, Elsevier 2015)

All Party Parliamentary Group on Skin, 'The Psychological and Social Impact of Skin Diseases on People's Lives' (APPGS, 2013) <www.appgs.co.uk/publication/view/the-psychological-and-social-impact-of-skin-diseases-on-peoples-lives-final-report-2013/>

Allport GW, *The Nature of Prejudice* (Addison-Wesley 1955)

Alopecia UK, 'Types of Alopecia' (Alopecia UK, undated), <www.alopecia.org.uk/Pages/FAQs/Category/types-of-alopecia> accessed 30 January 2019

Amundson R, 'Biological Normality and the ADA' in Pickering Francis L and Silvers A (eds), *Americans with Disabilities* (Routledge 2000)

Anastasiou D and Kauffman JM, 'The Social Model of Disability: Dichotomy between Impairment and Disability' (2013) 38 Journal of Medicine and Philosophy 441

Annual Population Survey, 'Disability and Employment, UK, 2019, 2020 and 2021 Editions' (Office for National Statistics – Annual Population Survey, 2020) <https://bit.ly/3Pm8Ibq> accessed 23 January 2024

Anonymous, 'Hair Loss Reversed in Alopecia Areata Sufferers' (BBC, 18 August 2014) <www.bbc.co.uk/news/health-28834058> accessed 30 January 2019

'The Obesity Pay Gap Is Worse Than Previously Thought' (2023) <https://econ.st/3TkkkwJ> accessed 2 January 2024

Anti-Bullying Alliance, 'Appearance-Targeted Bullying' (undated) <https://anti-bullyingalliance.org.uk/tools-information/all-about-bullying/at-risk-groups/appearance-targeted-bullying> accessed 6 December 2023

Arnadottir OM, *Equality and Non-discrimination under the European Convention on Human Rights*, vol 74 (International Studies in Human Rights, Martinus Nijhoff 2003)

'A Future of Multidimensional Disadvantage Equality?' in Arnadottir OM and Quinn G (eds) *The UN Convention on the Rights of Persons with Disabilities* (Martinus Nijhoff 2009)

Atkinson MJP, Diedrichs PCP and Garbett KMM, 'Evaluating a School-Based Intervention for Body Image (Dove Confident Me: 5-Part Body Confidence Workshops for Schools) among Adolescent Girls and Boys: Results from a Cluster Randomized Controlled Effectiveness Trial' (2017) 60 Journal of Adolescent Health S5

Bajorek Z and Bevan S, *Obesity Stigma at Work: Improving Inclusion and Productivity* (PURPOSE 2020)

Baker L and Gringart E, 'Appearance in Later Life' in Harcourt D and Rumsey N (eds), *The Oxford Handbook of the Psychology of Appearance* (Oxford University Press 2012)

Bankhead C, 'Tattoo Me: Tales of Regret and No Regrets' (Medpage, 2013) <www.medpagetoday.com/meetingcoverage/aad/37730> accessed 25 October 2023

Barmes L, *Bullying and Behavioural Conflict at Work: The Duality of Individual Rights* (Oxford University Press 2016)

'Equality Law and Experimentation: The Positive Action Challenge' (2009) 68 The Cambridge Law Journal 623

Barmes L and Malleson K, 'The Case for Caution in Making Social Class a Protected Characteristic under the UK's Equality Act 2010' (Oxford Human Rights Hub, 2023) <https://ohrh.law.ox.ac.uk/the-case-for-caution-in-making-social-class-a-protected-characteristic-under-the-uks-equality-act-2010/> accessed 3 August 2023

Barnard C, *Reflexive Law, Corporate Social Responsibility and the Evolution of Labour Standards: The Case of Working Time* (ERSC Centre for Business Research, University of Cambridge 2004)

Barnard C and Hepple B, 'Substantive Equality' (2000) 59 The Cambridge Law Journal 562

Barro RJ, 'So You Want to Hire the Beautiful. Well Why Not?' (Business Week) <https://scholar.harvard.edu/files/barro/files/98_0316_hire_bw.pdf> accessed 1 March 2018

Barth I and Wagner A-L, 'Physical Appearance as Invisible Discrimination' (2017) 4 International Perspectives on Equality, Diversity and Inclusion 127

Basire Y and Le Goffic C, 'To Be or Not to Be… Photoshopped?' (2018) 13 Journal of Intellectual Property Law & Practice 177

BBC, 'War on Plastic with Hugh and Anita' (BBC, 2020)

BCAP, 'The UK Code of Broadcast Advertising (BCAP Code) v12.2.52' (ASA, undated)

Beaver KM and others, 'Physical Attractiveness and Criminal Justice Processing: Results from a Longitudinal Sample of Youth and Young Adults' (2019) 26 Psychiatry, Psychology and Law 669

Bedell G, 'Girl, Interrupted' *The Guardian* (London, 5 May 2002) <www.theguardian.com/theobserver/2002/may/05/features.review27> accessed 15 August 2019

Bell M, *Racism and Equality in the European Union* (Oxford University Press 2008)

Benedi Lahuerta S, Rejchrt P and Patrick A, 'The UK Pay Transparency Regulations: Apparent Transparency without Accountability?' (2023) Legal Studies (Society of Legal Scholars) 1

Bennett C, 'At Long Last, a Newsreader Who Made Us Face Reality' *The Guardian* (22 November 2009) <www.theguardian.com/commentisfree/2009/nov/22/james-partridge-tv-newsreaders> accessed 8 November 2023

Berghs M, Atkin K and Graham H, 'Implications for Public Health Research of Models and Theories of Disability: A Scoping Study and Evidence Synthesis' (2016) NIHR Journals Library

Berry B, *Appearance Bias and Crime* (Cambridge University Press 2019)

The Power of Looks: Social Stratification of Physical Appearance (Ashgate 2008)

Bicchieri C, *Norms in the Wild: How to Diagnose, Measure, and Change Social Norms* (Oxford University Press 2017)

Bickenbach J, 'Disability Human Rights, Law and Policy' in Albrecht G, Seelman K and Bury M (eds), *Handbook of Disability Studies* (Sage 2001)

Black E, *War against the Weak: Eugenics and America's Campaign to Create a Master Race* (Four Walls Eight Windows 2003)

Black HC, 'Black's Legal Dictionary Online' (2019) <thelawdictionary.org.uk> accessed 18 March 2024

Blackham A, 'Abandoning Individual Enforcement? Interrogating the Enforcement of Age Discrimination Law' (2023) 43 Legal Studies (Society of Legal Scholars) 3

'Reflexive Change? A Quantitative Review of the Impact of the Equality Act 2010 on Age Equality Measures in Organizations' (2016) 16 International Journal of Discrimination and the Law 122

Reforming Age Discrimination Law: Beyond Individual Enforcement (Oxford University Press 2022)

Blake VK and Hatzenbuehler ML, 'Legal Remedies to Address Stigma-Based Health Inequalities in the United States: Challenges and Opportunities' (2019) 97 The Milbank Quarterly 480

Bocker A, 'Can Non-Discrimination Law Change Hearts and Minds?' (2020) 13 Erasmus Law Review 21

Bogart KR, Bryson BA and Harcourt D, 'Disclosing the Obvious: Psychosocial Implications of (Not) Explaining Facial Differences' (2023) 46 Body Image 91

Bogg A, 'Beyond Neo-Liberalism: The Trade Union Act 2016 and the Authoritarian State' (2016) 45 Industrial Law Journal 299

Bond BJ, 'The Development and Influence of Parasocial Relationships with Television Characters: A Longitudinal Experimental Test of Prejudice Reduction through Parasocial Contact' (2021) 48 Communication Research 573

Braun V and Clarke V, 'Using Thematic Analysis in Psychology' (2006) 3 Qualitative Research in Psychology 77

British Association of Dermatologists, 'Alopecia Areata' (BAD, July 2020) <www.bad.org.uk/shared/get-file.ashx?id¼68&itemtype¼document> accessed 9 February 2024

British Psychological Society, 'BPS Launches #Makeit10 Campaign' (2022) <www.bps.org.uk/psychologist/bps-launches-makeit10-campaign> accessed 25 October 2023

Broderick A, 'The Long and Winding Road to Equality and Inclusion for Persons with Disabilities' (PhD dissertation, Maastricht University 2015)

'A Reflection on Substantive Equality Jurisprudence' (2015) 15 International Journal of Discrimination and the Law 101

Brown A and Flint SW, 'Preferences and Emotional Response to Weight Related Terminology Used by Healthcare Professionals to Describe Body Weight in People Living with Overweight and Obesity' (2021) 11 Clinical Obesity e12470

Buck DW and Herbst KL, 'Lipedema: A Relatively Common Disease with Extremely Common Misconceptions' (2016) Plastic Reconstructive Surgery Global Open 1043

Bull R, 'The General Public's Reactions to Facial Disfigurement' in Graham JA and Kligman AM (eds), *The Psychology of Cosmetic Treatments* (Praeger 1985)

Bull R and Stevens J, 'The Effects of Facial Disfigurement on Helping Behaviour' (1981) 8 Italian Journal of Psychology 25

Bumiller K, *The Civil Rights Society: The Social Construction of Victims / Kristin Bumiller* (Johns Hopkins University Press 1988)

Burmeister JM and others, 'Reducing Obesity Stigma via a Brief Documentary Film: A Randomized Trial' (2017) 2 Stigma and Health 43

Cahners S, 'Young Women with Breast Burns: A Self-Help "Group by Mail"' (1992) 13 Journal of Burn Care and Rehabilitation 44

CAP, 'UK Code of Non-broadcast Advertising and Direct & Promotional Marketing (CAP Code) Edition 12 v12.2.88' (Advertising Standards Agency, 2014)

Carbonara E, 'Law and Social Norms' in Parisi F (ed), *The Oxford Handbook of Law and Economics* (Oxford University Press 2017)

CareerBuilder, 'Number of Employers Using Social Media to Screen Candidates at All-Time High, Finds Latest CareerBuilder Study' *PR Newswire* <https://prn.to/3IGytQ1> accessed 5 September 2023

Carlsson IK, Dahlin LB and Rosberg HE, 'Congenital Thumb Anomalies and the Consequences for Daily Life: Patients' Long-Term Experience after Corrective Surgery. A Qualitative Study' (2018) 40 Disability and Rehabilitation 69

Cavico FJ, Muffler SC and Mujtaba BG, 'Appearance Discrimination in Employment' (2012) 32 Equality, Diversity and Inclusion: An International Journal 83

Chambers C, *Intact: A Defence of the Unmodified Body* (Penguin Books 2022)

Changing Faces, 'Disfigurement in the UK' (Changing Faces, 2017)

'Evidence (EQD0131) (of Lords Select Committee on the Equality Act 2010 and Disability 2015)'

'I Am Not Your Villain: Equal Representation of Visible Difference in Film' (Changing Faces, undated) <www.changingfaces.org.uk/get-involved/campaign-with-us/i-am-not-your-villian/> accessed 7 December 2023

'Recruiting Someone Who Has a Visible Difference' (Changing Faces, undated) <www.changingfaces.org.uk/for-professionals/employers/training-guidance/fair-recruitment/accessed> accessed 25 March 2024

'Strategy Survey' (Changing Faces 2021)

'Training: Providing Good Customer Service to People with a Visible Difference' (Changing Faces, undated) <www.changingfaces.org.uk/for-professionals/employers/training-guidance/good-customer-service/> accessed 25 March 2024

'Visible Difference and Unconscious Bias Training' (Changing Faces, undated) <www.changingfaces.org.uk/for-professionals/employers/training-guidance/unconscious-bias-training/> accessed 25 March 2024

'What Is Visible Difference?' (Changing Faces, undated) <www.changingfaces.org.uk/about-visible-difference/what-is-visible-difference/> accessed 8 November 2023

Chen MKY and others, 'The Spectre of Visible Difference: Semiotics of Disfigurement and Moral Character in James Bond Films' (2022) 47 Clinical and Experimental Dermatology 767

Children's Commission, 'Young People with Eating Disorders on the Rise in England' (2023) <www.childrenscommissioner.gov.uk/media-centre/young-people-with-eating-disorders-on-the-rise-in-england/> accessed 8 December 2023

Chua LJ and Engel DM, 'Legal Consciousness Reconsidered' (2019) 15 Annual Review of Law and Social Science 335

Cialdini R and Goldstein N, 'Social Influence: Compliance and Conformity' (2004) 55 Annual Review of Psychology 591

CIPD, 'Inclusive Recruitment: Guide for Employers' (CIPD, 2022) <www.cipd.org/uk/knowledge/guides/inclusive-employers/#role-design-and-the-job-advert> accessed 24 October 2023

CIPD, 'Selection Methods' (CIPD, 24 November 2023) <www.cipd.org/uk/knowledge/factsheets/selection-factsheet/#7263> accessed 25 March 2024

Committee of Advertising Practice, 'ASA Adjudication on Yves Saint Laurent SAS t/a Saint Laurent Paris A15–292161' (ASA, 2015) <www.asa.org.uk/rulings/yves-saint-laurent-sas-a15-292161.html> accessed 11 March 2024

Committee on Advertising Practice, 'Social Responsibility: Body Image' (CAP, 2022) <www.asa.org.uk/advice-online/social-responsibility-body-image.html> accessed 8 March 2024

Committee of Advertising Practice and Broadcast Committee of Advertising Practice, 'Digitally Altered Images – Update Statement' (CAP / BCAP, 2023) <www.asa.org.uk/resource/digitally-altered-images-update-statement.html> accessed 11 March 2024

Corby S, William L and Richard S, 'Combatting Disability Discrimination: A Comparison of France and Great Britain' (2019) 25 European Journal of Industrial Relations 41

Cotterrell R, *Law, Culture and Society Legal Ideas in the Mirror of Social Theory* (Ashgate 2006)

The Sociology of Law: An Introduction (2nd edn, Butterworths 1992)

Cowan D, 'Legal Consciousness: Some Observations' (2004) 67 Modern Law Review 928

Craddock N and others, 'Can Big Business Foster Positive Body Image? Qualitative Insights from Industry Leaders Walking the Talk' (2019) 30 Body Image 93

Cranwell W, Sinclair R and Asfour L, 'Male Androgenetic Alopecia' (Endotext, 2023) <www.ncbi.nlm.nih.gov/books/NBK278957/> accessed 9 February 2024

Croley JA, Reese V and Wagner RF, 'Dermatologic Features of Classic Movie Villains: The Face of Evil' (2017) 153 JAMA Dermatology 559

Crossley M, 'Impairment and Embodiment' in Pickering Francis L and Silvers A (eds), *Americans with Disabilities* (Routledge 2000)

Crow L, 'Renewing the Social Model of Disability' (Roaring Girl Productions, July 1992) <www.roaring-girl.com/work/renewing-the-social-model-of-disability/> accessed 25 June 2019

Davies C and others, 'Bridging the Gap' (2016) 16 International Journal of Discrimination and the Law 83

Davis F, 'Deviance Disavowal: The Management of Strained Interaction by the Visibly Handicapped' (1961) 9 Social Problems 120

De Beco G, 'Is Obesity a Disability? The Definition of Disability by the Court of Justice of the European Union and Its Consequences for the Application of EU Anti-Discrimination Law' (2016) 22 Columbia Journal of European Law 381.

Deakin S, Mclaughlin C and Chai D, 'Gender Inequality and Reflexive Law: The Potential of Difference Regulatory Mechanisms' in Dickens L (ed), *Making Employment Rights Effective* (Hart 2012)

DEFRA, '10p Bag Charge Turns the Tide on Plastic Waste' (2022) <www.gov.uk/government/news/10p-bag-charge-turns-the-tide-on-plastic-waste> accessed 18 March 2024

Degener T, 'Disability in a Human Rights Context' (2016) 5 Laws 35

Dell L and Prior J, 'Evaluating a Schools' Service for Children with a Facial Disfigurement: The Views of Teaching and Support Staff' (2005) 20 Support for Learning 35

Denault V, 'Guilty or Innocent? In Virtual Courtrooms, the Absence of Non-verbal Cues May Threaten Justice' *The Conversation* (7 October 2020) <https://theconversation.com/guilty-or-innocent-in-virtual-courtrooms-the-absence-of-non-verbal-cues-may-threaten-justice-145371> accessed 21 November 23

Department for Work and Pensions, 'Disability Confident Employer Scheme' (2021) <www.gov.uk/government/collections/disability-confident-campaign> accessed 7 December 2023

'How to Sign Up to the Disability Confident Employer Scheme' (UK Government, 2019) <www.gov.uk/guidance/disability-confident-how-to-sign-up-to-the-employer-scheme#why-you-should-become-disability-confident> accessed 16 February 2024

Department for Work and Pensions and Disability Unit, *UN Committee on the Rights of Persons with Disabilities 2016 Inquiry – UK 2021 Follow-Up Report* (UK Government 2021)

Dion K, Berscheid E and Walster E, 'What Is Beautiful Is Good' (1972) 24 Journal of Personality and Social Psychology 28

Domoff SE and others, 'The Effects of Reality Television on Weight Bias: An Examination of *The Biggest Loser*' (2012) 20 Obesity 993

Downs AC and Lyons PM, 'Natural Observations of the Links between Attractiveness and Initial Legal Judgments' (1991) 17 Personality & Social Psychology Bulletin 541

Doyle L, Easterbrook MJ and Harris PR, 'Roles of Socioeconomic Status, Ethnicity and Teacher Beliefs in Academic Grading' (2023) 93 British Journal of Educational Psychology 91

Drage E and Mackereth K, 'Does AI Debias Recruitment? Race, Gender, and AI's Eradication of Difference' (2022) 35 Philosophy & Technology 89

Dror Y, 'Law and Social Change' (1958) 33 Tulane Law Review 787

Duchini E and others, 'Pay Transparency and Gender Equality' (2020) arXivorg

Dukes R and Kirk E, 'Law, Economy and Legal Consciousness at Work' (2022) 72 Northern Ireland Legal Quarterly 741

Efran MG, 'The Effect of Physical Appearance on the Judgment of Guilt, Interpersonal Attraction, and Severity of Recommended Punishment in a Simulated Jury Task' (1974) 8 Journal of Research in Personality 45

Egan K, Harcourt D and Rumsey N, 'A Qualitative Study of the Experiences of People Who Identify Themselves as Having Adjusted Positively to a Visible Difference' (2011) 16 Journal of Health Psychology 739

Eiserman W, 'Unique Outcomes and Positive Contributions Associated with Facial Difference: Expanding Research and Practice' (2001) 38 The Cleft Palate-Craniofacial Journal 236

Elliott L, 'What's So Scary about Disability?' (The Establishment, 2018) <https://theestablishment.co/whats-so-scary-about-disability/index.html> accessed 7 February 2024

Equality and Human Rights Commission, *Employment Statutory Code of Practice* (The Stationery Office Limited 2011)

Equality and Human Rights Commission, 'Our Litigation and Enforcement Policy 2019–2022' (EHRC, 2019) <www.equalityhumanrights.com/sites/default/files/our-litigation-and-enforcement-policy-2019-2022_0.pdf> accessed 7 November 23

Religion or Belief: Dress Codes and Religious Symbols (2018) <www.equalityhumanrights.com/guidance/religion-or-belief-workplace/religion-or-belief-dress-codes-and-religious-symbols> accessed 19 March 2024

Sexual Harassment and Harassment at Work (EHRC, 2020) <www.equalityhumanrights.com/sites/default/files/sexual_harassment_and_harassment_at_work.pdf> accessed 22 March 2024

Etcoff NL, *Survival of the Prettiest: The Science of Beauty* (Little, Brown 1999)

Etinson A, 'What's So Special about Human Dignity?' (2020) 48 Philosophy and Public Affairs 353

Evan WM, *Law and Sociology: Exploratory Essays / Edited by William M. Evan with a Foreword by Lehan K. Tunks* (Free Press of Glencoe 1962)

Evans L, 'Body Image Pledge' (undated) <www.drlukeevans.org.uk/body-image> accessed 7 December 2023

Ewick P, *The Common Place of Law: Stories from Everyday Life* (University of Chicago Press 1998)

Ezzati M and others, 'Height and Body-Mass Index Trajectories of School-Aged Children and Adolescents from 1985 to 2019 in 200 Countries and Territories: A Pooled Analysis of 2181 Population-Based Studies with 65 Million Participants' (2020) 396 The Lancet 1511

Face Equality International, 'Face Equality Is a Human Right' (Face Equality International, 2022) <https://faceequalityinternational.org/wp-content/uploads/2022/05/Face-Equality-is-a-Human-Right-Report.pdf> accessed 7 November 2023

Faces C, 'I Am Not Your Villain: Equal Representation of Visible Difference in Film' (undated) <www.changingfaces.org.uk/get-involved/campaign-with-us/i-am-not-your-villian/> accessed 8 September 2023

Fawkner H, 'Gender' in Harcourt D and Rumsey N (eds), *The Oxford Handbook of the Psychology of Appearance* (Oxford University Press 2012)

Fergus J, 'A Bookshelf in Your Job Screening Video Makes You More Hireable to AI' (2021) <www.inputmag.com/culture/a-bookshelf-in-your-job-screening-video-makes-you-more-hirable-to-ai> accessed 21 March 2024

Ford M, 'Employment Tribunal Fees and the Rule of Law: R (Unison) v Lord Chancellor in the Supreme Court' (2018) 47 Industrial Law Journal 1

Foulkes L and Stringaris A, 'Do No Harm: Can School Mental Health Interventions Cause Iatrogenic Harm?' (2023) 47 BJPsych Bulletin 267

Fredman S, *Discrimination Law* (2nd edn, Oxford University Press 2011)

'Emerging from the Shadows: Substantive Equality and Article 14 of the European Convention on Human Rights' (2016) 16 Human Rights Law Review 273

'The Public Sector Equality Duty' (2011) 40 Industrial Law Journal 405

'Substantive Equality Revisited' (2016) 14 International Journal of Constitutional Law 712

Freysteinson WM and others, 'Educating Nurses on Supported Mirror Viewing for Patients after Amputation and Other Visible Disfigurements' (2021) 46 Rehabilitation Nurse 43

Friedman LM, *Impact: How Law Affects Behavior* (Harvard University Press 2017)

Galanter M, *The Radiating Effects of Courts* (Empirical Theories of Courts, 1983)

'Why the Haves Come out Ahead: Speculations on the Limits of Legal Change' (2013) 85 Droit et société 575

Genetic and Rare Diseases Information Center, 'Wrinkly Skin Syndrome' (National Center for Advancing Translational Sciences, 2016) <https://rarediseases.info.nih.gov/diseases/273/wrinkly-skin-syndrome> accessed 1 February 2019

Gillig TK and Murphy ST, 'Fostering Support for LGBTQ Youth? The Effects of a Gay Adolescent Media Portrayal on Young Viewers' (2016) International Journal of Communication 3828

Ginsburg I and Link B, 'Psychosocial Consequences of Rejection and Stigma in Patients with Psoriasis' (1993) 32 International Journal of Dermatology 587

Giordano S, 'Understanding the Emotion of Shame in Transgender Individuals: Some Insight from Kafka' (2018) 14 Life Sciences, Society and Policy 23

Goffman I, *Notes on the Management of Spoiled Identity* (Penguin 1963)

Gooding C, *Disabling Laws, Enabling Acts: Disability Rights in Britain and America* (Pluto Press 1994)

Gouvier WD and others, 'Employment Discrimination against Handicapped Job Candidates: An Analog Study of the Effects of Neurological Causation, Visibility of Handicap, and Public Contact' (1991) 36 Rehabilitation Psychology 121

Government Equalities Office, 'Equality Act 2010: What Do I Need to Know? A Quick Start Guide to the Ban on Questions about Health and Disability during Recruitment' (UK Government, 2011) https://assets.publishing

.service.gov.uk/government/uploads/system/uploads/attachment_data/file/85013/employment-health-questions.pdf accessed 25 March 2024.

Gregory A, 'More than 42m UK Adults 'Will Be Overweight by 2040'" *The Guardian* (19 May 2022) <www.theguardian.com/society/2022/may/19/more-than-42m-uk-adults-will-be-overweight-by-2040> accessed 28 March 2023

Hamermesh DS, *Beauty Pays* (Princeton University Press 2011)

Harisha Y, 'I Felt Like the Fat Girl on *Love Island* and Was Killing Myself Doing Workouts to Slim My Legs, Says Shaughna Phillips' *The Sun* <www.thesun.co.uk/fabulous/13500351/shaughna-phillips-lipoedema-battle/> accessed 28 March 2023

Harris JE, 'The Aesthetics of Disability' (2019) 119 Columbia Law Review 895

Hartung F and others, 'Behavioural and Neural Responses to Facial Disfigurement' (2019) 9 Scientific Reports 8021

HC Deb (Standing Committee E) 7 February 1995, per David Hansen.

Hepple B, 'Enforcing Equality Law: Two Steps Forward and Two Steps Backwards for Reflexive Regulation' (2011) 40 Industrial Law Journal 315

'The New Single Equality Act in Britain' (2010) 5 The Equal Rights Review 11

Herring C, 'Does Diversity Pay?: Race, Gender, and the Business Case for Diversity' (2009) 74 American Sociological Review 208

Hinshaw SP, *The Mark of Shame: Stigma of Mental Illness and an Agenda for Change* (Oxford University Press 2006)

Hirsh CE and Louie P, 'Legal Consciousness, Mobilization, and Discrimination Disputes at Work', *The Oxford Handbook of Workplace Discrimination* (Oxford University Press 2018)

House of Commons Committee on Health and Social Care, 'The Impact of Body Image on Mental and Physical Health' (Second Report of 2022–2023, HC114).

House of Commons Women and Equalities Committee, 'Changing the Perfect Picture: An Inquiry into Body Image' (Sixth Report of Session 2019--2021, HC274)

'Enforcing the Equality Act: the Law and the Role of the Equality and Human Rights Commission' (Tenth Report of Session 2017–2019, HC1470)

House of Lords and House of Commons Joint Committee on Human Rights, 'Implementation Of the Right Of Disabled People to Independent Living' (23rd Report of Session 2010–2012, HL257 & HC 1074)

House of Lords Debate, 1995, vol 564, col 1642.

House of Lords Select Committee, 'The Equality Act 2010: The Impact on Disabled People' (Session 2015–2016, HL117)

Houston V and Bull R, 'Do People Avoid Sitting Next to Someone Who Is Facially Disfigured?' (1994) 24 European Journal of Social Psychology 279

Hughes J and others, 'South Asian Community Views about Individuals with a Disfigurement' (2009) 6 Diversity and Equality in Health Care 241

Humane Research Council, 'Study of Current and Former Vegetarians and Vegans: Initial Findings' (Faunalytics, 2014) <https://bit.ly/43qxBZq> accessed 19 December 2023

Hurstfield J and others, 'Monitoring the Disability Discrimination Act (DDA) 1995: Phase 3' (Disability Rights Commission, Department for Work and Pensions and the Equality Commission (Northern Ireland), 2004)

International Labour Organisation, 'Promoting Employment Opportunities for People with Disabilities: Quota Schemes' (2019) vol 1

Ishida Y and others, 'Skin Findings of Twenty-first Century Movie Characters' (2017) 32 Journal of the European Academy of Dermatology and Venereology

ITV News, 'Ex-CBeebies Presenter: 'Parents Criticised My Decision Not to Wear Prosthetic Arm''' (2017) <www.itv.com/news/2017-05-04/ex-cbeebies-presenter-cerrie-burnell-parents-rang-up-complaining-about-my-arm/> accessed 31 January 2019

James H, 'If You Are Attractive and You Know It, Please Apply: Appearance Based Discrimination and Employers' Discretion' (2008) 42 Valparaiso University Law Review 629

Jamrozik A and others, 'More Than Skin Deep: Judgments of Individuals with Facial Disfigurement' (2017) 13 Psychology of Aesthetics, Creativity, and the Arts 117

Jarvis A, 'James Partridge Obituary' The Guardian (London, 27 August 2020) <www.theguardian.com/society/2020/aug/27/james-partridge-obituary> accessed 6 December 2023

Javed S, 'Linda Evangelista Settles Lawsuit over Cosmetic Procedure That Left Her 'Permanently Deformed''' *The Independent* (20 July 2022) <www.independent.co.uk/life-style/fashion/linda-evangelista-coolsculpting-lawsuit-settle-b2127213.html> accessed 5 September 2023

Jones G and Stone D, 'Perceived Discomfort Associated with Working with Persons with Varying Disabilities' (1995) 81 Perceptual and Motor Skills 911

Jowett S and Ryan T, 'Skin Disease and Handicap: An Analysis of the Impact of Skin Conditions' (1985) 20 Social Science & Medicine 425

Judicial College, *Guidelines for the Assessment of General Damages in Personal Injury Cases*, vol 14 (Oxford University Press 2017)

Kahan DM, 'Gentle Nudges vs. Hard Shoves: Solving the Sticky Norms Problem' (2000) 67 The University of Chicago Law Review 607

Kanter AS, *The Development of Disability Rights under International Law* (Routledge 2015)

Kaplan M, *The Inclusion Dividend: Why Investing in Diversity & Inclusion Pays Off* (Bibliomotion 2013)

Kattlove J, 'Open Letter – The Impact of Portraying Villainous Character, Frank Nakai, with Scars in TV Series *Dark Winds*' (Face Equality International,

2022) <https://faceequalityinternational.org/2022/09/openletter-darkwinds/> accessed 8 November 23

Keegan N, 'Instagram Removed Photo of Boy with Facial Deformity for Violating 'Guidelines''' *The Sun* <https://nypost.com/2017/09/13/instagram-removed-photo-of-boy-with-facial-deformity-for-violating-guidelines/> accessed 17 October 2023

Kenealy P, Frude N and Shaw W, 'Influence of Children's Physical Attractiveness on Teacher Expectations' (1988) 128 The Journal of Social Psychology 373

Kent G and Keohane S, 'Social Anxiety and Disfigurement: The Moderating Effects of Fear of Negative Evaluation and Past Experience' (2001) 40 British Journal of Clinical Psychology 23

King B, 'Ladbrokes Claimed £102m Furlough Despite Online Boost' *BBC* (7 January 2022) <www.bbc.co.uk/news/business-59900249> accessed 16 February 2024

Kirby P, 'Battle Scars: Wonder Woman, Aesthetic Geopolitics and Disfigurement in Hollywood Film' (2020) 25 Geopolitics 916

Kirk E, 'Law and Legalities at Work: HR Practitioners as Quasi-Legal Professionals' (2021) 50 Industrial Law Journal 583

Kirk E and Busby N, 'Led Up the Tribunal Path? Employment Disputes, Legal Consciousness and Trust in the Protection of Law' (2017) 7 Onati Socio-Legal Series 1397

Kirkland A, 'Think of the Hippopotamus: Rights Consciousness in the Fat Acceptance Movement' (2008) 42 Law & Society Review 397

Kleck RE and Strenta A, 'Perceptions of the Impact of Negatively Valued Physical Characteristics on Social Interaction' (1980) 39 Journal of Personality and Social Psychology 861

Klecker C and Grabher GM, *The Disfigured Face in American Literature, Film, and Television* (1st edn, Routledge 2021)

Krawitz M, 'Beauty Is Only Photoshop Deep: Legislating Models' BMIs and Photoshopping Images' (2014) 21 Journal of Law and Medicine 859

Krieger LH, 'Afterword: Socio-Legal Backlash' (2000) 21 Berkeley Journal of Employment and Labor Law 476

Labour Party, 'Nothing about You, without You: A Manifesto with and for Disabled People' (2017) https://labour.org.uk/manifesto/a-more-equal-society/#fifth accessed 4 July 2018

Langlois JH, *Maxims or Myths of Beauty?: A Meta-analytic and Theoretical Review* (American Psychological Association 2000)

Lawrence J and others, 'Visible vs Hidden Scars and Their Relation to Body Esteem' (2004) 25 Journal of Burn Care and Rehabilitation 25

Lawson A, 'Disability and Employment in the Equality Act 2010: Opportunities Seized, Lost and Generated' (2011) 40 Industrial Law Journal 359

Lawson A and Beckett AE, 'The Social and Human Rights Models of Disability: Towards a Complementarity Thesis' (2021) 25 The International Journal of Human Rights 348

Le Défenseur des droits, 'Decision MLD-2014-147 of 3 November 2014 on Discriminatory Recruitment Procedures in Relation to the Physical Appearance of Candidates' <https://juridique.defenseurdesdroits.fr/index.php?lvl=notice_display&id=12325> accessed 7 December 2023

Le Défenseur des Droits et L'Organisation Internationale du Travail, '13e barometre: La perception des discriminations dans l'emploi' (Defenseur des Droits, 2020)

Le Monde, 'French Court Backs Miss France Beauty Contest against Feminists' (Le Monde, Paris) <https://bit.ly/3VsxR84> accessed 22 March 2023

Levin S, 'A Beauty Contest Was Judged by AI and the Robots Didn't Like Dark Skin' *The Guardian* (8 September 2016) <https://bit.ly/3TBBQxH> accessed 5 September 2023

Lewis P, 'Disability Discrimination Act: 1995 and Now' (House of Lords Library, 2020) <https://lordslibrary.parliament.uk/disability-discrimination-act-1995-and-now/> accessed 14 February 2024

Lien Y-Y and others, 'Challenging Mental Illness Stigma in Healthcare Professionals and Students: A Systematic Review and Network Meta-analysis' (2021) 36 Psychology & Health 669

Lopez J, 'Unconscious Bias Training' (UK Parliament, HCWS652, 15 December 2020) <https://questions-statements.parliament.uk/written-statements/detail/2020-12-15/hcws652> accessed 7 December 2023

Lucy W, 'Abstraction and the Rule of Law' (2009) 29 Oxford Journal of Legal Studies 481

Luis S and Palma-Oliveira J, 'Public Policy and Social Norms: The Case of a Nationwide Smoking Ban among College Students' (2016) 22 Psychology, Public Policy, and Law 22

Lustgarten L, 'Problems of Proof in Employment Discrimination Cases' (1977) 6 Industrial Law Journal 212

Macgregor FC, 'Facial Disfigurement: Problems and Management of Social Interaction and Implications for Mental Health' (1990) 14 Official Journal of the International Society of Plastic Surgery 249

'Social and Psychological Implications of Dentofacial Disfigurement' (1970) 40 The Angle Orthodontist 231

MacKinnon CA, *Sexual Harassment of Working Women: A Case of Sex Discrimination* (Yale University Press 1979)

'Substantive Equality Revisited: A Reply to Sandra Fredman' (2016) 14 International Journal of Constitutional Law 739

'Where #MeToo Came From, and Where It's Going' *The Atlantic* (24 March 2019) <www.theatlantic.com/ideas/archive/2019/03/catharine-mackinnon-what-metoo-has-changed/585313/> accessed 17 October 2023

Madera JM and Hebl MR, 'Discrimination against Facially Stigmatized Applicants in Interviews: An Eye-Tracking and Face-to-Face Investigation' (2012) 97 Journal of Applied Psychology 317

Malek H, *Phipson on Evidence* (19th edn, Sweet and Maxwell, 2017)

Malleson K, 'Diversity in the Judiciary: The Case for Positive Action' (2009) 36 Journal of Law and Society 376

'Equality Law and the Protected Characteristics' (2018) 81 Modern Law Review 598

Manfredi S, Vickers L and Clayton-Hathway K, 'The Public Sector Equality Duty: Enforcing Equality Rights through Second-Generation Regulation' (2018) 47 Industrial Law Journal 365

Masnari O and others, 'Self- and Parent- Perceived Stigmatisation in Children and Adolescents with Congenital or Acquired Facial Differences' (2012) 65 Journal of Plastic, Reconstructive & Aesthetic Surgery 1664

Mason A and Minerva F, 'Should the Equality Act 2010 Be Extended to Prohibit Appearance Discrimination?' (2022) 70 Political Studies 425

Matthews A, Costa B and Harcourt D, '"Scars: How Our Wounds Make Us Who We Are": Improving Appearance-Based Stigma, Conceptualisation of Beauty and Body Esteem through a Documentary' (2023) 9 Scars, Burns and Healing

McAdams RH, *The Expressive Powers of Law: Theories and Limits* (1st edn, Harvard University Press 2015)

McComb SE and Mills JS, 'A Systematic Review on the Effects of Media Disclaimers on Young Women's Body Image and Mood' (2020) 32 Body Image 34

McCrudden C, 'Human Dignity and Judicial Interpretation of Human Rights' (2008) 19 European Journal of International Law 655

McDonald JJ, 'Lookism: The Next Form of Illegal Discrimination' (Bloomberg Law Reports, 2010) <www.fisherphillips.com/en/news-insights/lookism-the-next-form-of-illegal-discrimination.html> accessed 8 December 2023

McLaughlin C, 'Equal Pay, Litigation and Reflexive Regulation: The Case of the UK Local Authority Sector' (2014) 43 Industrial Law Journal 1

McPhail D and Orsini M, 'Fat Acceptance as Social Justice' (2021) 193 Canadian Medical Association Journal E1398

McTigue P, 'From Navas to Kaltoft' (2015) 15 International Journal of Discrimination and the Law 241

McWilliam Reynolds A, 'What New Research about the Impact of COVID-19 on Charities' (Charities Commission, 2021) <https://charitycommission.blog.gov.uk/2021/10/28/what-new-research-tells-us-about-the-impact-of-covid-19-on-charities/> accessed 16 February 2024

Mehic A, 'Student Beauty and Grades under In-Person and Remote Teaching' (2022) 219 Economics Letters 110782

Merry SE, *Getting Justice and Getting Even: Legal Consciousness among Working-Class Americans / Sally Engle Merry* (University of Chicago Press, 1990)

Meyerson MD, 'Resiliency and Success in Adults with Moebius Syndrome' (2001) 38 The Cleft Palate-Craniofacial Journal 231

Middlemiss S, 'Protection against Discrimination on the Ground of Looks? Primmer v Mayflower Kebabs Ltd', Employment Law, Issue 80, October 2007

Minerva F, 'The Invisible Discrimination before Our Eyes: A Bioethical Analysis' (2017) 31 Bioethics 180

Moss TP and Rosser B, 'Adult Psychosocial Adjustment to Visible Differences: Physical and Psychological Predictors of Variation' in Rumsey N and Harcourt N (eds), *Oxford Handbook of the Psychology of Appearance* (Oxford University Press 2012)

Murgia M, 'Emotion Recognition: Can AI Detect Human Feelings from a Face?' *Financial Times* (London, 12 May 2021) <www.ft.com/content/c0b03d1d-f72f-48a8-b342-b4a926109452> accessed 7 December 2023

Murrar S and Brauer M, 'Entertainment-Education Effectively Reduces Prejudice' (2018) 21 Group Processes & Intergroup Relations 1053

Nadler J, 'Expressive Law, Social Norms, and Social Groups' (2017) 42 Law & Social Inquiry 60

Nadler J and Bilz K, 'Law, Moral Attitudes, and Behavioral Change' in Zamir E and Teichman D (eds), *The Oxford Handbook of Behavioral Economics and the Law* (Oxford University Press 2014)

Naqvi H and Krysia S, 'Culture and Ethnicity' in Rumsey N and Harcourt D (eds), *The Oxford Handbook of the Psychology of Appearance* (Oxford University Press 2012)

Newell R and Marks I, 'Phobic Nature of Social Difficulty in Facially Disfigured People' (2000) 176 The British Journal of Psychiatry: The Journal of Mental Science 177

Nussbaum MC, *Creating Capabilities: The Human Development Approach* (Harvard University Press 2011)

Women and Human Development: The Capabilities Approach, vol 3 (1st edn, Cambridge University Press 2000)

O'Connell R, 'The Role of Dignity in Equality Law: Lessons from Canada and South Africa' (2008) 6 International Journal of Constitutional Law 267

O'Dea Z and Southcott J, 'My Mummy Has a Hole in Her Face: Living with Facial Eye Disfigurement' (2023) 28 Qualitative Report 1

Office for Disability Issues, 'Equality Act 2010: Guidance on Matters To Be Taken into Account in Determining Questions Relating to the Definition of Disability' (HM Government 2011)

Oliver M, *Understanding Disability* (2nd edn, Palgrave Macmillan 2009)

Oliver M, Sapey B and Thomas P, *Social Work with Disabled People* (Macmillan 2012)

International Labour Organisation, 'Promoting Employment Opportunities for People with Disabilities' (2019) 1

Osez Le Feminisme, 'Décision Justice MISS France' (2023) <https://osezlefeminisme.fr/decision-justice-miss-france/> accessed 8 December 2023

Oxford Dictionaries Online, https://en.oxforddictionaries.com/definition/disfigurement accessed 29 April 2019

Palacio RJ, *Wonder* (Penguin Books 2020)

Parnell J, 'Promoting Acceptance of Diverse Appearances in Primary School-Aged Children' (PhD, UWE 2021)

Parry S and others, 'Interventions to Reduce Mental Illness Stigma and Discrimination at the Person-Level for Individuals and Small Groups' in Vogel DL and Wade NG (eds), *The Cambridge Handbook of Stigma and Mental Health* (Cambridge University Press 2022)

Partridge J, *Changing Faces: The Challenge of Facial Disfigurement* (Penguin Books 1990)

Patzer G, 'Improving Self-Esteem by Improving Physical Attractiveness' (1997) 9 Journal of Esthetic Dentistry 44

Pittenger JB and Baskett LM, 'Facial Self-Perception: Its Relation to Objective Appearance and Self-Concept' (1984) 22 Bulletin of the Psychonomic Society 167

Priestley M, 'We're All Europeans Now! The Social Model of Disability and European Social Policy' in Barnes C and Mercer G (eds), *The Social Model of Disability: Europe and the Majority World* (The Disability Press 2005)

Probst C and others, 'Socioeconomic Differences in Alcohol-Attributable Mortality Compared with All-Cause Mortality: A Systematic Review and Meta-Analysis' (2014) 43 International Journal of Epidemiology 1314

Puhl RM and Heuer CA, 'Obesity Stigma: Important Considerations for public Health' (2010) 100 The American Journal of Public Health 1019

Pulver A, 'BFI to Refuse Funding for Films with Facially-Scarred Villains' *The Guardian* (29 November 2018) <www.theguardian.com/film/2018/nov/29/bfi-to-refuse-funding-for-films-with-facially-scarred-villains> accessed 8 November 2023

Quinn BA, 'The Paradox of Complaining: Law, Humor, and Harassment in the Everyday Work World' (2000) 25 Law & Social Inquiry 1151

Quinn G, 'Report of the Special Rapporteur on the Rights of Persons with Disabilities on Artificial Intelligence and the Rights of Persons with Disabilities' (United Nations, 2021)

Rankin M and Borah G, 'Perceived Functional Impact of Abnormal Facial Appearance' (2002) 111 Plastic & Reconstructive Surgery 2140

Restricted Growth Association, 'About Restricted Growth' (RGA, undated) <https://rgauk.org/about-restricted-growth> accessed 29 April 2019

Rhodes D, *The Beauty Bias* (Oxford University Press 2010)

Rhodes G, 'The Evolutionary Psychology of Facial Beauty' (2006) 57 Annual Review of Psychology 199

Rhodes T and others, 'Prevalence of Male Pattern Hair Loss in 18–49 Year Old Men' (1998) 24 Dermatologic Surgery 1330

Ringel W, 'Non-discrimination, Accommodation, and Intersectionality under the CRPD: New Trends and Challenges for the UN Human Rights System' (2017) 20 Max Planck Yearbook of United Nations Law Online 98

Robinson E, 'Psychological Research on Visible Differences in Adults' in Lansdown R and others (eds), *Visibly Different* (Butterworth-Heinemann 1997)

Romaniuc R, 'What Makes Law to Change Behavior? An Experimental Study' (2016) 12 Review of Law & Economics 447

Rumsey N and Harcourt D, 'Body Image and Disfigurement: Issues and Interventions' (2004) 1 Body Image 83

Rumsey N and others, 'Altered Body Image: Appearance-Related Concerns of People with Visible Disfigurement' (2004) 48 Journal of Advanced Nursing 443

Rumsey N, Bull R and Gahagan D, 'The Effect of Facial Disfigurement on the Proxemic Behaviour of the General Public' (1982) 12 Journal of Applied Social Psychology 137

Sarwer DB and others, 'The Psychosocial Burden of Visible Disfigurement Following Traumatic Injury' (2022) 13 Frontiers in Psychology 979574

Saunders H, *Appearance, Harassment and the Equality Act 2010* (UCL UK Labour Law Blog 2022)

'Difficult Distinctions in Anti-discrimination Law: Disfigurement, Appearance and Disability' (2020) 20 International Journal of Discrimination and the Law 21

'The Invisible Law of Visible Difference: Disfigurement in the Workplace' (2019) 48 Industrial Law Journal 487

Savin J, 'The Men from the 'Four Lads in Jeans' Meme Discuss the Down Sides of Going Viral' *Cosmopolitan* (January 2021) <www.cosmopolitan.com/uk/entertainment/a35249416/four-lads-jeans-meme/> accessed 13 March 2024

Schauer F, *The Force of Law* (Harvard University Press 2015)

Schvey NA and others, 'The Influence of a Defendant's Body Weight on Perceptions of Guilt' (2013) 37 International Journal of Obesity 1275

Schweik SM, *The Ugly Laws: Disability in Public* (New York University Press 2009)

Selensky JC and Carels RA, 'Weight Stigma and Media: An Examination of the Effect of Advertising Campaigns on Weight Bias, Internalized Weight Bias, Self-Esteem, Body Image, and Affect' (2021) 36 Body Image 95

Shakespeare T and Watson N, 'The Social Model Of Disability: An Outdated Ideology?' in Barnartt S and Altman B (eds), *Exploring Theories and*

Expanding Methodologies: Where We Are and Where We Need to Go To, vol 2 (Emerald Group Publishing Limited 2001)

Shakespeare T, *Disability Rights and Wrongs Revisited* (2nd edn, Routledge 2014)

Sharratt ND and others, 'Becoming Known: Disclosure and Exposure of (In) Visible Difference' (2020) 5 Stigma and Health 413

'Understandings and Experiences of Visible Difference and Romantic Relationships: A Qualitative Exploration' (2018) 27 Body Image 32

Sholli S, 'Daniel Barnett Reacts to 'Bizarre' Tribunal Ruling that Calling Man Bald Is Sex Harassment' (LBC, 2022) <https://bit.ly/4cdsGih> accessed 9 February 2024

Short Reads, 'The Dartmouth Scar Experiment: Revealing the Power of 'Victim Mindset'' *medium.com* <https://bit.ly/3Tlwplq> accessed 8 February 2024

Slater A, Guest E and Treneman-Evans G, 'Utilising Social Media to Increase Acceptance of Appearance-Altering Conditions: A Two-Part Experimental Study' (2023)

Smart C, *Feminism and the Power of Law* (Routledge 1989)

Smith MR, *A Comparative Analysis of the Criminal and Civil Justice Systems in England and Wales* (1st edn, Manchester University Press 2017)

Solanke I, *Discrimination as Stigma* (1st edn, Hart 2016)

Stevenage SV and McKay Y, 'Model Applicants: The Effect of Facial Appearance on Recruitment Decisions' (1999) 90 British Journal of Psychology 221

Stewart JE, 'Appearance and Punishment: The Attraction-Leniency Effect in the Courtroom' (1985) 125 The Journal of Social Psychology 373

Steyn J, 'Pepper v Hart: A Re-examination' (2001) 21 Oxford Journal of Legal Studies 59

Stone A and Fisher V, 'Changing Negative Perceptions of Individuals with Facial Disfigurement: The Effectiveness of a Brief Intervention' (2020) 42 Basic and Applied Social Psychology 341

Stone A and Wright T, 'When Your Face Doesn't Fit: Employment Discrimination against People with Facial Disfigurements' (2013) 43 Journal of Applied Social Psychology

Stone E, Stone D and Dipboye R, 'Stigmas in Organizations: Race, Handicaps and Physical Unattractiveness' in Kelley K (ed), *Organizational Psychology* (Elsevier 1992)

Sumner W, *Folkways: A Study of the Sociological Importance of Usages, Manners, Customs, Mores, and Morals* (Dover 1906)

Sunstein CR, 'On the Expressive Function of Law' (1996) 144 University of Pennsylvania law review 2021

Svegar D, 'What Does Facial Symmetry Reveal about Health and Personality?' (2016) 47 Polish Psychological Bulletin 356

Tankard ME and Paluck EL, 'The Effect of a Supreme Court Decision Regarding Gay Marriage on Social Norms and Personal Attitudes' (2017) 28 Psychological Science 1334

Tartaglia A and others, 'Workplace Discrimination and Disfigurement: The National EEOC ADA Research Project' (2005) 25 Work 57

Tausel S, 'Writing against the Stigma: Facial Disfigurement in R.J. Palacio's Wonder' in Klecker C (ed), *The Disfigured Face in American Literature, Film and Television* (Routledge 2021)

Teubner G, 'After Privatization? The Many Autonomies of Private Law' (1998) 51 Current Legal Problems 393

Thompson A and Kent G, 'Adjusting to Disfigurement: Processes Involved in Dealing with Being Visibly Different' (2001) 21 Clinical Psychology Review 663

Toubon J, 'Décision-cadre n°2019-205 relative aux discriminations dans l'emploi fondées sur l'apparence physique' (Defenseur des droits 2019)

Trades Union Congress, 'Technology Managing People: The Worker Experience' (2020)

Tranter B and Grant R, 'A Class Act?: Social Background and Body Modifications in Australia' (2018) 54 Journal of Sociology 412

Tyler TR, *Why People Obey the Law* (Princeton University Press 2021)

Ulen, T, 'The Importance of Behavioral Law in Eyal Zamir and Doron Teichman', *The Oxford Handbook of Behavioral Economics and the Law* (1st edn, Oxford University Press 2014)

UN Committee on the Rights of Persons with Disabilities, *General Comment No. 6 on Equality and Non-discrimination* (United Nations 2018)

United Kingdom Government, 'Response to the Report by the United Nations Committee on the Rights of Persons with Disabilities under Article 6 of the Optional Protocol to the Convention' (2017) 3 CRPD/C/17.R.3.

United Nations, *The Convention on the Rights of Persons with Disabilities Training Guide* (United Nations 2014)

United Nations Committee on the Rights of Persons with Disabilities, 'Inquiry Concerning the United Kingdom of Great Britain and Northern Ireland Carried Out by the Committee under Article 6 of the Optional Protocol to the Convention Report of the Committee' (2016) CRPD/C/15/R.2/Rev.1

Urwin P and Latreille PL, 'Experiences of Judicial Mediation in Employment Tribunals' in Roche WK, Teague P and Colvin AJS (eds), *The Oxford Handbook of Conflict Management in Organizations* (1st edn, Oxford University Press 2014)

US Equal Employment Opportunity Commission, 'ADA Charge Data by Impairments/Bases – Merit Factor Resolutions (Charges Filed with EEOC) FY 1997 – FY 2022' (undated) <https://bit.ly/43kwmeb> accessed 8 November 2023

'Interpretive Guidance of Title 1 of the Americans with Disabilities Act' (as amended) <www.law.cornell.edu/cfr/text/29/appendix-to_part_1630> accessed 18 March 2024

Vo LT, 'A More Attractive Look at Physical Appearance-Based Discrimination: Filling the Gap in Appearance-Based Anti-discrimination Law' (2002) 26 Southern Illinois University Law Journal 339

Waddington L, 'Saying All the Right Things and Still Getting It Wrong' (2015) 22 Maastricht Journal of European and Comparative Law 576

Wagner, A, Can Britain "Ignore Europe on Human Rights?" (UK Human Rights blog, 23 October 2011)

Wardle C and Boyce T, *Media Coverage and Audience Reception of Disfigurement on Television* (Cardiff University / The Healing Foundation 2009)

Wasserman D, 'Stigma without Impairment' in Francis LP and Silvers A (eds), *Americans with Disabilities* (Routledge 2000)

Waterfield B and Huggler J, '"I Don't Feel My Weight Is a Big Problem," says Dane in EU Obesity Ruling' *The Telegraph* (24 May 2019) <https://bit.ly/48Y2Xrt> accessed 24 May 2019

Watson G, 'Elephant Man City Statue Plan Faces 'Freak Show' Criticism' *BBC News* <www.bbc.co.uk/news/uk-england-leicestershire-51012975> accessed 8 September 2023

Watson N, 'Well, I Know This Is Going to Sound Very Strange to You, but I Don't See Myself as a Disabled Person: Identity and Disability' (2002) 17 Disability & Society 509

Weisbuch M, Pauker K and Ambady N, 'Subtle Transmission of Race Bias via Televised Nonverbal Behavior' (2009) 326 Science 1711

Westen P, 'The Empty Idea of Equality' (1982) 95 Harvard Law Review 537

Widdows H, 'Be Ashamed of Body Shaming' (Sussex Publishers LLC, 2020) <https://bit.ly/3Pm9y84> accessed 10 January 2020

'Everyday Lookism' (undated) <www.everydaylookism.com/> accessed 8 June 2023

'Lookism: The Last Acceptable Discrimination' (Appearance, Identity and the Law Conference, Queen Mary University of London, 7 September 2022)

Perfect Me: Beauty as an Ethical Ideal (Princeton University Press 2018)

World Health Organisation, 'Weight Bias and Obesity Stigma: Considerations for the WHO European Region' (undated) <www.euro.who.int/__data/assets/pdf_file/0017/351026/WeightBias.pdf> accessed 24 May 2019

Woodhams C and Corby S, 'Defining Disability in Theory and Practice: A Critique of the British Disability Discrimination Act 1995' (2003) 32 Journal of Social Policy 159

Workman C and others, 'Evidence against the "Anomalous-Is-Bad" Stereotype in Hadza Hunter Gatherers' (2022) 12 Scientific Reports 8693

Yoshino K, 'The Pressure to Cover' *New York Times* (New York, 15 January 2006) <www.nytimes.com/2006/01/15/magazine/the-pressure-to-cover.html> accessed 25 October 2023

Zanga G and De Gioannis E, 'Discrimination in Grading: A Scoping Review of Studies on Teachers' Discrimination in School' (2023) 78 Studies in Educational Evaluation 101284

Zebrowitz LA and McDonald SM, 'The Impact of Litigants' Baby-Facedness and Attractiveness on Adjudications in Small Claims Courts' (1991) 15 Law and Human Behavior 603

Zephaniah B, *Face* (Bloomsbury 1999)

Zerebecki BG and others, 'Can TV Shows Promote Acceptance of Sexual and Ethnic Minorities? A Literature Review of Television Effects on Diversity Attitudes' (2021) 15 Sociology Compass

Zucchelli F and others, 'Men's Experiences of Alopecia Areata: A Qualitative Study' (2022) 9 Health Psychology Open

INDEX

CAMBRIDGE BIOETHICS AND LAW

Books in the Series

Marcus Radetzki, Marian Radetzki and Niklas Juth *Genes and Insurance: Ethical, Legal and Economic Issues*

Ruth Macklin *Double Standards in Medical Research in Developing Countries*

Donna Dickenson *Property in the Body: Feminist Perspectives*

Matti Häyry, Ruth Chadwick, Vilhjálmur Árnason and Gardar Árnason *The Ethics and Governance of Human Genetic Databases: European Perspectives*

J. K. Mason *The Troubled Pregnancy: Legal Wrongs and Rights in Reproduction*

Daniel Sperling *Posthumous Interests: Legal and Ethical Perspectives*

Keith Syrett *Law, Legitimacy and the Rationing of Health Care: A Contextual and Comparative Perspective*

Alasdair Maclean *Autonomy, Informed Consent and Medical Law: A Relational Change*

Heather Widdows and Caroline Mullen *The Governance of Genetic Information: Who Decides?*

David Price *Human Tissue in Transplantation and Research: A Model Legal and Ethical Donation Framework*

Matti Häyry *Rationality and the Genetic Challenge: Making People Better?*

Mary Donnelly *Healthcare Decision-Making and the Law: Autonomy, Capacity and the Limits of Liberalism*

Anne-Maree Farrell, David Price and Muireann Quigley *Organ Shortage: Ethics, Law and Pragmatism*

Sara Fovargue *Xenotransplantation and Risk: Regulating a Developing Biotechnology*

John Coggon *What Makes Health Public?: A Critical Evaluation of Moral, Legal, and Political Claims in Public Health*

Mark Taylor *Genetic Data and the Law: A Critical Perspective on Privacy Protection*

Anne-Maree Farrell *The Politics of Blood: Ethics, Innovation and the Regulation of Risk*

Stephen W. Smith *End-of-Life Decisions in Medical Care: Principles and Policies for Regulating the Dying Process*

Michael Parker *Ethical Problems and Genetics Practice*

William W. Lowrance *Privacy, Confidentiality, and Health Research*

Kerry Lynn Macintosh *Human Cloning: Four Fallacies and Their Legal Consequence*

Heather Widdows *The Connected Self: The Ethics and Governance of the Genetic Individual*

Amel Alghrani, Rebecca Bennett and Suzanne Ost *Bioethics, Medicine and the Criminal Law Volume I: The Criminal Law and Bioethical Conflict: Walking the Tightrope*

Danielle Griffiths and Andrew Sanders *Bioethics, Medicine and the Criminal Law Volume II: Medicine, Crime and Society*

Margaret Brazier and Suzanne Ost *Bioethics, Medicine and the Criminal Law Volume III: Medicine and Bioethics in the Theatre of the Criminal Process*

Sigrid Sterckx, Kasper Raus and Freddy Mortier *Continuous Sedation at the End of Life: Ethical, Clinical and Legal Perspectives*

A. M. Viens, John Coggon and Anthony S. Kessel *Criminal Law, Philosophy and Public Health Practice*

Ruth Chadwick, Mairi Levitt and Darren Shickle *The Right to Know and the Right Not to Know: Genetic Privacy and Responsibility*

Eleanor D. Kinney *The Affordable Care Act and Medicare in Comparative Context*

Katri Lõhmus *Caring Autonomy: European Human Rights Law and the Challenge of Individualism*

Catherine Stanton and Hannah Quirk *Criminalising Contagion: Legal and Ethical Challenges of Disease Transmission and the Criminal Law*

Sharona Hoffman *Electronic Health Records and Medical Big Data: Law and Policy*

Barbara Prainsack and Alena Buyx *Solidarity in Biomedicine and Beyond*

Camillia Kong *Mental Capacity in Relationship: Decision-Making, Dialogue, and Autonomy*

Oliver Quick *Regulating Patient Safety: The End of Professional Dominance?*

Thana Cristina de Campos *The Global Health Crisis: Ethical Responsibilities*

Jonathan Ives, Michael Dunn and Alan Cribb *Empirical Bioethics: Theoretical and Practical Perspectives*

Alan Merry and Warren Brookbanks *Merry and McCall Smith's Errors, Medicine and the Law* (second edition)

Donna Dickenson *Property in the Body: Feminist Perspectives* (second edition)

Rosie Harding *Duties to Care: Dementia, Relationality and Law*

Ruud ter Meulen *Solidarity and Justice in Health and Social Care*

David Albert Jones, Chris Gastmans and Calum MacKellar *Euthanasia and Assisted Suicide: Lessons from Belgium*

Muireann Quigley *Self-Ownership, Property Rights, and the Human Body: A Legal Perspective*

Françoise Baylis and Alice Dreger *Bioethics in Action*

John Keown *Euthanasia, Ethics and Public Policy: An Argument against Legislation* (second edition)

Amel Alghrani *Regulating Assisted Reproductive Technologies: New Horizons*

Britta van Beers, Sigrid Sterckx and Donna Dickenson *Personalised Medicine, Individual Choice and the Common Good*

David G. Kirchhoffer and Bernadette J. Richards *Beyond Autonomy: Limits and Alternatives to Informed Consent in Research Ethics and Law*

Markus Wolfensberger and Anthony Wrigley *Trust in Medicine: Its Nature, Justification, Significance, and Decline*

Catriona A. W. McMillan *The Human Embryo in vitro: Breaking the Legal Stalemate*

Benjamin Peter White and Lindy Willmott (editors) *International Perspectives on End-of-Life Law Reform: Politics, Persuasion and Persistence*

Carolyn Adams, Judy Allen and Felicity Flack *Sharing Linked Data for Health Research: Toward Better Decision Making*

Emily Postan *Embodied Narratives: Protecting Identity Interests through Ethical Governance of Bioinformation*

Jaime Lindsey *Reimagining the Court of Protection: Access to Justice in Mental Capacity Law*

Marcelo Corrales Compagnucci, Michael Lowery Wilson, Mark Fenwick, Nikolaus Forgó and Till Bärnighausen *AI in eHealth: Human Autonomy, Data Governance and Privacy in Healthcare*

Steph Jowett *Consent for Medical Treatment of Trans and Gender Diverse Youth*

Julia Duffy *Mental Capacity, Dignity and the Power of International Human Rights*

Cressida Aukland *Values and Disorder in Mental Capacity Law*

Margaret Sleeboom-Faulkner *Regulatory Violence: The Global Dynamics of Regulatory Experimentation in Biomedicine and Health*

Printed by Integrated Books International,
United States of America